Volume 10, Issue 1/2 Double Issue March/June 2006

Vogue

Special Double Issue
Edited by Becky Conekin and
Amy de la Haye

Fashion Theory

The Journal of Dress, Body & Culture

Fashion Theory: The Journal of Dress, Body & Culture

Editor
Dr. Valerie Steele
Director
The Museum at the Fashion Institute of Technology, E201
Seventh Avenue at 27th Street
New York, NY 10001-5992
USA
Fax: +1 212 924 3958
e-mail: valerie@fashiontheory.com

Book Reviews Editor
Christopher Breward
Research Department
Victoria and Albert Museum
South Kensington
London SW7 2RL

Exhibitions Reviews Editor
Alexandra Palmer
Royal Ontario Museum
100 Queen's Park, Toronto
Ontario M5S 2C6, Canada
Fax: +1 416 586 5877
e-mail: alexp@rom.on.ca

Please send all books for review to the Book Reviews Editor

Aims and Scope
The importance of studying the body as a site for the deployment of discourses is well-established in a number of disciplines. By contrast, the study of fashion has, until recently, suffered from a lack of critical analysis. Increasingly, however, scholars have recognized the cultural significance of self-fashioning, including not only clothing but also such body alterations as tattooing and piercing. *Fashion Theory* takes as its starting point a definition of "fashion" as the cultural construction of the embodied identity. It aims to provide an interdisciplinary forum for the rigorous analysis of cultural phenomena ranging from footbinding to fashion advertising.

Anyone wishing to submit an article, interview, or a book, film or exhibition review for possible publication in this journal should contact Valerie Steele (at the address listed to the left) or the Editorial Department at Berg (1st Floor, Angel Court, 81 St Clements Street, Oxford, OX4 1AW, UK; e-mail: enquiry@bergpublishers.com).

Notes for Contributors can be found at the back of the journal.

ISSN: 1362-704X
www.fashiontheory.com

Ordering Information
By mail:

Four issues per volume.

Customer Services
Turpin Distribution
Stratton Business Park
Pegasus Drive
Biggleswade
SG18 8QB
UK

One volume per annum.

2006: Volume 10

By fax: +44 (0) 1767 601640

By telephone: +44 (0) 1767 604951

By e-mail: custserv@turpin-distribution.com

Free online subscription for print subscribers. Full color images available online. Access your electronic subscription through www.ingenta.com or www.ingentaselect.com

Inquiries

Editorial: Kathryn Earle, Managing Editor, e-mail: kearle@berg1.demon.co.uk

Production: Ian Critchley, e-mail: icritchley@bergpublishers.com

Advertising + subscriptions: enquiry@bergpublishers.com

Subscription Rates:
Institutional base list subscription price: £125.00, US$225.00.

Individuals' subscription price: £45.00, US$75.00.

Reprints of Individual Articles
Copies of individual articles may be obtained from the Publishers at the appropriate fees. Write to: Berg, 1st Floor, Angel Court, 81 St Clements Street, Oxford, OX4 1AW, UK.

Printed in the United Kingdom.
MARCH/JUNE 2006

Indexed by the IBSS (International Bibliography of Social Sciences); the DAAI (Design and Applied Arts Index); ARTbibliographies Modern; H.W. Wilson Art Index and H.W. Wilson Omnifile Index; the Anthropological Index Online (AIO) of the Royal Anthropological Institute of Great Britain and Ireland; Sociological abstracts; ISI Web of Science/Arts & Humanities Citation Index and ISI Current Contents Connect/Arts & Humanities (THOMSON); and the MLA (Modern Language Association) Bibliography

Page 13

Page 39

Page 73

Page 97

Page 127

Page 153

Page 175

Page 225

Page 259

Contents

CALL FOR PAPERS

Fashion Theory (Berg Publishers) would like to publish a special issue on Eco-fashion, to be edited by Regina A. Root. All topics related to the subject of dress and the environment are invited; the issue will integrate both local and global perspectives. Topics might include the recycling of textiles or trash in dress; fashion that advocates social change (towards sustainable economies that are beneficial to the environment – from The Body Shop concept to Carlos Miele's creations incorporating the handiwork of Brazilian women's cooperatives that establish living wages); eco-tourist style and adventure gear; cultural histories of "natural" looks, fabrics and designs; dress and ecological utopia. Please submit a two-page abstract, bibliography, and a curriculum vitae before November 1, 2006, to Dr. Regina A. Root, Modern Languages and Literatures, College of William and Mary, P.O. Box 8795, Williamsburg, VA 23187-8795 (USA) or email your submission to raroot@wm.edu

Fashion Theory, Volume 10, Issue 1/2, pp. 5–6
Reprints available directly from the Publishers.
Photocopying permitted by licence only.
© 2006 Berg.

Foreword

Vogue is the world's oldest fashion magazine. The first edition was published in America in 1892 and there are now 16 *Vogues* across the world—the latest addition to the family being Chinese *Vogue*, launched in September 2005.

Over the years much has been written about *Vogue*, the title and the brand, in part because *Vogue* is so much more than a magazine. Through its pages you can see the role fashion and style has played in the wider world and the many ways in which those facets have reflected what is happening economically, socially, culturally, and artistically.

This special issue forms the first academic scrutiny of the magazine in its historical and international context, using *Vogue* as both subject and source to examine such subjects as Sexual Subculture in the 1920s to *Vogue*'s role in Russia over the past seven years.

I am delighted to introduce and support this interesting and illuminating project.

Alexandra Shulman, Editor of British Vogue

Fashion Theory, Volume 10, Issue 1/2, pp. 7–12
Reprints available directly from the Publishers.
Photocopying permitted by licence only.
© 2006 Berg.

Introduction

In his article for this volume, the art historian Christopher Reed writes of 1920s British *Vogue* under editor Dorothy Todd, arguing that as it was "too posh for social historians, too popular for specialists in literature and art," it has "slipped from critical view, overlooked altogether or obscured in condescending stereotypes about fashion magazines." When we exclude scholars of fashion theory and history, including the astute readers of *Fashion Theory*, it seems we can extend Reed's contention to *Vogue* magazine generally.[1] Unlike another Condé Nast publication, *Vanity Fair*, or even the American Book of the Month Club, *Vogue* has not attracted the scholarly attention it deserves.[2] It is our intention that the articles which follow will help redress this. In this Special Issue the writers, scholars, and curators have employed a range of methodologies and ask a wide variety of questions. Having done so, they illustrate just how much *Vogue* magazine can add to our knowledge of the past and the present, as well as that of various national fashion cultures.

Beginning at the beginning, with the first *Vogue*, American *Vogue* (1892), Alison Matthews David examines its "early attempts at self-definition," revealing fascinating insights into gender and race attitudes, New York's fashion geography, and changing constructs of American identity in the "Gilded Age" at the turn of the twentieth century. Christopher Reed picks up the story of British *Vogue*, charmingly nicknamed "Brogue," in a unique phase of the magazine's history between 1922 and 1926, under the editorship of Dorothy Todd. As Reed fascinatingly reveals, Todd incorporated the "amusing style," "queer" attitudes, and literary and artistic modes of Bloomsbury's "inkyllectuals" into the pages of "Brogue," making it resemble *Vanity Fair* more often than American or French *Vogue* of the period. Reed's final assessment of Todd's magazine is that "with other writers for British *Vogue* in the 1920s, she created a magazine that continues to offer attentive readers the queer pleasures of androgynous fashion, campy wit, and visual extravagance that are some of the pleasures of sexual subculture." In the next piece, entitled "'We Are Fatally Influenced by Goods Bought in Bond Street': London, Shopping, and the Fashionable Geographies of 1930s *Vogue*," Bronwen Edwards employs an interdisciplinary approach, including mapping and issues of place, both key concerns of historical geographers, to provide a stimulating reading of British *Vogue* in the decade after the "lofty," "crop-headed, double-breasted" Miss Todd. Edwards's article provides insights into the differences between the national versions of *Vogue* in New York, Paris, and London, as well as how these cities were portrayed in fashion terms. Historian Becky Conekin then traces Lee Miller's career with *Vogue* as model, photographer, and WWII correspondent, from New York to Paris and finally London, between 1927 and 1953. The different incarnations of Lee Miller, along with *Vogue* magazine, allow us to further our understandings of the history of surrealism, fashion photography, and modeling, as well as some of the darker moments of the Second World War and the constrained world of recovering Britain after the war.

Whereas these four scholars unpack various aspects of *Vogue*'s history in its first-half century, the curator and dress historian Amy de la Haye approaches from the opposite direction, analyzing how British *Vogue* has engaged with the history of fashion. She assesses how the magazine has reported on fashion exhibitions, as well as the dress worn by celebrity guests at their private-view parties, held at London's Victoria and Albert Museum between 1971 and 2004. In striking contrast to the pristine new season's garments, presented by *Vogue* in the context of consumption, de la Haye focuses on fashion that is presented for contextual interpretation. A suit designed by Chanel in 1937–1938 and worn by Diana Vreeland is the case study that allows her to explore the implications of re-presenting historical dress and its accompanying biographical story on the glossy pages of this preeminent fashion magazine.

Although sociologist Agnès Rocamora's article also, of course, examines *Vogue*'s glossy pages, they are quite different ones from those turned by de la Haye. Rocamora's focus is the readers' letters section of French *Vogue* that ran from 1996 to 2001. She assesses how the reader's voice was appropriated to represent the magazine and its readership. Her argument is that this section shifted the magazine away from the realm of consumption toward that of enlightened debate, allowing French *Vogue* to represent itself as a platform for critical discussion in line with the ideal of the public sphere—that quintessential space for the rational exchange of ideas. The readers' letters section also served to promote the belief, conveyed throughout the magazine, that in France, fashion is high art.

"In Russia, at Last and Forever" is the title of Djurdja Bartlett's analysis of the first seven years of Russian *Vogue* (launched 1998). She observes that: "The arrival of *Vogue* announced a change in the politics of style, imagery, gender representations, and consumption practices. However, the Russian version of *Vogue* was itself influenced by the former socialist cultural patterns." Given Russia's unstable economy and absence of sophisticated fashion traditions, the survival of Russian *Vogue* was perhaps a most surprising success story. Drawing on her PhD research into how socialist countries have variously responded to fashion, as well as interviews with Editors Anna Harvey and Aliona Doletskaya, especially for this article, Bartlett analyses the strategies and negotiations that made this success possible.

Starting from the assertion that fashion text is clearly the key to understanding fashion, yet generally neglected by fashion scholars, Anna König sets out to identify the most distinctive and enduring elements of fashion text in British *Vogue* between 1980 and 2001. A close analysis of content, tone, lexicon, and cultural references allows her to uncover patterns of continuity and change across the period and from there to discuss broader cultural issues pertaining to the language of fashion, as well as 'the textual constructions of the fashion world.'

The ninth article in this volume takes us to Japan. Its author, Brian Moeran, teaches in the Department of Intercultural Communication and Management at the Copenhagen Business School. In "Elegance and Substance Travel East: *Vogue Nippon*," Moeran uses content analysis of seven issues from 2002, supplemented by a dozen in-depth interviews with Japanese fashion magazine readers, to "focus on Japanese *Vogue* as both cultural product and commodity." His aim was "to highlight the relationship between editorial and advertising matter" and "to take into account the total social processes surrounding the production, representation, circulation, and reception of Japanese *Vogue*."

The final article, written by Judith Clark, takes the form of an interview with Anna Piaggi, Creative Consultant to Italian *Vogue*, and Luca Stoppini, the magazine's Creative Director. Clark's purpose is to examine Piaggi's influential, thematic, *Doppie Pagine* (Double Pages). In her afterword, the author draws fascinating parallels with Piaggi's working methodology and that seen in the art historian Aby Warburg's unfinished work, *Mnemosyne Atlas* (1866–1929). In turn, Clark is reflective about how Piaggi's work has informed her own curatorial fascination with "instinctive work" and installation design.

We close this Special Issue with timelines of *Vogue's* nineteen international publications, from American *Vogue* in 1892 to the most recent edition in 2005 Chinese *Vogue*. These have been meticulously researched and compiled by Janine Button, Library and Archive Manager at London's Vogue House, and now form a standard reference point.

It was Janine's enthusiasm for this project, from the very outset, that enabled so many of our writers to enter the company library at Vogue House in London's Hanover Square. Rather than staring at electronic screens and zooming directly to specific references, we have savored the scholarly, haptic—and even olfactory—pleasures of leafing through back issues of international *Vogue* magazines—magazines explored, handled, and enjoyed by so many readers before us. The fascinating destinations to which our many diversions have taken us have, of course, inspired us and will, we hope, in turn spawn new research outcomes.

At Vogue House we would also like to acknowledge Alexandra Shulman's support of this project and her permission for us to use the many striking, beautiful, and fascinating images from British *Vogue,* which illustrate this Special Issue. For their enthusiasm, skillful negotiations and valuable time given to facilitate them, we are most grateful to Harriet Wilson, Director of Editorial Administration and Rights, and her Assistant, Nicky Budden. We are also grateful to Harriet, Janine, and Nicky for putting our writers in touch with their international colleagues and endorsing our project, which has made possible the publication of images from Russia, America, Italy, Japan, and France.

At the London College of Fashion, University of the Arts, we thank Sandra Holtby, Helen Thomas, Rob Lutton, Yejide Akinade, and Nick Sargent. We would also like to thank our Readers for their time and thought-provoking suggestions.

Becky Conekin and Amy de la Haye

Notes

1. As Anna König explains in her piece for this volume, "even when academic texts such as Paul Jobling's *Fashion Spreads* (1999) look at print representations of fashion, the focus is on images." His is, of course, an important contribution to the scholarly study of fashion magazines, but here we aim to take just one fashion magazine, *Vogue*—which many would agree is international fashion's preeminent magazine—and examine it from many different directions: historically, its text, image, editors, star contributors, its relationship to fashion cities, its readers, as well as what makes its different national versions distinct.

2. Michael Murphy (1996) has written of how *Vanity Fair* between 1914 and 1936 was a key proponent of modernism for American readers and Janice Radway (1996) has devoted almost 500 pages to the study of the Book of the Month Club in America, contending that it helped to define and create a serious "middlebrow" reading culture and continues to do so today. See Reed's article and its list of references for the scholarly pieces that have been written on *Vogue* to date.

Coming in September 2006...

'At last
a work that deals not
only with the history of
footwear, but also with its
cultural significance.
This volume helps transform the
shoe from a mundane object of
everyday use into something of
great social and
psychological power.'
Manolo Blahnik

SHOES

A HISTORY FROM SANDALS TO SNEAKERS

Edited by Giorgio Riello and Peter McNeil

⊛BERG

www.bergpublishers.com

Fashion Theory, Volume 10, Issue 1/2, pp. 13–38
Reprints available directly from the Publishers.
Photocopying permitted by licence only.

Vogue's New World: American Fashionability and the Politics of Style

Alison Matthews David

Dr. Alison Matthews David is a lecturer in the History of Textiles and Dress at the University of Southampton, UK. She has published on nineteenth and early twentieth-century-fashion in Europe and is currently working on several projects, including research on military camouflage and fashion during World War I and a book entitled *Fashion Victims: Death by Clothing* for Berg Publishers.
alisonmd@soton.ac.uk

Avoir la Vogue: In authoritate esse

Nicot, *Trésor de la langue française*, 1606

Despite the French connotations of its title, the first *Vogue* was an inherently American cultural phenomenon. It began in New York in 1892 as social gazette for a Eurocentric elite and became a more professional and self-confidently patriotic publication under the directorship of Condé Nast, who purchased it in 1909. Although *Vogue* has always maintained its aloofness as an elite women's publication, this article links the magazine with the geographical and social conditions of its production. The magazine carefully negotiated the urban and demographic fabric of Manhattan at a period when concepts of national and gender identity were undergoing a radical transformation. In the face of mass immigration and the rise of new models of womanhood during the late nineteenth and early twentieth centuries, early *Vogue* adopted a largely conservative stance. However, as the magazine's editorial staff and market audience changed during its first three decades, *Vogue* began to renounce the snobbery of the social networks of the Gilded Age (the period from 1870 to 1914). While it maintained privileged ties to Europe, it also began to embrace more populist understandings of "authentic" American taste and style in dress. This new nationalism included a greater acceptance of mass-produced and branded goods, an attitude which typifies American fashion design and production in the twentieth century.

The period from 1870 to 1914, known as America's "Gilded Age," saw the rise of corporate capitalism alongside an emphasis on the branding and marketing of commodities—from chocolate to magazines. While American companies like Kodak and Coca-Cola celebrated their homegrown roots, in the fashion world French chic monopolized the market. The real innovation of *Vogue* was that it established the US as an authoritative voice in the realm of high fashion, a domain where the US had previously been a net importer and follower of Parisian couture trends. The rise of American fashion journalism coincided with New York's increasing importance as a producer of luxury womenswear for the American market. After Condé Nast purchased the magazine in 1909, *Vogue* embarked upon an era of cultural imperialism which exported American fashion writing through British (1916), French (1920), and even Argentinean (1924) editions. Yet throughout its history, *Vogue*'s relationship with Europe was complex and fraught with contradictions. Like the American people, who felt ambivalent toward the countries they had emigrated from, *Vogue* had to steer a difficult course between fostering patriotic pride and keeping its readers abreast of the latest trends from the Continent. *Vogue*'s office, located in the midst of New York's luxury shops, publishing houses, and garment factories, became a geographical hub linking the old and new worlds of fashion.

Over a century after *Vogue* was first launched, America's fashionable landscape has altered almost unrecognizably. The early readers of *Vogue* reinforced their social status by traveling to Europe to fill their trunks with extravagant gowns purchased in Parisian couture houses. These houses have now lost much of their American clientele, and high-powered New York businesswomen, who have become style icons in their own right, often favor native-born designers such as Donna Karan and Calvin Klein over the luxurious creations of, for example, Christian Lacroix or John Galliano. The streamlined style and practical elegance of American fashions owe more to the aesthetics of mass-produced goods than to the decorative profusion and exquisite workmanship of traditional European haute couture. This article explores some of the underlying reasons for this shift from an elitist Eurocentrism to a more populist understanding of "authentic" American taste and style in dress.

In the past decade, critical literature on the production, consumption, and theory of fashion has grown exponentially (Troy 2003; Crane 2000; Bruzzi and Church Gibson 2000; Carter 2003; Kawamura 2004). Sociologists, semioticians and feminist critics have produced an extensive body of scholarship on magazines and the women's press (Beetham 1996; Kitch 2001; Jobling 1999). Social, economic, and labor historians, along with cultural geographers, have contributed to an equally significant volume of work on the urban garment trades and immigrant labor (Green 1997; Breward 2004). While bringing these literatures into productive dialogue is a far greater project than the scale of this article permits, I hope to sketch out some intersections between the production, marketing, and consumption of American fashion. The trajectory I trace examines *Vogue*'s early attempts at self-definition, its shifting attitudes toward gender and race in the US at the turn of the century, the geographical migrations of *Vogue*'s office within Manhattan from 1892–1929, and the magazine's increasing professionalism and emphasis on branding and advertising under the ownership of Condé Nast. Changing historical understandings of "American" identity are central to this narrative.

Defining *Vogue*

Self-definition has always been crucial to *Vogue*. In its inaugural issue, the first editor printed a dictionary definition of the term used for its title, appropriating what was originally a French term for its American readership. The entry was directly cut and pasted from the recently published American *Century Dictionary* of 1889. It states that the term was most commonly used in the phrase "*in vogue*: as, a particular style of dress was then *in vogue*."[1] This popular understanding of the term had the advantage of making the figurative literal. When readers flicked through the pages of the magazine they would expect to find the appropriate dress or opinions they were looking for *in Vogue*. This pun often finds its way into the editorial content itself. To choose only one example, in 1916 the editor confidently claimed that "The best-dressed women choose their wardrobes by one infallible rule: if it's in *Vogue*, it's smart" (*British Vogue*, September 15, 1916: table of contents).

Yet throughout its first thirty years of existence, the magazine's erudite editorship and illustrators consistently played on the original French meaning of the word *vogue*. *Vogue* is a maritime term. The first dictionary of the Académie Française (1694) defines *vogue* as the impulsion or movement of a galley or other ship by the force of rowing. By the

Figure 1
"Vogue, The Ancient Mariner,
Charts the Sea of Fashion."
Illustration by Janet Blossom,
American *Vogue*, August 1,
1925.

late eighteenth century, it had taken on its current meaning and vogue
and fashion are listed as synonyms (Féraud 1787–8). During its first ten
years, the magazine frequently featured coverage of modern yachting
events and dress while recalling the earlier meaning of the word through
a sixteenth- or seventeenth-century galleon it called "The Good Ship
Vogue."[2] This form of navigation recalled the arrival of America's first
white explorers and colonists, from Christopher Columbus's voyage of
"discovery" to the landing of the *Mayflower*. It also emphasized the
magazine's role as a bearer of fashion news from European shores before
the age of air travel. This metaphor is expressed in Janet Blossom's 1925
illustration entitled "*Vogue*, the Ancient Mariner, Charts the Sea of
Fashion" (Figure 1).

With the Wind of Desire filling its sails, the Good Ship *Vogue* sets its sails, journeying from the Empire of the Past at the upper left to the Unknown Land Called Future at the upper right of the image. During the course of its travels it navigates the turbulent Current of Fashion, avoiding such deadly hazards as the Rocks of Self-Indulgence, Showy Shallows, Whirlpool of Everyone Else's Advice, and the dragon-like Monster Expense. It steers its course close to the Island of the Blessed where passengers might visit the Paradise of the Well-Dressed and the Empire of the Mode passing through Style City or the Archipelago of Charming Accessories. This illustration highlights how maritime metaphors are particularly apt for fashion as they capture the constant flux of trends and styles as well as the ebb and flow of fashion cycles.[3] On a more political level, the prestige of this "ancient" galleon and its allusions to early migration offers a stark contrast in 1925 to the modern steamers landing at Ellis Island with more recent and less fortunate immigrants to US shores. This illustration alludes to the commercial and geographical importance of New York, which served as a point of exchange between commodities and people traveling between the old and new worlds (Breward 2003:194).

1892 and the Appearance of an American "Debutante"

Vogue's snobbish Eurocentrism set it apart from the burgeoning mass press of the time, which proudly proclaimed its homegrown American roots. Part of this contrast can be explained by examining its editor and readership. While less expensive magazines *Ladies' Home Journal* and *Munsey*'s were aimed at a largely rural middle-class public based in the Midwest and western states, *Vogue*'s cosmopolitan, urban Manhattan address allowed it to bridge the gulf between US and Europe, while catering to an upper-class New England public. The first issue of American *Vogue* came out on December 17, 1892 in Manhattan. Its editor was Arthur Turnure, a Princeton graduate who had some experience of publishing. He called wealthy friends and fashionable relatives to his aid. The stockholders (over 250 people) included all of New York's leading lights, the so-called "four hundred" who formed its most elite social circle, many of whom were descended from seventeenth-century Dutch immigrants and called "Knickerbockers." Others were of Anglo-Saxon stock, but had almost equally prestigious lineage and could trace their ancestry back to colonial times.[4] They included Peter Cooper Hewitt, Mrs. Stuyvesant Fish, Everetta C. Whitney and Cornelius Vanderbilt. The magazine's purported audience was this circle itself, and it made no apologies for its elitist tone and content. As Turnure wrote on the first editorial page:

A foreign critic of American society has said that in no monar-
chical country is the existence of aristocracy so evident as in the
republic of the United States. That with us class distinctions are
as finely drawn, social aspirations as pronounced, and snobbishness as prevalent as in any nation that confers titles and ignores
the principle of equality. This assertion is unquestionably true.
Society, if it is to exist at all, must have its marks and limitations.
(*Vogue*, December 17, 1892: 2)

At the same time it argued that "American society enjoys the distinction
of being the most progressive in the world...," its aristocracy founded
in "reason and developed in natural order." This quote captures the
inherently contradictory nature of American democracy during the late
nineteenth century. Though this period was dubbed the Gilded Age
for the vast fortunes won by oil barons, railroad tycoons and large-
scale industrialists, it was also an era when both traditional elites and
the nouveaux riches wished to reinforce their distance from poorer
and more recent immigrants to the US. This cachet was reinforced by
importing luxury goods from Europe.

The French author and social commentator Paul Bourget traveled to
the US in 1894 and was invited into vacation homes at Newport, Rhode
Island. Newport, the vacation destination of wealthy Manhattanites,
was frequently mentioned in the pages of *Vogue* in the 1890s. Bourget
stated that the décor of Newport houses betrayed:

...a constant, tireless effort to absorb European ideas... It is in
Europe that the silk of these stuffed chairs and these curtains was
woven; in Europe that these chairs and tables were turned. The
silverware came from Europe, and this dress was woven, cut,
sewn in Europe; these shoes, stockings, gloves came from there.
"When I was in Paris"; "Then we go to Paris"; "We want to go
to Paris to buy our gowns." These expressions continually recur
in conversation... (Bourget 1895: 51)

The elite's emphasis on Old Europe and Parisian gowns took on new
urgency in a milieu where new patterns of European immigration
were radically changing the demographic profile of the US. Between
1880–1920, Irish, German, and Scandinavian immigrants were joined
by a "new" and less welcome influx of southern Italians and Eastern
European Jews (Binder and Reimers 1995: 114–148).[5] In 1892, the
same year that saw the founding of *Vogue*, immigration authorities set
up New York's Ellis Island to filter the arrival of steerage passengers
through a single port. This immigration pattern is inseparable from
the development of the garment trades in New York and from the consistently anti-immigration and anti-mass-production stance adopted by
early *Vogue*.

Vogue's emphasis on imported European couture garments and sneering attitude toward cheap goods and labor concealed the fact that America's real fashion expertise lay in clothing its masses in inexpensive suits and workwear made from basic fabrics such as denim and calico. By the 1890s, half of the male population wore ready-made suits (Welters and Cunningham 2005: 2). In the womenswear sector, garment manufacture was concentrated in New York. *Vogue*'s celebration of its exclusive ties with French couture and English tailoring belies its dependence on the local products and expertise of immigrant retailers, tailors, and dressmakers. Many of these dressmakers and department store entrepreneurs had immigrated earlier in the century and were of German Jewish origin. They tended to employ more recently arrived Eastern European Jews in their workshops, and statistics show that by the turn of the century, Jews constituted three-quarters of the 300,000-strong labor force in the garment industry and six out of every ten Jewish workers earned their livelihood through the production of clothing (Binder and Reimers 1995: 122; Daniels 1990: 226).[6] Though these firms traded on their importation of "Parisian" models, couture gowns were often simply window dressing to draw in customers for garments copied from French models and made locally, with or without the authorization of the couturiers. As early as the late 1880s, there was a market for counterfeit couture dresses from the Parisian House of Worth and when Paul Poiret arrived in the US for a promotional tour in 1913, he was "astonished" to see shop windows filled with "Poiret" gowns, which he had not designed (Troy 2003: 25, 232–3). Though the editorial copy of *Vogue* stresses its internationalism, its advertisements reveal its local roots. The firms advertised are all based in New York, which was increasingly becoming a center for high-end womenswear production. In 1899, 65 percent of the total value of American-made womenswear was produced in New York, while by 1925, the total had reached an astonishing 78 percent (Green 1997: 48).

In its first decade, *Vogue* deliberately turned a blind eye to all but the uppermost echelons of the garment trade at its back door, in part because it considered itself more of a social gazette than a trade paper. While Turnure's proclamation in the first issue stresses the "progressive" meritocracy of American society, he also clearly calls for a reinforcement of class boundaries, boundaries that by definition had ethnic connotations. In an 1897 editorial, *Vogue* criticized "sentimentalists" who opposed restrictions on immigration and suggested that the US should no longer be the "refuge of all the oppressed peoples of the world":

> The lot of those whose lives are unhappily cast in the countries of Europe, (where, between overpopulation and grinding taxation, the poorer classes hopelessly struggle for bare existence), is truly deplorable; but, after all, that is a matter for which nature and their governments are responsible and however philanthropic

even a rich nation like the United States may be, it cannot under-
take to protect all nationalities from the inevitable effects of their
own folly in bringing into the world ten mouths when there is
sufficient food for but one; nor can we set up an asylum for all
peoples who are oppressed by their governments (*Vogue*, January
7, 1897: n.p.).

This text suggests not only concern over uncontrolled population
growth amongst the poorest populations of immigrants but a fear that
these oppressed people would neither understand nor respect American
forms of democratic government. Later, more specifically anti-Semitic
editorials were to single out Jewish men as "immigrant shirks" who,
unlike true Americans, sent their women to work outside the home
(American *Vogue*, August 10, 1905: n.p.).[7] *Vogue*'s scorn of New York's
immigrant populations masked the city's reliance on the expertise of
certain segments of this very population for its economic profitability in
the garment trades, especially in high-end womenswear production. A
study of the geographical migrations of *Vogue* headquarters demonstrates
that the publication tried to divorce itself from any associations with
mass-production and garment manufacture in Manhattan.

Vogue Moves Uptown

Vogue's attitude toward "new" Americans must be seen in the context of
geographical shifts in late nineteenth-century Manhattan. Using the tools
of mapping and cultural geography, this section considers the changing
locations of *Vogue* headquarters from 1892–1929. When examining
the migrations of the *Vogue* offices during its first few decades, it becomes clear that its movements were tied to shifting patterns in both
the manufacturing and retailing sectors. Though *Vogue* headquarters
were always situated in fashionable retail districts, before 1910 these
districts were never far from the sites of garment production, which
were moving northward and turning increasingly toward high-end
womenswear production.

The magazine's first home was just north of Union Square, which
at that time formed part of elegant New York's shopping district. This
area was popularly known as Ladies' Mile and compared to similar
areas in European capitals, including the Rue de la Paix in Paris and
Regent Street in London. It was bordered by 14th Street to the south,
23rd Street to the north, Sixth Avenue to the west and Broadway to
the east. It was also in close proximity to, but not surrounded by, the
garment district at that time, which was concentrated below 14th Street
on the Lower East Side (just east of Broadway) until the early twentieth
century (Rantisi 2004: 90). As wealthy residents of New York moved
uptown (northward), the luxury retail trade followed them and garment

manufacturers began to move northward and westward, occupying the Ladies' Mile, which was becoming somewhat more down-at-the-heels in the first decade of the twentieth century. Elegant shops moved to the 30s, 40s, and even 50s along Fifth Avenue, which replaced Broadway as an opulent shopping street (Milbank 1989: 62). *Vogue* followed this trend, moving northward up to 29th Street and Fifth Avenue by 1901 and all the way up to 34th Street and Fifth Avenue between 1902–4. It followed a similar trajectory to one of *Vogue*'s important early advertisers, the firm of B. Altman. Benjamin Altman began his career in the heart of the garment district in 1864 and moved northward from Third avenue and 10th Street to Sixth Avenue and 18th Street in the early 1870s, then in 1876 he moved into new premises on the western border of fashionable Ladies' Mile at Sixth Avenue and 21st Street. He stayed there for thirty years, but when high-end retail moved ever further uptown, he relocated in 1906 to a renaissance building occupying an entire city block at 34th Street and Fifth.[8]

In 1905, a need for more office space sent *Vogue* back southward into one of the new "skyscrapers" being erected in downtown New York: the seventeen-floor marble Aeolian building at the busy intersection between Fifth Avenue, Broadway, 23rd Street and Madison Square. By this time, *Vogue* would have found many of its advertisers had deserted this formerly elite shopping district and the garment district was beginning to encroach on these retail spaces, now occupying loft spaces in midtown Manhattan. In reaction, commercial interests tried to stop the "invasion" of sewing machines and to "segregate" retail from the manufacturing trade. By 1913, the Fifth Avenue Association, composed of retailers, hoteliers, and other property owners, was lobbying for a sweatshop-free zone in midtown Manhattan (Green 1992: 226). As if to remove it from the taint of manufacture, in 1911 Condé Nast made the biggest move that *Vogue* had yet seen, taking his flagship magazine twenty-six city blocks northward to 49th Street, thus geographically distancing it from the orbit of the garment trades. It was never to descend below 42nd Street again, but remained in the newly elegant areas surrounding Fifth Avenue, firmly allying itself with the retail and advertising sectors.[9]

Consumption, Class, and Gender in Early *Vogue*

This physical mapping of *Vogue* is inseparable from the magazine's ideological response to shifting concepts of gender and class in the 1890s. American elites, whose taste had been formed during the second half of the nineteenth century, looked back with longing to France and its aristocratic traditions in architecture, fashion, and décor. Yet among the broader base of American society there had always been resistance to this servile imitation of French fashions, which were censured for being undemocratic and inherently un-American. Socialist communities had long favored versions of "authentic" American reform dress. The notorious trousered Bloomer costume is but one example of the garments imagined by women living in mid-nineteenth-century America. Though it was worn only by a brave few, it embodied the principles of class and gender equality (Fischer 2001). In 1856, the journalist Mary Fry called for a form of American costume that would challenge French supremacy. In "Let Us Have a National Costume," published in *The Ladies' Repository*, she wrote:

> In matters of dress the French took the lead, and the rest of the enlightened world, regardless of health, climate, comfort, or even modesty, acquiesced in all humility… But all must see that it is at war with our form of government, to be dependent on the nod of a foreign aristocracy for the form and material of our dress. (Fry in Johnson, Torntore and Eicher 2003: 79)

Her criticism is directed at what she calls the "exclusive class" who spent money gained through American entrepreneurship during the gold rush on ruinously expensive imported fashions rather on than fostering national industry. A truly "national costume" would not only promote patriotism and the American economy, but efface the distinctive sartorial practices of different classes and ethnic groups, dress practices which marked them out visually from their peers. While the term "melting pot" was not coined until Israel Zangwill's play of 1908, mass-produced American design marketed commodities around Anglo-Saxon ideals of the hygienic, comfortable, and efficient body (Forty 1986: 244). In fashion design, this emphasis on streamlined practicality even begins to find its way into elite constructions of femininity at the *fin de siècle*.

Although the women of American high society found it desirable to travel to the fashion houses of London and Paris for their gowns if they could afford the expense, the consumption practices of this exclusive or "leisure class" as defined by Thorstein Veblen in his *Theory of the Leisure Class* (1899) cannot be mapped unproblematically onto the readership of early *Vogue*. While many members of the first editorial board belonged to the well-heeled and flamboyantly leisured ranks of yacht racers, polo players and foxhunters, nineteenth-century women had a more complex role as bearers of class status through fashionability than Veblen's theories would suggest.

As Rebecca Kelly argues, many of the generation of debutantes who were in their youth in the 1890s were raised in the context of the college-educated New Woman and absorbed the lessons of dress reform movements. Dedication to the principles of these movements, which included wearing clothing that was light, comfortable, and hygienic, meant no longer slavishly following Parisian haute couture. Women's colleges in particular fostered classically informed ideals of healthful beauty and fashions designed according to rational principles (Cunningham 2003: 139). In a detailed case study of the fashion purchases of a Gilded Age mother and daughter, Kelly traces a nuanced story of generational differences in the consumption of female elites in the US of the late nineteenth century (Kelly 2005: 9–32). Ella King married in 1875 into a respectable old New England family. Her trousseau and subsequent wardrobe were acquired in Paris at the most expensive couture houses, including the famous Worth and Doucet. Her daughter Gwendolyn came out as a debutante in 1896 and belonged to the audience early *Vogue* sought to reach. Her Parisian wardrobes came instead from the couture houses of Raudnitz, Huet, and Chéruit, who catered to a more youthful clientele.

In Gwendolyn's married life, which coincided with the early years of the twentieth century, she began to favor more practical garb, including tailored suits. To her couture-clad mother's horror, she supplemented her wardrobe with American-made accessories and shirtwaists bought at New York department stores, such as Lord and Taylor, Wannamaker's and Altman's. This reliance on both European and American sources for an upper-class woman's wardrobe is reflected on the pages of early *Vogue*. Weekly features like "Smart Fashions for Limited Incomes" and advertisements for department stores hint at the New Woman's consumption practices and her desire for "value for money." Yet the many advertisements for New York-based milliners, tailors and furriers like Bergdorf & Voigt suggest the continued importance of the luxury trades in the city. At this period, when the Parisian gown still commanded cultural capital, retailers were careful to promote their imported fabrics, "French bonnets" and new stocks of "robes et manteaux." Despite the rhetoric of importation, the actual wardrobes of women like Gwendolyn King hint at a moment when mass-produced shirtwaists, sportswear, and streamlined styles became the hallmark of American women who valued comfort and practicality over "high" fashion. These new elites held more positive views regarding the convenience and affordability of mass-produced goods than their Knickerbocker or Old New England ancestors, who continued to privilege European luxury imports. The artwork and content of *Vogue* suggest additional ways in which traditional class and gender roles were being contested in 1890s America.

Vogue's Image

The magazine's first cover presented the publication in the guise of a young socialite. Its caption reads "*Vogue*—A Debutante." From its inception, *Vogue* magazine was embodied in the form of a youthful woman. By imagining her as a debutante, *Vogue* likened itself to a young, vulnerable but wealthy Anglo-Saxon Protestant woman, calling on its

readers to chaperone or squire her in their social circles. The content of
early *Vogue* was clearly aimed at both a male and female readership,
with popular columns such as "As Seen by Him" aimed at improving
American men's dress sense and social etiquette. The first years included
special issues on leisure-class pursuits like yachting, golfing, hunting,
and polo, but by 1895 the magazine was already becoming a more
feminized and specifically fashion-oriented publication.

While the "college girl" featured prominently in its pages, the magazine did not adopt a consistent position on gender roles during its
first decade. The content of *Vogue* at this time embodies increasingly
contradictory ideals of femininity in the late nineteenth century, which
saw a new breed of liberated, athletic "New Women" like Gwendolyn
King rub shoulders with a more traditional model of obedient, decorative
womanhood epitomized by a previous generation of late Victorians like
her mother Ella. *Vogue*'s content appealed to both audiences. In 1898
Vogue celebrated the "fitness of dress" espoused by the modern young
wearer of streamlined and practical "jackets and skirts," while other
editorials urged readers to remember that "ladies, without aspirations
along radical lines, or college educations, or conventions, or clubs"
should be "entitled to as much respect as their more brilliant latter-day
sisters" (American *Vogue*, February 7, 1895: n.p. and December 10,
1896: n.p.). Therefore *Vogue* aimed to cater to both modern women
confident in their American identity, and traditionally minded readers
eager for news of high fashion and elaborate ceremonial wear imported
from the Continent. The first published index hints at this wide spec-
trum of readers, featuring articles on "Social Topics—Independent
Careers and the Girl Graduate" and "Smart Fashions for Limited
Incomes" for younger or less well-off readers, rubbing shoulders with
"Paris Correspondence" and "Coiffures from Paris" (American *Vogue*,
July 2, 1896: n.p.). This multiplicity of voices is not surprising in a
magazine with a staff composed of a mixture of young male Ivy League
graduate writers and young women from more modest backgrounds,
like the future editor Edna Woolman Chase. She was typical of the
new population of working women flocking to New York to take up
clerical and sales posts, a self-proclaimed "country girl" with no college
education, who was eighteen in 1895 when she joined the staff of
Vogue in the lowly subscriptions department. She wrote: "I envied the
debutantes—I was their age—but I knew that I would never be one and
if I ever expected to have any money I must set about earning it" (Chase
1954: 4). She soon started writing fashion news and eventually, under
Condé Nast, was appointed to the magazine's editorship. Though she
was a complete outsider to the social circles she wrote about in *Vogue*'s
early years, Chase's common sense and humble background were to
prove instrumental in marketing the cachet and fashions of the leisured
classes to a broader audience of urban working women in the early
twentieth century.

Mass and Class Publications

At the time that *Vogue* was founded, a profound shift was taking place in the publishing world. In the 1890s, magazines began to rely on advertising as their primary source of income. While earlier periodicals generated revenue from subscription and newsstand sales, the new breed of mass publications actively solicited advertising dollars.[10] As a deliberately dilettantish "quality class" social gazette with a small circulation, *Vogue* still relied on its readers for its income. Despite the fact that they were charged four times as much for an annual subscription than the middle-class audience of the *Ladies' Home Journal*, the magazine frequently found itself in debt. The independent and opinionated tone of its early features on fashion and beauty highlight *Vogue*'s aloofness from the world of crass commercialism. For example, on January 11 and 18, 1894, *Vogue* published two dress models intended as an "Object Lesson for Stout Women." These texts and accompanying sketches offer fashion tips for clothing a short, wide body far from the lean, athletic ideal of the Gibson Girl of the late nineteenth century. Chase later wrote that: "Once Vogue showed two or three dresses for stout women, but we were so shaken by the experience that we haven't repeated it in fifty-seven years" (Chase 1954: 26). Another editorial attacks the false promises offered by the cosmetics industry: "Woman's skin is the source of much anguish of mind, torture of body, depletion of purse, and the occasion of much misplaced confidence on the one hand; and on the other a constant promoter of mendacity and quackery" (American *Vogue*, February 4, 1897: n.p.). This editorial criticizing women's use of beauty aids is unimaginable in twenty-first-century *Vogue*, yet despite these moments of revolt, *Vogue* was shifting its focus from social reportage to traditional elite fashion journalism. This process was accelerated under the stewardship of Condé Nast, who ushered in a new era of professionalism and international expansion.

Condé Nast and the Branding of *Vogue*

After Arthur Turnure died in 1906, the magazine went through a series of amateur hands from the magazine's original social circles. Condé Nast purchased *Vogue* in 1909, when it was a weekly black-and-white fashion publication with a readership of only 14,000. Its new proprietor had no practical experience of, and little interest, in the fashion trade except as a way of generating income. An American with French and German ancestry, Nast was a rising star in the publishing and advertising industries. He had already turned *Collier's Magazine* into a success and was ready to try his hand at new ventures. Nast bought the magazine largely because he was interested in *Vogue*'s pattern service, which sold paper patterns of the latest styles (Emery 1999:

242).[11] Pattern companies such as *Demorest*, *Butterick*, *McCall*'s and *Harper*'s were well established and most were tied to their own fashion publication (Emery 1999: 242). They were particularly popular in the US, where rapid expansion and geographical distance made it difficult for many women to keep up with fashion except by mail-order patterns and home dressmaking. Nast was also instrumental in modernizing the magazine. He brought it into line with other successful publishing ventures and in just over a decade, circulation went from 14,000 to 150,000 while advertising revenue soared from $76,111 to two million dollars (Robinson 1923: 170). With many new brands of cosmetics and slimming products advertised in its pages, the era of editorials featuring dresses for stout women and tirades against makeup was unfortunately over. Nast had harnessed *Vogue*'s upper-class cachet in order to market luxury goods such as imported perfumes and automobiles to a broader public. The social gazette that had once scorned mass immigration and manufacture had become a mass-produced commodity in its own right.

Vogue's Cover Girl

Condé Nast modernized other aspects of the magazine, including its graphic presentation. A year after he bought the magazine, he replaced the black-and-white line drawings and occasional photographs on its covers with commissioned, signed lavish full-color reproductions of painted illustrations to attract attention on the newsstands. As an advertising man, he understood the value of having a visual brand or logo and Nast revived the original *Vogue* trademark, a "distinguished little sketch" which "immediately became known as the *Vogue* girl. This design, or variations of it, is always associated with the publicity connected with the magazine" (Robinson 1923: 74). The *Vogue* girl was the creation of the first art director, Harry McVickar, a French-trained illustrator and clubman who belonged to New York's highest circles. Attired in a fancy-dress outfit with fashionable leg-of-mutton sleeves, the *Vogue* girl sported the letter "V" on her skirt and bodice, reinforcing her identity as the icon of the magazine. This use of images to promote brand names was becoming increasingly common in American commodity culture. In 1914, Edward Rodgers, a popularizer of new advertising techniques, explained that in the case of Baker's chocolate, twenty-five percent of women designated the product not by its name but by its packaging showing, "… 'the chocolate with the Quaker lady', 'with the Dutch lady', 'with the Puritan girl', or in some similar fashion" (Rodgers 1914: 69).

Like the Baker's chocolate icon who is alternately Quaker, Dutch or Puritan, readers could interpret the *Vogue* girl in different registers. Her nationality was deliberately ambiguous and she might be a French

Figure 2
Eighteenth-century *Vogue* girl. Color illustration by Frank Leyendecker. First appeared on the cover of American *Vogue* on March 1, 1911. This version was reproduced as the cover of British *Vogue*'s Spring Fashion Forecast number on February 1, 1917.

shepherdess or a young American woman dressed for a costume ball. The *Vogue* girl had appeared sporadically in the period from 1893–1908, but Nast moved her from the inside pages of the magazine to a starring role on its cover.

When Frank Leyendecker featured her on the cover of early March 1911, she was by no means a rank debutante (Figure 2). With Condé Nast's editorship, the *Vogue* girl began to appear frequently on and in *Vogue*. Earlier covers included Gale Porter Hoskins' vulnerable-looking waif of October 1909 and Harry Morse Meyers' version of March 1, 1910. However, Leyendecker's 1911 version was to prove the most popular and was adopted as the masthead until 1920.

By choosing the *Vogue* girl for its brand image, Nast made a direct appeal to upper-class readers' fantasies. Leyendecker's illustration embodies complex layers of historical revivalism. Her unearthly ivory skin, snow-white wig, tiny waist, voluptuous bosom, and elaborate dress belong to an impossibly feminine china figurine. She is a Watteau shepherdess come to life, though her actions retain the mechanical stiffness of a doll. She steps forward and raises her skirts to make a curtsey. She is stage-lit from below, and she casts a sly glance at her audience. Though she is richly attired in an eighteenth-century guise, she seems to make an obeisance to her audience, performing for their pleasure. She is *Vogue* magazine personified, metaphorically bowing down before her readers. Like the *Vogue* girl, fashion was unabashedly gendered feminine, as were the eighteenth century and rococo taste. Yet this seemingly innocuous candy-box figurine had specific class and ethnic connotations in an American context.

Eighteenth-century-inspired costumes were very popular in the US from the 1850s until the early twentieth century.[12] Dressing up in "colonial," loosely eighteenth-century outfits was most popular with elite New England Yankees. During the American Civil War, society women frequently dressed up as colonials for balls, fairs and charity kitchens to raise money for the Union army (Gordon 1993: 109–139).[13] While nouveaux riches invested a great deal of money in their costumes, it was even more prestigious to don an actual eighteenth-century or Empire gown passed down by one's ancestress. In an era when old New England families were increasingly interested in marking their difference from more recent immigrants and showy nouveaux riches, heirlooms allowed women to display their more ancient genealogical pedigrees and national identities on their bodies (Gordon 1993: 129). This fanaticism for historical costume continued into the twentieth century and the *Vogue* girl's ability to personify both the European "shepherdess" and the Yankee Lady made her a perfect signifier of both European cachet and American heritage.

In *Vogue*'s special Fancy Dress issue of December 1913, the author suggests that while Arabian Nights themes pioneered by Poiret were all the rage, Leyendecker's "Lady *Vogue*… [made] a charming model for her who would be an XVIII coquette" (American *Vogue*, December 15, 1913: 21–6).[14] She served as a pivot between Old World and New World fashions, when a socialite dressed up as the *Vogue* girl presided over *Vogue*'s "Fashion Fête" of American fashions held at the Ritz-Carlton in 1914, in 'the exquisite panniered costume' drawn from Leyendecker's illustration (Chase 1954: 106). This fashion show, the first to feature the creations of American designers, was organized at a moment when *Vogue* feared that the outbreak of World War I would cut off New York's supplies of French couture designs. It also marks the moment when American fashion began to assume increasing importance on the pages of *Vogue*. The following year, pressure from outraged Parisian

Figure 3
Miss Miriam Sears playing the role of Leyendecker's *Vogue* girl. American *Vogue*, August 15, 1917.

(Left) Miss Miriam Sears, daughter of Mr. Richard D. Sears, appeared as the Leyendecker Vogue Girl. The Vogue Girl and her six attendant Vogue covers were the treasure sought throughout the play

couturiers prompted *Vogue* to stage a similar, if apparently less successful "French Fashion Fête" in order to smooth ruffled feathers.

The *Vogue* girl's popularity endured throughout the nineteen teens, as the 1917 Boston performance of a play for charity called *Pleasure Island* suggests. In *Pleasure Island*, society ladies and their daughters dressed up to present *tableaux vivants* of famous *Vogue* covers. Leyendecker's theatrical cover girl made a perfect star in the colonial charity mode. She was played by a white-wigged Miss Miriam Sears, who was photographed curtseying, like the original, for the pages of the magazine (Figure 3). Few young women of the period had the economic means to dress up in such a fanciful costume, and this image operates both as an assertion of the upper-class status of its readers and as a perfect opportunity to reiterate the cachet of its brand through the now well-established image of the *Vogue* girl.

The Ascendancy of New York and the Demise of the *Vogue* Girl

Like any magazine dedicated to changing styles, the *Vogue* girl had to keep up with the times and she was refashioned during the late nineteen teens and twenties. From the Frenchified American taste expressed by Leyendecker's work, *Vogue* now turned to French illustrators such as Georges Lepape for many of its covers. Lepape's *Vogue* girl of September 15, 1920 ushered in a new decade of streamlined design and dress. (Figure 4) The *Vogue* girl had changed her image: she was no longer a

Figure 4
Modern *Vogue* girl. Color
illustration by Georges Lepape,
American *Vogue*, September
15, 1920.

mincing fantasy of the past but a resolutely contemporary woman at the
height of 1920s fashion.

Part of this shift can be explained by the increasing internationalism
and cultural imperialism of the magazine itself. *Vogue* had gone from
being an importer to an exporter of fashion news. Nast not only launched
a British edition in 1916, but in 1920 purchased and started publishing
an American version of Lucien Vogel's luxury French magazine, the
Gazette du Bon Ton. He also renamed and launched the *Jardin des
Modes* in Paris (Seebohm 1982: 133–4). While *Vogue* still bowed down
to French fashion artistry in its selection of a French illustrator for the
cover, the issue's contents in the 1920s show a decided shift toward

Figure 5

Thirtieth anniversary cover. Color illustration by Georges Lepape and Pierre Brissaud, American *Vogue*, February 1, 1923.

coverage of New York's own fashions and designers. This bias toward local industry reflects anti-European sentiment in the wake of the World War I.

The increasing emphasis on American fashions coincided with *Vogue*'s thirtieth birthday, when it published its most comprehensive anniversary edition (Figure 5). It appeared in the US on January 1, 1923, on February 1 in the UK and March 1 in France. The cover shows Leyendecker's *Vogue* girl descending from the heavens in a stylish apotheosis. The original debutante, Miss 1892, and a short-skirted, bobbed Miss 1922, offer her a cake topped with thirty candles. However, this issue also marks the decline in the use of the *Vogue* girl as a suitable logo. Like Ladies' Mile before her, Lady *Vogue* was being sullied by the encroachment of manufacturers.

Soon after Nast had assumed the editorship, the masthead proclaimed that the magazine was copyrighted and registered in the US patent office. He reminded readers that the *Vogue* Company was responsible only for the publication itself and *Vogue* Dress Patterns, and had not dirtied its hands in the commercial fray of manufacturing and merchandising (American *Vogue*, November 15, 1914: 51). This was his response to the increasing piracy of the magazine's name and artwork. In the 1920s clothing companies continued to steal the *Vogue* brand name in order to sell their products. In 1924, *Vogue* took the hatmakers Thompson-Hudson to court for using not only the name "vogue" for their hat labels, but the capital letter "V" and the "V-Girl" as well. *Vogue* lost the case: the courts saw it not as unfair competition but as "healthy growth." *Vogue* did not itself make hats, therefore the hatmaker was not in direct competition for clients with the magazine. Its use of the image did not make the plaintiff any poorer (*Columbia Law Review* 1925: 199–204). This lack of protection against those who appropriated the "V-Girl" symbol may have convinced *Vogue* to drop her as a symbol, though other factors certainly contributed. While reportage on the latest Paris fashions continued to play an important role in the magazine's copy, New York assumed a new confidence in itself as a center of art, culture, fashion, and finance in the 1920s. At the same time, the face of the New York garment industry was changing. While the production of workwear and menswear was relocated to other cities during the 1920s, the costliest lines of womenswear were increasingly designed and manufactured in New York. This high-end ready-to-wear transformed the consumption practices of female elites. Even Bergdorf Goodman, who specialized in custom-made clothing, started to sell ready-made goods in the 1920s (Green 1997: 47). In response to changes in upper-end manufacturing and the retail landscape of America's fashion capital, well-heeled female consumers in the 1920s often spurned the sartorial rituals of their mothers and grandmothers, who had flocked to Europe to fashion themselves into an elite. For this new generation, who embraced the convenience of mass-produced goods, a trip to the Paris couture houses was no longer an obligatory rite of passage. The simplified, easily reproduced styles and comfortable sportswear preferred by many young women in the 1920s have come to typify American fashion in the twentieth century. Designs by Donna Karan, Calvin Klein, and Ralph Lauren epitomize the "comforting but conservative inclusiveness" of styles which seek to reconcile fractured New World identities under the heading of "Americanness" (Breward 2003: 205). They deliberately gloss over the class and ethnic distinctions that early *Vogue* was so keen to reinforce.

Figure 6
Hundredth anniversary cover.
Color photograph by Patrick
Demarchelier, American *Vogue*,
April 1992.

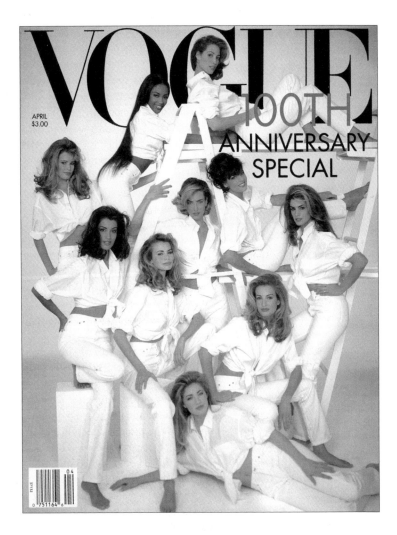

Hundredth Anniversary Issue

In the century since its debut, Vogue has thoroughly embraced American
fashion. *Vogue*'s hundredth anniversary issue was published in April
1992. Fashion illustration had long since disappeared from the covers
of American *Vogue* and the eighteenth-century coquette did not feature
at all in the magazine's self-commemoration. However, the *Vogue* girl
had been replaced by an even more potent embodiment of idealized
femininity, the supermodel or, in this case, supermodels (Figure 6). On its
anniversary cover, *Vogue* featured the ten most important supermodels
of the 1990s, each one presumably representing a decade of the magazine's existence. These were Naomi Campbell, Cindy Crawford, Linda
Evangelista, Yasmeen Ghauri, Elaine Irwin, Karen Mulder, Tatjana

Patitz, Claudia Schiffer, Niki Taylor, and Christy Turlington. Though the photographer who orchestrated the shoot, Patrick Demarchelier, was French, six of the models were born in North America. They perch on the planks and ladders in white shirts and jeans, their poses on this informal scaffolding more reminiscent of a construction worker's fantasy than a socialite's ball. Though this image stresses the casual simplicity of American fashion, gathering these international queens of the runway together for a fashion shoot was "a logistical nightmare" which took three months of meshing schedules (American *Vogue*, April 1992: 138). Booking the models, of course, cost more than supplying them with the inexpensive clothing on their backs. While *Vogue* claims to be showing the "newest way" of wearing a great American classic by tying the shirts at the waist, the fashions are by Gap, one of the most popular and populist of clothing companies. The models are carbon copies wearing identical outfits that could be purchased by anyone at one of Gap's its 3,000 stores worldwide. This lack of individualism would have horrified the Manhattan elite of a century ago, who sought out exclusive and exotic attire to reinforce their social status.

By 1992, *Vogue* was celebrating the homegrown tradition of mass-produced, androgynous, generic jeans and plain cotton shirts manu-factured in standardized sizes, over the traditional Parisian model of feminine luxury, clothed in silk satin and chiffon. Yet despite its global branding, *Vogue*, like the US itself, has always been a cultural hybrid, combining European and American esthetics while concealing the conditions and sites of the manufacture of its commodities. This cover reunites the artistic direction of a French fashion photographer with a product designed in New York and most likely manufactured abroad in Latin American or Asian sweatshops. In contemporary America, status is defined and produced by a new kind of celebrity generated by fashion's image and merchandising sectors. This hundredth anniversary cover reflects the increasingly global scale of geographical and economic divisions separating the design, marketing, and manufacturing of fash-ion while bringing it under the ever-expanding aegis of Condé Nast's publishing empire.

In 1992, the year *Vogue* celebrated its hundredth anniversary, Gap became the second-largest selling apparel brand in the world (Milestones, www.gapinc.com). It is now common to see Gap advertisements on the pages of international editions of *Vogue*. The presence of Gap on the pages of *Vogue* exemplifies the homogenizing sociopolitical force of twentieth-century American design, which has deliberately effaced structural inequalities of geography, class, and race (Forty 1986: 245). In its first three decades, *Vogue* played an increasingly central role in promoting this ongoing process in the field of fashion. The period from 1892–1923 saw *Vogue* headquarters relocate from downtown to uptown Manhattan, a move that took it farther from centers of garment production and immigration. At the same time, its cover design (as embodied in the radically different *Vogue* girls of Leyendecker and Lepape), its editorial content, and its advertising policies evolved considerably. From an amateur, Eurocentric social gazette that focused on fantasies of the colonial past, *Vogue* became a professional, self-confident mass-circulation magazine with its gaze resolutely fixed on a modern, streamlined American future.

Acknowledgments

Unless otherwise stated, all quotes are from the American edition of *Vogue*. This article is dedicated to my mother, Julia Matthews, for her indefatigable help in locating the earliest *Vogues*. Janine Button provided cheerful and invaluable assistance at the *Vogue* archive in London and I wish to thank Lara Perry, Lesley Miller, Carrie Lambert, Kristin Schwain, Wayne Morgan, Cynthia Cooper, Eric Segal, Jonathan White, Hilary Davidson, Irene Wu, Line Christensen, and Becky Conekin for their help and suggestions.

Notes

1. Chase states that it was the first editor, Mrs. Redding, who chose this title for the magazine while leafing through the pages of the dictionary (Chase 1954: 27).
2. See for example the galleon in the March 4, 1893 issue, flying a banner from its mast with "Vogue la galère!" or "Come what may!" inscribed upon it, the special "Yachting Number" of 24 June, 1893 and the nautical cover of 27 August, 1896 for one of the many examples of maritime-themed illustrations.
3. In this constantly changing world, *Vogue* positions itself as the navigator, the ancient mariner who charts these treacherous seas for the benefit of its less experienced passengers and brings them the wisdom of his experience.
4. Though early Dutch and British immigrants from the seventeenth and eighteenth centuries had assumed social prominence by the late nineteenth century, most of the original immigrants had come from humble stock and the majority were farmers, soldiers, and craftsmen (Binder and Reimers 1995: 13).
5. See "Jews and Italians in Greater New York City, 1880 to World War I" in Binder and Reimers 1995: 114–148.
6. Ten percent of skilled Eastern European immigrants may have been tailors, though immigrants no doubt knew that this was one of the trades which would help them gain admittance to the country at Ellis Island.

7. Another article from the same year stresses the impossibility and undesirability of social equality in America. It opposes teaching needless social "accomplishments" to the working classes in public schools. See "Impossible Democracy," American *Vogue*, October 26: 1905 (n.p.).

8. B. Altman Dry Goods Store, www.nyc-architecture.com.

9. *Vogue*'s current headquarters at 43rd and seventh Avenue, now renamed Fashion Avenue, finds it once again just north of New York's contemporary garment district, which works largely in pattern- and sample-making for the high-end market, and outsources much of cutting and sewing to outlying boroughs or overseas (Rantisi 2004: 101).

10. *The Ladies' Home Journal* may have been the first magazine to use different cover illustrations with each issue and cleverly interspersed advertising with editorial content instead of placing it at the beginning and end (Ohmann 1996: 28 and Schneirov 1994).

11. *Vogue*'s issue of February 20, 1901 printed a photograph of its patterns salesroom and cordially invited its "patrons to visit the Pattern Room" to view its model spring and summer patterns. The salesroom was located at 3, West 29th Street.

12. They appear in publications such as *Weldon's Practical Fancy Dress* as Dolly Varden, Dresden or Watteau Shepherdess outfits. For wonderful Victorian versions of eighteenth-century fancy dress see Cooper 1997.

13. These theatrical events were extremely popular and attracted large audiences, though the actors tended to come from social elites, while uncostumed audiences admired the lavish dress worn by their local leaders. One reporter sarcastically remarked that a dozen of the gowns worn at one charity event cost more than the net profits of the evening (Gordon 1993: 109–139).

14. Also suggested is a "*Vogue* girl" with five Vs pinned to her costume and "her great-grandmother" Lady *Vogue* painted on her petticoat in a rather fantastic interpretation of genealogy (Rittenhouse 1913: 21-26).

15. Although Gap headquarters is located in San Francisco, its design teams are based in New York. It is careful to point out that it is an "apparel retailer" rather than a "garment manufacturer."

References

American *Vogue*. 1892. Vol. 1, No. 1, December 17.

American *Vogue*. 1897. January 7.

"Appropriation of Trade Symbols by Noncompetitors," *Columbia Law Review* xxv: 199–204.

Beetham, M. 1996. *A Magazine of Her Own? Domesticity and Desire in the Woman's Magazine, 1800–1914*. London: Routledge.

Binder, Frederick and David Reimers. 1995. *All the Nations Under Heaven: An Ethnic and Racial History of New York City*. New York: Columbia University Press.

Bourget, P. 1895. *Outre-Mer: Impressions of America*. London: T. Fisher Unwin.

Breward, C. 2003. *Fashion*. Oxford: Oxford University Press.

—— 2004. *Fashioning London*, Oxford: Berg.

Bruzzi, Stella and Pamela Church Gibson. 2000. *Fashion Cultures: Theories, Explanations and Analysis*. London: Routledge.

Carter, M. 2003. *Fashion Classics from Carlyle to Barthes*. Oxford: Berg.

Chase E. W. and I. 1954. *Always in Vogue*. London: Victor Gollancz.

Cooper, C. 1997. *Magnificent Entertainments: Fancy Dress Balls of Canada's Governors General, 1876–1898*. Hull: CMC.

Crane, D. 2000. *Fashion and Its Social Agendas*. Chicago: Chicago University Press.

Cunningham, P. 2003. *Politics, Health and Art: Reforming Women's Fashion, 1850–1920*. Kent: Kent State University Press.

Daniels, Roger. 1990. *Coming To America: A History of Immigration and Ethnicity in American Life*. New York: Harper Collins.

Emery, J. 1999. "Dreams on Paper: A Story of the Commercial Pattern Industry," in B. Burman (ed.), *The Culture of Sewing*, pp. 235-253. Oxford: Berg.

Féraud, J.-F. 1787–8. *Dictionaire critique de la langue française*. Marseille: n.p.

Fischer, G. 2001. *Pantaloons and Power: Nineteenth-Century Dress Reform in the United States*. Kent: Kent State University Press.

Forty, A. 1986. *Objects of Desire: Design and Society, 1750–1980*. London: Thames and Hudson.

Fry, M. 2003. "Let Us Have a National Costume," in Kim Johnson, Susan Torntore and Joanne Eicher (eds). *Fashion Foundations: Early Writings on Fashion and Dress*, pp. 77–81. Oxford: Berg.

Green, N. 1992. "Sweatshop Migrations: The Garment Industry Between Home and Shop," in David Ward and Oliver Zunz (eds), *The Landscape of Modernity: New York City, 1900–1940*, pp. 213–32. Baltimore: Johns Hopkins University Press.

—— 1997. *Ready-to-Wear and Ready-to-Work*. Durham: Duke University Press.

Gordon, B. 1993. "Dressing the Colonial Past: Nineteenth-Century New Englanders Look Back," in Susan Voso Lab and Patricia Cunningham (eds), *Dress in American Culture*, pp. 109–139. Bowling Green: Bowling Green State University Press.

"Immigrant Shirks." 1905. American *Vogue*, August 10.

Jobling, P. 1999. *Fashion Spreads: Word and Image in Fashion Photography since 1980.* Oxford: Berg.

Kawamura, Y. 2004. *Fashion-ology.* Oxford: Berg.

Kelly, R. 2005. "Fashion in the Gilded Age: A Profile of Newport's King Family," in L. Welters and Patricia Cunningham (eds), *Twentieth-Century American Fashion,* pp. 9–32. Oxford: Berg.

Kitch, C. 2001. *The Girl on the Magazine Cover: The Origins of Visual Stereotypes in the American Mass Media.* Chapel Hill: University of North Carolina.

Milbank, C. 1989. *New York Fashion: The Evolution of American Style.* New York: Harry N. Abrams.

Nast, C. 1915. "To Protect Vogue's Originality," *Vogue,* November 15: 51.

Ohmann, R. 1996. *Selling Culture: Magazines, Markets and Class at the Turn of the Century.* London: Verso.

Rantisi, N. 2004. "The Ascendance of New York Fashion," *International Journal of Urban and Regional Research* 28 (1): 86–106.

Rittenhouse, A. 1913. "On with the Masque!" *Vogue,* December 15: 21–26.

Robinson, Walter, 1923. "And Now the Makers of Vogue: The First Thirty Years," *Vogue,* January 1: 74–77; 166; 170.

Rodgers, E. 1914. *Good Will, Trade Marks and Unfair Trading.* Chicago: A.W. Shaw.

Seebohm, C. 1982. *The Man Who Was Vogue.* London: Weidenfeld and Nicolson.

Schneirov, M. 1994. *The Dream of a New Social Order: Popular Magazines in America, 1893–1914.* New York: Columbia University Press.

"The Next Four Numbers of *Vogue,*" 1916. British Vogue, September 15: contents page.

Troy, N. 2003. *Couture Culture.* Cambridge, MA: MIT.

Welters, Linda and Patricia Cunningham. 2005. *Twentieth-Century American Fashion.* Oxford: Berg.

Fashion Theory, Volume 10, Issue 1/2, pp. 39–72
Reprints available directly from the Publishers.
Photocopying permitted by licence only.
© 2006 Berg.

A *Vogue* That Dare Not Speak its Name: Sexual Subculture During the Editorship of Dorothy Todd, 1922–26

Christopher Reed

Christopher Reed is Chair of the Art Department at Lake Forest College. His books are *A Roger Fry Reader*, the anthology *Not at Home: The Suppression of Domesticity in Modern Art and Architecture* (both 1996), and *Bloomsbury Rooms: Modernism, Subculture, and Domesticity* (2004). He has also published widely on issues of sexual identity and contemporary art and design.
reed@ifc.edu

We sat in the meadow and discussed the future of Miss Todd... [S]he has got the sack from *Vogue*, which, owing to being too highbrow, is sinking in circulation... Nast, when threatened with an action [for breach of contract], retorted that he would defend himself by attacking Todd's morals. So poor Todd is silenced since her morals are of the classic rather than the conventional order.

> Vita Sackville-West to Harold Nicolson, September 24, 1926, describing a visit with Virginia Woolf (in Luckhurst, *Bloomsbury in Vogue*)

When Miss Todd came to see, us, when Miss Todd came to see, us,
when Miss Todd came to see, us.
When Miss Todd came to see us.
Who need never be mentioned.

Gertrude Stein, A Novel of Thank You[1]

Discussed, silenced, never mentioned again: this sequence of attitudes almost too perfectly encapsulates the view from the "highbrows"—novelists, poets, and artists—toward Dorothy Todd, the remarkable editor of British *Vogue* between 1922 and 1926. Subsequent scholarship, by exaggerating and reifying the perspectives of brows high and low, has only deepened the silence. Too posh for social historians, too popular for specialists in literature and art, Dorothy Todd's *Vogue* has slipped from critical view, overlooked altogether or obscured in condescending stereotypes about fashion magazines. Perhaps she brought it on herself. Failure has few friends, and Dorothy Todd ultimately failed in her ambitious effort to create a magazine that broke the boundaries that protected (and still, to a large extent, protect) art from fashion, intellectuals from popular culture, masculinity from femininity, and heteronormativity from queerness of all kinds.

The quick history of Dorothy Todd's involvement in British *Vogue* is this. In 1916, *Vogue* publisher Condé Nast, faced with American paper shortages and restrictions on overseas shipping caused by World War I, initiated a British edition, which his New York staffers called, after the truncated name used in overseas cable communications, "*Brogue*." Appointed *Brogue*'s first editor, Todd was removed to Nast's headquarters for six years so that, in the words of her powerful New York counterpart, Edna Woolman Chase, "she might acquaint herself more thoroughly with our policies and format" (Chase 1954: 151). But the submission of Todd's *Brogue* to the accents of New York's *Vogue* did not go according to plan. Chase's memoir, *Always in Vogue*, describes with surprised dismay how a "literary and artistic bent" made "Dorothy," on her return to London in 1922, take to the "super-civilized, exotic, somewhat self-conscious milieu" of Bloomsbury "like a duck to water" (1954: 151). Acknowledging that during Todd's era, "many distinguished members of what was widely referred to as the 'inkyllectuals' appeared in British *Vogue*," Chase cancels this dubious accomplishment with the pronouncement: "Fashion Miss Todd [she is no longer Dorothy] all but eschewed, and our service features—Seen in the Shops, Smart Fashions for Limited Incomes, the Hostess and Beauty articles—were given short shrift" (1954: 151-2). "The atmosphere she created was lofty and she was browsing happily in rich pasture," Chase concludes, "unfortunately from our point of view, it was the wrong one" (1954: 152). Todd was fired in 1926 and Chase, by her own account, dissuaded Nast from closing British *Vogue* only by installing herself at the helm to "get our British edition back into the *Vogue* formula" (152). The limited historical commentary on this episode has followed Chase's autobiography, attributing Todd's determination to make British *Vogue* an avant-garde forum to the quirks of her personality, and adding, as if they were unrelated data, the claim that, "The morally rigorous Mrs. Chase also disapproved strongly of Miss Todd's personal proclivities, which were overtly homosexual" (Seebohm 1982 125) and the point that British *Vogue* under Todd's editorship adopted many attributes of *Vogue*'s rival within Condé Nast's New York headquarters, *Vanity Fair*. This essay's exploration of the "rich pasture" where Todd trespassed starts by recognizing it as the point where these apparent tangents intersect.

My focus on the relationship between what scholars characterize as Todd's "transformation of Condé Nast's product—a women's magazine whose staple elements were high society, the rich and famous, plus high fashion—into a review for the *avant-garde*" and accounts of her appearance as "a short, square, crop-headed, double-breasted, bow-tied lady" (Luckhurst 1998: 3) clearly raises broad issues of gender and sexuality, class and mass culture, and the relationship of all these to definitions of modernity in the 1920s. The intervening eighty years have imposed (to maintain the pasture metaphor) thick sediments of cliché and presumption over the rich soil of the 1920s, a remarkably inventive era when the hierarchies now associated with modernism had yet to acquire their authority. To attempt to return to the 1920s on its own terms is to discover a culture flourishing with many of the transgressive pleasures—of wit, mass culture, self-conscious performativity—that post-modernism later claimed for itself in contrast to the ossified modernism of the intervening years.

This case has been made in relation to *Vanity Fair*, which from 1914 to 1936 embodied the style of what might be called the long 1920s. Challenging the myth that modernism held itself always above the taint of commerce, Michael Murphy argues that, although *Vanity Fair* "*became* modernism for many of its readers," their experience "was most evocative of precisely the qualities that current critical convention asks us to *dissociate* from modernism" (1996: 64). Our attitude, Murphy says, is "not only a crude underestimation of the past," but, in assuming that postmodernists "have now all learned to deal with the problems of art's commodification in duly sophisticated and enlightened ways,… also implies a dangerous overestimation of the present" (1996: 66). To appreciate what Todd attempted at British *Vogue*, therefore, one might begin with the models for modern magazines she encountered in Condé Nast's New York offices around 1920.

In 1913, Nast, who had made *Vogue* a thriving business since acquiring it in 1909, bought *Dress*, a competing fashion magazine for women, and *Vanity Fair*, a failing Broadway gossip sheet. A few issues of his new combined journal struggled under the title of *Dress and Vanity*

Fair, but when Nast hired Frank Crowninshield, the art editor of *The Century*, who had earned an avant-garde reputation by defending the modern art in the 1913 Armory Show, the new editor shortened the title, dropped women's fashions, and remade *Vanity Fair* as a magazine that he promised Nast would "cover the things people talk about at parties—the arts, sports, theater, humor, and so forth" (in Amory and Bradlee 1960: 7). By the time Dorothy Todd arrived for training in New York, *Vanity Fair*'s self-described "cheerful" blend of saucy cartoons, modern graphics, poems by the likes of Djuna Barnes and Gertrude Stein, articles on avant-garde music, art, and literature, along with regular features on theater, cars, golf, and men's fashions, had made it the preeminent journal for and about the American avant-garde and its patrons. Although it could never challenge *Vogue*'s consistently huge profits, *Vanity Fair* quickly became Condé Nast's most prestigious title.

   The rivalry between *Vogue* and *Vanity Fair* is exemplified in the career of another notable Condé Nast employee named Dorothy, who overlapped with Todd's time in New York. Dorothy Rothschild, better known as Dorothy Parker, was hired by *Vogue* in 1915. By 1917, however, her irreverent articles on "Interior Desecration" and photo captions like "Brevity is the Soul of Lingerie" had revealed, as Crowninshield put it, that "fashion would never become a religion with her." The result was that "Mrs. Chase, the Editor of Vogue, turned her over to my tender care" (Crowninshield 1944: 197). Crowninshield recalled that Parker "also confessed to having been a little overawed by the nobility of the language used by the *Vogue* Editors. 'To whom should one properly address oneself for towels?' 'How could Mrs. Astor think chinchilla appropriate for mourning?'" (1944: 197). In contrast, Crowninshield, a bachelor who enjoyed tweaking Chase's refined sensibilities, noted proudly that Parker thrived amid "the diversified and unpredictable goings on... at *Vanity Fair*," which he described as "a combined club, vocal studio, crap game, dance-hall, sleeping lounge, and snack bar (to make no mention of derisive whistlings, paper darts, and charades)" (1944: 201).[2] It was during this period that the raucous literary lunches enjoyed by Parker and her *Vanity Fair* colleagues made famous the so-called Round Table at the Algonquin Hotel restaurant down the street from Condé Nast's headquarters.

   Contrasts between the stuffy propriety of *Vogue* and the high jinks at *Vanity Fair* were strongly inflected by gender, though these dynamics were more complex than a simple opposition of conventional femininity and masculinity. Chase's grandiose propriety, so easy for her *Vanity Fair* counterparts to mock, only partially masked her enormous ambition and superior business acumen. Equally ambivalently, *Vanity Fair*'s avant-garde attitude was not the machismo of Hemingway's novels, Mies van der Rohe's buildings, or other manifestations of what became canonic modernism, but rather the modernist subcurrent I have called—drawing terminology from British writings about interior design in the

1920s in *Vogue* among other sources—the "Amusing Style" (C. Reed 2004: 236–37). Closely related to the phenomenon Ann Douglas calls —after Dorothy Parker—"mongrel Manhattan" (1995: 5), this critic-ally neglected mode of modernism developed within burgeoning urban subcultures: the racial mixing of jazz clubs, the gender mixing of boyish flappers and their androgynous consorts, the "camp" mixing of high and low associated with homosexuals.[3] Parker's feature on "Interior Desecration" riled *Vogue*'s advertisers and flustered Chase with allu-sions to hysterical, effeminate interior decorators (Meade 1988: 42), but such references were welcome at *Vanity Fair*, where Crowninshield encouraged Parker's production of blank-verse "Hate Songs" that skewered, among other current phenomena, the young men she called "Sensitive Souls":

> Who do interior decorating for Art's sake ...
> They look at a woman, languorously, through half closed eyes,
> And tell her, in low, passionate tones,
> What she ought to wear.
>
> (In Crowninshield 1944: 198)

Edmond Wilson (1975), who worked at *Vanity Fair* in 1920, com-plained in his diaries of the "homosexual element" in the office, "which Crowninshield accepted and ignored" (39), and by the 1930s, the maga-zine was covering drag performers during the so-called "pansy craze" (Chauncey 1994: 316, 327–28). But it would be anachronistic to see in *Vanity Fair* manifestations of the essentialized "gay" or "lesbian" identi-ties developed in the mid-twentieth century. When Parker characterized her *Vanity Fair* colleagues fondly as "four young men who go to pieces easily. Even when they're in the best of health, you have to stand on their insteps to keep them from floating away" (in Kerth 1995), her imputation of flightiness was not code for homosexuality, but a per-formance of irreverent gender-reversal consonant with a widespread rejection of sexual norms among the "modern" young men and women of the 1920s. Gender-bending codes of dress and deportment at *Vanity Fair*'s offices complemented an editorial policy that, as announced in Crowninshield's first issue in March, 1914, promised: "For women we intend to do something in a noble and missionary spirit, something which, so far as we can observe, has never been done for them by an American magazine. We mean to make frequent appeals of their intellects... we hereby announce ourselves as determined and bigoted feminists" (in Amory and Bradlee 1960: 13). By 1918, when Parker succeeded P. G. Wodehouse in the traditionally masculine role of theater critic, she presented herself to *Vanity Fair*'s readers as "a tired businesswoman... seeking innocent diversion" (in Meade 1988: 45).

Although Parker left Condé Nast early in 1920 when the acerbic wit of her reviews—"'The House Beautiful' makes the play lousy" and "If you don't knit, bring a book"—provoked Broadway advertisers to demand her dismissal, Todd, during her New York apprenticeship, was clearly enthralled by *Vanity Fair*, both as a magazine and an editorial milieu. Todd's blend of women's fashion with avant-garde culture at British *Vogue* was, therefore, both less and more than the eccentric departure from a Condé Nast formula that commentators following Chase have described. On the most basic level, Todd simply offered the smaller British market a fusion of Nast's two flagship products in one publication. Though British *Vogue* shared covers and fashion features with its New York namesake, it took other articles, illustrations, and cartoons from *Vanity Fair*.[4] Nast endorsed this strategy as "in keeping with the present economic stress" and "apparent taste" of postwar Britain (in Luckhurst 1998: 18), and sent *Vanity Fair*'s business manager, Albert Lee, to London to assist Todd. When his New York magazines suffered economic reversals during the Depression, moreover, he followed a similar model, merging them under the *Vogue* title. Although "in the Twenties the British edition was not intended to be the advanced literary and artistic review she was turning out," Chase grudgingly acknowledges, "after *Vogue* absorbed *Vanity Fair*, we have, within limits, used features in line with the kind of thing Dorothy was promoting" (1954: 152). *Vanity Fair* was never as consistently queer as British *Vogue*, however, and the impact of its merger with its staider, stronger New York rival was minimal and short-lived (G. Douglas 1991: 126–28). The far more interesting implication of Todd's editorial guidance in the 1920s was that her mix of models created a magazine that brought its readership of British women a vision of modernity defined not only by new trends in hemlines, but by new claims for women as both consumers and producers of avant-garde culture (Mahood 2002), including radical challenges to conventions of gender and sexuality.

My claims go further than—or contradict outright—other scholars' presentations of Todd's era at British *Vogue*. The tendency cited by Michael Murphy to overvalue critical turns associated with postmodernism by stereotyping modernist culture and those who produced it is evident in, for instance, denunciations of Todd and the Bloomsbury writers she commissioned for their "silent collusion in the promotion of a heteronormative agenda" at *Vogue*, where "nothing that evinced a homoerotic sensibility" is claimed to have appeared in the pages (Garrity 1999: 35).[5] In a decade when men were regularly prosecuted for "unnatural acts" and British courts prohibited distribution of Radclyffe Hall's novel, *The Well of Loneliness*, for depicting lesbian mores, no mass-circulation magazine could have announced homosexuality with the blatancy apparently required by some recent arbiters of sexual politics. Subtler scholars, however, have elucidated the homoeroticism in Virginia Woolf's writings for *Vogue* (Luckhurst 1998: 9) and on fashion more generally (Cohen 1999, 2005) to create a more nuanced account of both Todd and her writers. This article follows a path pointed out by Lisa Cohen (1999), the subtlest of recent readers of Todd's *Vogue*, whose sensitive essay on Woolf's "frock consciousness" in an earlier issue of this journal demonstrates how careful readings of fashion can register expressions of sexual identity characterized by their obscurity.[6]

Cohen's efforts to "see through the unsigned prose" in *Vogue* in order to perceive "Todd's editorial hand" in articles like "Fashions for Spinsters" (169) encouraged my quest to outline the editorial sensibility that, for instance, under the wicked pseudonym of Polly Flinders, celebrated the modern artist Marie Laurencin as "the sister of Sappho" (*Vogue*, late January 1925: 40). A caption under one painting of frolicking females notes that in the "new poetic world" of Laurencin's imagination, "There are slim girls…, horses, dogs, and birds, but never a man" (Early December 1924: 70).[7] A similar sensibility illustrated a feature on decorative screens with an example depicting the type of modern masculine horsewoman in breeches and top hat known in Paris as "une Amazonne" (Late September 1924: 42), and commissioned an article on Geneviève Prémoy, "The Amazon Who Fought For Louis XIV in the Guise of a Man and Won Glory in the Wars" (Early September 1925: 53, 80). The selection of photographs for the regular theater feature "Seen on the Stage" betrays a related fascination with actresses in masculine costume, among them, in the words of a caption, "The Beautiful Varda" in her "dangerously attractive" tuxedo (Early August 1925: 55).[8] (Figure 1).

The fluidity of gender and eroticism is especially clear in *Vogue*'s cartoons on modern mores. These regularly lampoon courtship and marriage, with an array of effeminate men avoiding or failing at heterosexual coupling. In "A Bachelor at Bay" by the female cartoonist called Fish, for instance, Jasper spurns female advances in order to stay home, draped on a chaise longue, reading French books, most prominently the controversial 1922 novel *La Garçonne*, about a modern businesswoman's many love affairs, both hetero- and homoerotic (Early May 1925: 72) (Figure 2). Conversely, a cartoon about an "aged millionaire who hated his relations because they were younger than he," and therefore sent them the most inappropriate Christmas gifts he could imagine, centers on his mannish great-niece in a tuxedo-styled pajama suit puffing happily on her cigars and composing her thank-you note: "…the smokes are the best I have ever hit" (Early December 1925: 84) (Figure 3). Even more explicitly referencing the possibility of erotic attraction between women is "A Rather Vicious Circle," which (in addition to recalling a sobriquet for the Algonquin round table) includes among its frustrated romantic attachments the dreams of a seventeen-year-old girl for Adelaide, "her convent friend and one person she has ever loved" (Early March 1925: 48) (Figure 4).

Figure 1
The "Beautiful Varda." Early
August 1925: 55. British *Vogue*.

(Above) Jeanne de Casalis is now playing lead in "Mixed Doubles," with which the Criterion is keeping up its reputation as the home of first-rate farce. She combines immense vitality with delicate artistry

British *Vogue* drew much of its fashion copy from Condé Nast's New York and Paris offices, and these features reflect less of Todd's influence.[9] One exception was the choice of "Dora Stroeva, the famous French cabaret singer" to illustrate a feature, "The Small Neat Coiffure is the Favorite of the Mode" (Late December 1923: 55) (Figure 5); Stroeva was known for her performances at lesbian-themed evenings at the "Boeuf sur le toit" nightclub in Paris, where she accompanied herself, like a man, on her guitar (Pénet 2003). *Vogue* noted the guitar-playing when she was pictured again six months later (Late July 1924: 25). Though the feature on hairstyles left readers to their own conclusions (or fantasies) about this elegant, butch woman with short hair and mannish clothes, British *Vogue* during Todd's era suggested a significant subcultural context for advice such as "the flat, boyish locks of the shingled head make the simplest and neatest coiffure that can be imagined" (Late December 1923: 55).

Vogue's frequent allusions to styles and mores associated with emerging sexual subcultures not only kept insiders abreast of developments in

Figure 2
"A Bachelor at Bay," drawn
by FISH. Early May 1925: 72.
Fish/British *Vogue*.

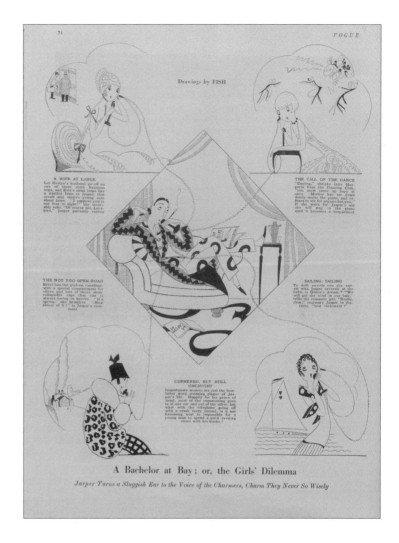

these communities, but encouraged a wider audience of fashionable women to identify with a "modern" openness to new ideas. Unsigned editorials widened the definition of "fashion" to "Zeitgeist" or simply "change." "Vogue has no intention of confining its pages merely to hats and frocks," announced one editorial. "In literature, drama, art and architecture, the same spirit of change is seen at work" (Early April 1925: xiv). This spirit of change extended to "fashions in religion, in philosophy, in literature, and the arts," which "do not change as quickly as they do in millinery, but they change quite quickly enough" (Early February 1924: 49). Noting that "the young find mental dowdiness ridiculous" while "the old call mental *chic* immoral" (Early February 1924: 49), *Vogue*'s editorials consistently interpellated "you, dear

Figure 3
"Inappropriate Presents,"
drawn by Charles Martin. Early
December 1925: 84. Charles
Martin/British *Vogue*.

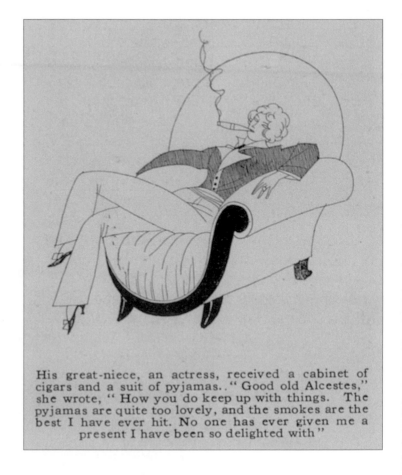

His great-niece, an actress, received a cabinet of
cigars and a suit of pyjamas.."Good old Alcestes,"
she wrote, "How you do keep up with things. The
pyjamas are quite too lovely, and the smokes are the
best I have ever hit. No one has ever given me a
present I have been so delighted with"

reader of the younger generation" as part of an "us who belong, thank
goodness! to the Twenties." With the "moral indignation" of "old
ladies" dismissed as "secretly begotten of envy" for the "emancipated"
young, *Vogue* defined generational identification as a matter of attitude
not age: "Why should one be thirty? Many women who were in their
cradles at the time of the Franco-Prussian War are not thirty yet" (Early
February 1923: 37). And the magazine was, of course, essential to
achieving and maintaining youth:

> There are now so many excellent reasons—besides the tango—for
> not growing old. But if anyone should some morning unawares
> discover symptoms of old age creeping upon her... one of the
> first things the patient should do is to send out for a copy of
> *Vogue*. This has been found efficacious in even the worst cases
> of confirmed middle age, and taken regularly will prevent any
> danger of a recurrence of the malady. By this means old age can

Figure 4
"A Rather Vicious Circle,"
drawn by Charles Martin.
Early March 1925: 48. Charles
Martin/British *Vogue*.

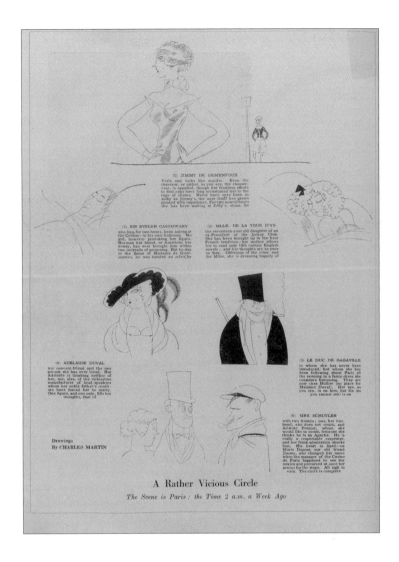

be postponed till so late in life that it becomes quite unnoticeable (Early November 1925: xlvii).

Born in 1883, Todd was not quite a Franco-Prussian war-baby, but her identification with the youth of the 1920s was manifestly a matter of attitude. Her editorship was a partnership—sexual as well as professional—with a woman who rose from being Todd's assistant to become *Vogue*'s Fashion Editor, Madge Garland. Todd and Garland shared a flat in Chelsea, described by Virginia Woolf in 1928 as "incredibly louche: Todd in [men's] sponge bag trousers, Garland in pearls and silk" (1977: 501). Novelist Rebecca West contrasted the

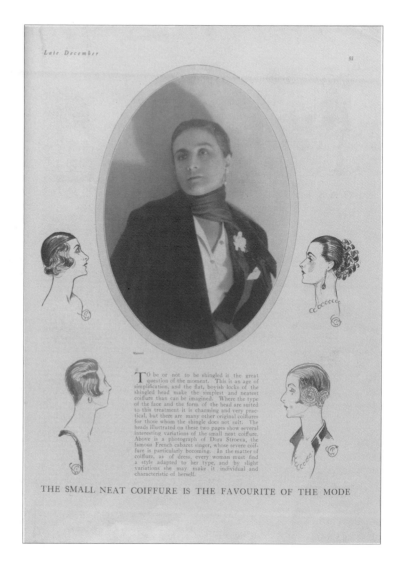

Figure 5
"The Small Neat Coiffure is the Favourite of the Mode," with photograph of Dora Stroeva. Late December 1923: 55. Manuel/British *Vogue*.

appearance of Todd, "a fat little woman, full of genius," with Garland, "a slender and lovely young woman, who could have been a model," but assessed them both as great Editors: "Together these women changed *Vogue* from just another fashion paper to being the best of fashion papers and a guide to the modern movement in the arts ... they brought us all the good news about Picasso and Matisse and Derain and Bonnard and Proust and Jean Cocteau and Raymond Radiguet and Louis Jouvet and Arletty and the gorgeous young Jean Marais" (in Noble 1972: 90).

West's list of the "good news" British *Vogue* announced, links heavy hitters of the modernist art canon to icons of queer culture, with special emphasis on sexy stars of the French stage and screen whose performances of desire and desirability inverted conventions of active men pursuing passive women. West's tribute is less a record of fact, however, than an evocation of effect, for the stars she names are from a later era. Jean Marais made his first film in 1933, long after Todd's time at *Vogue*, while Arletty's famous role as the sexually aggressive Garance in *Les Enfants du Paradis* dates from 1945, though this film's archaic style recalls the silent films that began to be reviewed in Todd's era (Hankins 2004: 450–506). What the mid-century film stars West cited had in common, however, was that they embodied queerness in the mass-cultural imagination created by the movies the way the stage performers who animated the pages of *Vogue* did for theater audiences in the mid-1920s. In *Vogue*, the butch elegance of "The Beautiful Varda" and Dora Stroeva was complemented by actors Dorothy Parker would undoubtedly call sensitive: the effete Ernest Thesiger (Early April 1925: 72) (Figure 6), the androgynous "ingénu" Tom Douglas (Early October 1924: 90) (Figure 7) and the foppish young John Gielgud.

Readers could also look to *Vogue*'s theater pages for images of handsome actors and male dancers in various stages of undress. One striking image produced by *Vogue*'s London photographers presents Rudolph Valentino scantily clad in a skintight faun costume (with a remarkably phallic tail), recalling Vazlav Nijinski's scandalously sexual role in the Russian Ballet's prewar *Après-Midi d'un Faune* (Late October 1924: 36)[10] (Figure 8). Since nothing links Valentino to this ballet in the text, the photograph simply confirms the actor's inheritance of the retired dancer's reputation for transgressive erotic appeal at a time when the Russian Ballet was increasingly associated with homosexual subculture (Latimer 1999). The current stars of the Russian Ballet were also regularly pictured in *Vogue* with captions describing their "perfect physique" (Late December 1924: 51) and emphasizing the influence of Serge Diaghileff, whose propensity for bedding his leading men was widely rumored. A drawing selected to represent the young Russian Ballet composer Dukelsky in a "We Nominate for the Hall of Fame" feature in 1925 offers *Vogue*'s clearest visual suggestion of homosexual intimacy: the musician is paired with the poet and librettist Boris Kochno so as to suggest a domestic couple, both men apparently clothed in dressing gowns, one carrying a puppy (Late October 1925: 58)[11] (Figure 9).

Theater and literature, during Todd's era at *Vogue*, were the purview of Raymond Mortimer, whose signed columns—another innovation borrowed from *Vanity Fair*, in contrast to the anonymous authority of *Vogue*'s fashion pages—offered readers a consistent attitude identified as that of irreverent youth.[12] "Belonging as I do to the generation of which Edith, Osbert, and Sacheverell Sitwell are brilliant representatives," begins a column trumpeting recent acclaim for these often-derided authors, "once more the old have to confess that they were in the wrong. And that is very good for the old, as anyone young will tell you" (Early

Figure 6
"Seen on the Stage" with
photograph of Ernest Thesiger.
Early April 1925: 72. Maurice
Beck and Macgregor/British
Vogue.

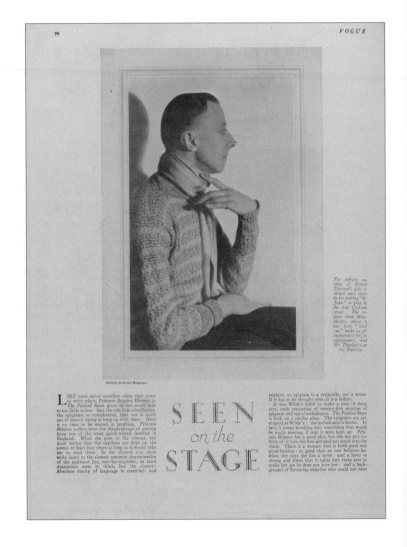

July 1924: 49). Another column opens: "Nice people will only like one of these books, the first. But all five will interest the sophisticated young, the amateurs of new things, those who find our age entertaining and those who are teased by a nostalgia for the exotic. This is a warning" (Early December 1924: 71).

The nostalgia that teased this not-old, not-nice generation was a specific historical legacy looking back through the Aesthetes to the free-thinking eighteenth-century *philosophes*. "I sometimes wish I had been born in 1868: it must have been such fun to be young in the Nineties," begins another of Mortimer's columns, which goes on to cite Oscar Wilde and Aubrey Beardsley as exemplary of a movement that "was for

Figure 7
"Young Talent on the London Stage," with photographs of Tom Douglas and Mollie Kerr. Late January 1925: 60. Maurice Beck and Macgregor/British *Vogue*.

the most amusing in the most boring of all possible worlds." Mortimer singles out Wilde in particular, because "he defined an attitude to life" in which "Pleasure...is something more than a mere relaxation, and it needs education and taste to really enjoy oneself... And for this, all his faults of style, whether in living or writing, will be forgiven him, at any rate by the younger generation" (Early March 1925: 49). Others in this Aesthetic legacy included Marcel Proust, "the greatest novelist of his time" (Late August 1925: 55) and Arthur Rimbaud, whose poems, Mortimer proudly announced in the opening line of another column, first appeared in *Vogue* in 1886 (Late July 1924: 45). Looking farther into history, Mortimer asserted, "Intelligent persons today feel

Christopher Reed

Figure 8
Rudolph Valentino. Late
October 1924: 36. Maurice
Beck and Macgregor/British
Vogue.

enormously in sympathy with the eighteenth century. The Victorian Age seems a curious intervening backwater." *Vogue*, therefore, offered readers frequent short biographies, by Mortimer, Francis Birrell, and Richard Aldington, of underappreciated French aristocrats and their consorts. European "civilization has never reached a higher level than it did in eighteenth-century France," *Vogue* announced. "Men cultivated the feminine graces and women the masculine accomplishments. They met on equal terms. In this world the only object was to amuse and be amused" (Late February: 35, 80).

An analogous modern sensibility now relished a new translation of *Les Liaisons Dangereuses* as much as it enjoyed the novels of frequent

Figure 9
"We Nominate for the Hall of Fame," Dukelsky, drawn by Pruna. Late October 1925: 58. Pruna/British *Vogue*.

Vogue contributor Aldous Huxley, whose books, Mortimer claimed, serve as a generational litmus test marking "fundamentally opposed philosophies of life":

> The older generation, for the most part, detests Mr. Huxley. If you have a trace of Victorianism in you, if you have any respect for conventions, if you are a churchwarden, a member of the Primrose League, an optimist, a sentimentalist, an admirer of Mr. Galsworthy or the Royal Academy, you will disapprove of Mr. Huxley as much as of the Bolsheviks, cubism, cocktails, shingled hair and psychoanalysis. If, on the other hand, you use the word "respectable" as a term of abuse, if you hate Dickens, Switzerland, the nineteenth century, and all organized attempts to improve mankind, if you like saxophones, foreigners, Baroque architecture, the Steinach operation and a pronounced *maquillage*, then it is almost certain you will be an admirer of Mr. Huxley's writings" (Late June 1924: 46).

Mortimer's catalog of generational differences avoids explicit reference to homosexuality, even as it insists on openness to new ideas about gender (androgynous "shingled" hair and pronounced makeup) and sex (psychoanalysis and the Steinach operation, which was the Viagra of its day). Far more free-floatingly "queer" than the competing medical essentialism of "homosexual," the attitude performed in Mortimer's literature columns echoed one of Huxley's characters, whom he quoted approvingly for referring to "'the best of indoor sports'—love-making" (Late February 1925: 41). This attitude appreciates the "picturesque eroticism" of the "already forgotten" Pierre Loti (Late September 1926: 57) and identifies with the racy life described in the novels of Paul Morand, "the suavest guide to our contemporary Arabian Nights" (Early December 1924: 71). Mortimer also updated his readers on the recent publications of certain French authors: André Gide, who is "fascinated by whatever is illicit" (Late September 1926: 57); Jean Cocteau, "a dilettante so brilliant that he gives new meaning to the word" (Late December 1924: 50), Raymond Radiguet, Cocteau's "disciple, a boy" (Early August 1924: 33), and René Crevel (Early December 1924: 124).

In historical retrospect, Mortimer's columns read as a guide to an emerging queer literary canon, and, combined with the photographs and cartoons in British *Vogue*, make the magazine an exhilarating, sometimes moving, record of a subculture developing around ideals of transgressive erotics and playful androgyny. Although these qualities resonate with aspects of the post-"gay/lesbian" queerness that emerged in the final decades of the twentieth century, this earlier manifestation was also strongly defined by the social and legal constraints of Britain in the 1920s, which required that expressions—and thus experiences—of minority sexual identity be tempered through the ambiguities of inference and innuendo, and distanced both in time and place. Mortimer's columns consistently locate the most transgressive performances of sex and gender elsewhere: in history, in France, often doubly distanced by being in French history—somewhere beyond the reach of current British law and custom. When, in 1926, Mortimer wrote a pamphlet arguing that marital love could be deepened by extramarital sex, Leonard Woolf deemed it too radical even for the Hogarth Press, which had been publishing translations of Sigmund Freud for four years (Nicolson 1992:138–39). No wonder that when Mortimer's *Vogue* column announced the philosophy, "Lacking sensuality, without sensibility, we are without soul. The more we are voluptuous, the more we are intelligent! ... I parody Descartes' saying, 'I love, therefore I am. When I love no more, I am no longer,'" these words were not only attributed to the recently deceased Anatole France, but quoted in French, without translation (Early January 1925: 49 [my translation]).[13]

Today we can confirm the suggestions of queer subculture implied in *Vogue*'s pages by turning to letters, diaries, and memoirs that offer glimpses into the biographies of the magazine's writers and editors. These documents find both Mortimer and Todd living the queer high life on holidays to the Riviera, posing for photographs with friends in the nude, dining with Cocteau and Crevel.[14] Mortimer turns up in the letters of his lover Harold Nicolson, who groused about Mortimer's effeminate "*tapette* side" to his wife, the novelist and occasional *Vogue* contributor Vita Sackville-West, who, at the time, was exercising her own rights within their remarkable open marriage by flirting with Virginia Woolf, another *Vogue* writer (in Nicolson 1992: 150). The handsome and charming George "Dadie" Rylands appears in Woolf's diaries, not only as her introduction to Todd, but also as the object of Mortimer's unrequited infatuation (Woolf 1978: 266, 319). This context provides a reference for the allusion, in one of Mortimer's literature columns, to "the young men, at once so elegant and so intellectual, whose fastidiousness and sophistication make King's the object of alarmed admiration to the mere Oxonian" (Late June 1924: 46). It also helps explain how, before Rylands's poetry and book reviews first appeared in *Vogue* (Early September 1924: 30; Late October 1924: 40, 96), his image appeared as an anonymous Cambridge undergraduate in magnificent drag as the Duchess of Malfi, photographed by Cecil Beaton (his first picture for *Vogue*) to accompany an ecstatic description by an unsigned reviewer (Early April 1924: 55, 84) keen to fan the flames of rivalry with Oxford men who performed women's roles in undergraduate plays (Early July 1924: 35).[15]

Some sense of the social milieu *Vogue*'s staff created may be gleaned from the diary of a surprisingly easily scandalized young Cecil Beaton, which describes a costume party thrown by Todd and Garland at which the choreographer Frederick Ashton performed extravagant impersonations of famous ballerinas: "the sort of thing one is ashamed of and only does in one's bedroom in front of large mirrors when one is rather excited and worked up" (in Kavanagh 1996: 74). Clive Bell's letters describe a party at Mortimer's eccentrically decorated residence (illustrated in *Vogue* as "A Bachelor Flat in Bloomsbury" [Late April 1925: 44]) as "a regular bugger gathering with a smattering of English…girls and a few American sapphists" which he fled on the arrival of "a party of boxers" (in C. Reed 2004: 236). Virginia Woolf's account of another party, this one given by Edith Sitwell for Gertrude Stein, captures both the exhilaration and the constraints of this subculture. Woolf found herself, her diary records, proposing "wildly, fantastically" that the Hogarth Press should publish Todd's memoirs, "which she accepts!" (1980: 89). A letter written immediately after this encounter, however, acknowledges that the "squalor" that made Todd's story interesting also made it unpublishable.[16] The ambivalent mix of fascination and repulsion expressed even by insiders from Beaton to Bloomsbury reflects the risks of *Vogue*'s high-wire act, as its writers demanded attention (but not too much!) for a vision of modernity that included new (but not too specified!) erotic and emotional ideals.

At a time when queerness was experienced and expressed through implication and innuendo, *Vogue* offered attentive readers not only rosters of images and names associated with the emerging queer subculture of the 1920s, but, more importantly, tutorials in how to recognize and take queer pleasures. Training audiences in new ways of reading was a constant preoccupation during Todd's years at *Vogue*. Some of these lessons were quite literal: instructions for the appreciation of "Modern Free Verse," for instance (Late September 1925: 57, 90; Early December 1925: 95, 130). Edith Sitwell's two essays on Gertrude Stein demonstrate how such lessons in reading modern prose could imply broader assertions of identity. Sitwell's first article contrasts Stein with two other female novelists: "Katherine Mansfield's style is pellucid beyond measure," she says, and Dorothy Richardson's "is a warm household style, . . . seldom telling you anything." Stein's "strange, wild" writing, by implication, eschews conventions of both clarity and feminine association with domesticity (Early October 1924: 81). Sitwell's second essay makes these implications explicit. Stein's importance, Sitwell says, lies in her revivification of "our language," in which words are conventionally "grouped together in little predestined families, bloodless and timid." Stein "breaks down the predestined groups of these words, their sleepy family habits" (Early October 1925: 73). Stein's work, for Sitwell, is a harbinger of the future; she has "gone so far ahead of our time that she is almost out of sight" (73). And like Mortimer, who proclaimed his identification with the Sitwells' generation, she divides readers into two camps. The same sentence appears in both Sitwell's essays on Stein's writing: "Either one understands it, or one doesn't." Allying herself with the forward-looking moderns, Sitwell annouces, "I have come to understand most of it . . . after a year's hard work" (Early October 1924: 81). The secret, she explains, is that Stein "lets each man have his own experience, and she is reticent about hers, except to people whose experience has been the same as hers" (81).

To read Stein properly, in sum, is to assert a shared identity ("people whose experience has been the same as hers") that affirms one's own life against conventions of language that would require one to be "pellucid"—seen into, understood—and, or perhaps as, familial: to be defined as a wife, a sister, a daughter. Stein's emancipation into anti-familial mystery is connected, in Sitwell's description, to a blurring of gender boundaries. The phrase "Each man his own experience" also appears in both Sitwell's articles on Stein, where, given her focus on women writers, it cannot be simply an unconscious lapse into the generic masculine. Stein, of course, claimed, "Pablo [Picasso] and Matisse have a maleness that belongs to genius. Moi aussi, perhaps" (in Benstock 1986, 189), and this identity was visually suggested in the Man Ray photograph *Vogue* ran on the page facing Sitwell's first article, in which Stein, with short hair and mannish clothes, dominates four other far more feminine-looking "Women of Distinction in Literature." Neither Sitwell nor *Vogue*'s caption writers announce identification with Stein as a lesbian (no critic addressed Stein's lesbianism in print during her lifetime). Far more typically of *Vogue* and queer culture of the 1920s, Stein appears here exemplifying a sensibility that shatters conventional notions of gender, not in the interests of either a specific lesbian identity or a vague universalism, but as a subcultural identity, a mode of being modern.

Tutorials in another form of queer perception were regularly provided by *Vogue* theater coverage, which inducted readers into the sensibility now identified by the term "camp." The caption under a photograph of the French revue star Delysia includes the reader in a "we" who "adore her because she is amusing. A past mistress of innuendo, she can make any line comic" (Late April 1925: 78). A review of an "atrociously con-structed" melodrama divides the audience (again) in two. Followers of "the reports of *crimes passionels* in the Sunday papers" will naively "adore" the play. "Highly sophisticated persons with a taste for parody," however, will understand why, when, at the play's climax, the extravagant leading lady, Violet Vanbrugh, with her "sonorous, tre-mendous voice" adopts "the tone of Lady Macbeth crying 'Give me the daggers'" to "boom out with the awful threat, 'I will show him his birth certificate,'" it is "no wonder there are titters in the stalls" (Early February 1924: 41). If half of camp sensibility is to find humor in conventional performances of extreme pathos, the other half is to recognize the pathos in what is conventionally thought humorous.[17] Thus the "magnificently accomplished American" vaudevillian Sophie Tucker is hailed for "suggesting beneath a Gargantuan humour the tragic trend in life" (Late November 1925: 83). This subtext, according to two similar notices in *Vogue*'s theater columns around Christmas 1925, links Tucker to the legacy of the late music-hall star Marie Lloyd, whose performances of bawdy innuendo onstage complemented a highly publicized life of romantic disappointment and scandal (Late November 1925: 83; Late January 1926: 82).

The paradox inherent in educating mass audiences to the sensibilities and vernaculars of subcultures is fundamental to modernity. This imbrication of the mass media with specifically modern subcultures has been noted in relation to both avant-garde (Murphy 1996) and queer identity (Castiglia and Reed 2004). Under pressure from New York to increase circulation, Todd and her staff struggled over this contradiction between mass audience and subcultural sensibility. An editorial near the end of Todd's time at *Vogue* purports to be a letter from "Jane Rustington," a conveniently named subscriber in "a little country town" who offers detailed advice on how to read *Vogue*: "I find Vogue simply invaluable in keeping me in touch with current movements," Jane reports, "there are very few issues that do not contain something that will set our brains working and our tongues wagging… I find myself able to discuss 'what's on' with a knowledge that no country cousin could hope to achieve without the guidance of *Vogue*" (Late May 1926: lv). Appended to a lengthy discourse on how to clip and file fashion illustrations, this seems a superficial bid for *Vogue*'s culture coverage as relevant to the rustics.

A far more provocative essay in this mode is a "Seen on the Stage" column presented as a girlish letter between sisters: "To Susan in the country from Constance in town." The girls' cousin Roderick, it transpires, is *Vogue*'s theater critic ("Fancy our having a relative who writes for *Vogue*. I know how this will thrill you."). Roderick "has been an *angel*," Constance reports, squiring his wide-eyed cousin "to all the plays he was going to criticize. Of course, he is terribly highbrow and clever, but so *good* and *kind* that I have enjoyed every moment." In the ensuing play-by-play account, the exuberant, naive taste of young Susan exactly correlates with that of highbrow Roderick—although Constance has fewer qualms about admiring more than the acting ability of "Henry Ainley (whose photograph we have cut out so often)" and "Ivor Novello, who is so handsome." Together Constance and Roderick were bored by "the ordinary acting of Shakespeare," preferring "when all the children at Aunt Agatha's Christmas party did the fairy scenes from the *A Midsummer Night's Dream*." Both "enjoyed ourselves tremendously" at farces, one of which reminded Roderick of those he had seen in Paris, while the other prompted him to comment, "It was always an agreeable chance to go to a play that was evidently written by a grown-up person." Both were "rather vague" about *Exiles* by James Joyce, "who wrote that big square blue book, *Ulysses*, which Aunt Grimstone threw into the fire," although Roderick was more articulate in saying that "the style suffered from false *naïveté*." Both admired the coherence of the ensemble in Chekov's *Three Sisters*, and once Roderick had explained that the producer ensures such aesthetic unity, Constance was quick to recognize the producer's hand in a production of *The Jealous Wife* put on by her cousin's "great friend," Bonamy Dobrée, at the working-class East London College. Constance's letter concludes by reporting that she told Roderick that "as soon as I got home I was really going to read a great deal," and announcing that she no longer looked forward "to the Hunt Ball as much as I had expected. I have got to prefer intellectual conversation" (Early March 1926: 58, 88, 90). Behind this fantasy of a meeting of the minds between *Vogue*'s thirty-ish male culture writers and simple country girls—"It is wonderful how we always agree," Constance effuses—lies Mortimer's reiterated assertions of a younger generation united in its scepticism about established values and open-minded enough to enjoy being shocked.[18]

As Constance is imagined here, she discomfits Roderick only once. But that instance is significant. When Roderick condescendingly warns her against excessive reading, saying that "nobody went down so well with men as a girl who was both intelligent and ill-informed," Constance reports that she responded, "that I did not wish to go down with men, but to be a genuine companion to a really clever man like him. At this he blushed quite crimson" (90). Roderick's crimson suggests more than a blush of pleasure. Constance's earnest feminism perhaps shames the sexist condescension in his Wildean remark. Constance's naive heterosexism perhaps blinds her to the implications of emulating Wilde. Perhaps both.[19] Or perhaps, like Wilde's young heroines, Constance is not as earnestly naive about Roderick as she seems. But for whatever reason, their modernisms do not ultimately meld. Even in this fantasy of *Vogue*'s theater critic, the disjunction between the avant-garde aesthetics associated with an urban subculture and a mass-market readership, foundered over what could be said about sexuality. This returns us to where this essay began: to the question of the failure of Dorothy Todd's *Vogue* to sustain itself within the specific context of Condé Nast's corporate structure and the general context of British culture in the 1920s.

Solid facts about *Vogue*'s revenue and readership are hard to come by, as financial and circulation numbers were secret. The editorial model Todd followed, however, was poorly conceived to raise profits. Edmund Wilson recalls that in 1920 in New York, "*Vanity Fair* was always 'in the doghouse' as the money-losing member of the Nast group, of which *Vogue* was the great success" (Wilson 1975: 35). Though *Vanity Fair* never matched American *Vogue*'s circulation or revenue, however, it sustained itself in the American economic boom of the 1920s. The same period saw wages (measured against inflation) fall in Britain, however (D. Reed 1997: 171), and the memoirs of the magazine's business manager Harry Yoxall quantify Edna Woolman Chase's claim that Nast's British title was "losing Condé a great deal of money" with the impressive figure of a £25,000 loss for 1923 (Chase 1954: 152–3; Yoxall 1966: 124). Todd confronted this challenge by halving the cover price (Early September 1923) and inaugurating an editorial campaign asserting, "Every page of *Vogue* shows you how to save money by spending it to advantage" (Late October 1923: iv). Circulation rose, albeit slowly, under her stewardship, and a survey of readers found *Vogue* among the top three magazines read by middle-class women in 1927 (White 1970: 118).[20] Chase's claim that Todd's "determination to twist *Vogue* into what it was not" meant that "advertising fell off by the pageful," is disproved simply by looking at extant issues of the magazine, and, although Chase claims credit for setting British *Vogue* on the road to profitability, it continued to lose money during her editorship, only turning a profit in 1929, and then not from the magazine, but from associated fashion pattern books (Yoxall 1966: 124).[21] What precipitated Todd's firing is, thus, unclear. Nast was certainly losing money on British *Vogue* and circulation had dipped during the months before her dismissal because of the General Strike, but the business manager's diary records his surprise at Todd's dismissal, noting that "It followed a letter of mine, in which I complained of her prolonged absence at a crucial time, with all her fashion staff too, but the letter was only one of many such that I have written and I never expected such drastic consequences" (in Luckhurst 1998: 20).

Even harder to assess is *Vogue*'s influence on its readers. If the queer lives of *Vogue*'s celebrity contributors are only fragmentarily reflected in the historical record, how much more obscure are the lives of its readers. Cecil Beaton, who began his undergraduate years in 1922 determined to become, in his own words, "a rabid aesthete with a scarlet tie, gauntlet gloves, and hair grown to a flowing length," recalled that, "At Cambridge each issue of *Vogue* was received as an event of importance" (1951: 39–40). But apart from Beaton's small circle and the fictional Jane Rustington and country Constance, the only records of readers come in lists of prizewinners for two contests, one from the start of Todd's editorial career, the other a few weeks after it ended. The first lists twelve readers, ranging from a Dutch Baronness to a Miss H. Wolfe who gave her address as The Lyceum Club, Piccadilly. Unsurprisingly middle class (the non-urban addresses are houses with names, and the addresses in London are quite respectable), half the readers are identified as "Miss" (Late February 1923: 49).[22] The second contest had only four winners, but the circumstances of their subscriptions were offered: Mrs. Millicent Rymond of Birmingham had read *Vogue* "for years," Mr. J. E. Sussex of West Norwood, London, reported that the "ladies" of his family had been reading *Vogue* for just a year, while Miss M. Callender-Rule of Edinburgh and Miss Joan Bircumshaw of London claimed, respectively, five and eight years of readership (Late January 1927: 74). The intriguing suggestion that at least half of *Vogue*'s regular readers were unmarried women—some unmarried well into adulthood—allows at least the speculation that the insights the magazine offered into the nascent sexual subcultures of the 1920s were not wasted.

Approached with an open mind today, Dorothy Todd's *Vogue* seems remarkably queer. Flipping though its pages, one wonders—as with jazz hits of the 1920s like "Masculine Women, Feminine Men," plays like Noel Coward's 1932 *Design for Living*, movies like Alla Nazimova's 1923 *Salome*, derived from Beardsley's illustrations[23]—how did they get away with it? Of course they didn't. Period recordings of the song, both British and American, cut off after the first verse, avoiding the couplets "Auntie is smoking, rolling her own/ Uncle is always buying cologne" and "You go give your girl a kiss in the hall/ Instead you find you're kissing her brother Paul."[24] Coward's play was banned when it was first produced and substantially rewritten for the film version (his riskier 1926 *Semi-Monde* was never produced during his lifetime). Nazimova's film was censored and ruined her financially (Russo 1981: 27–29).

So too, after Todd was fired by Condé Nast, those, like Virginia Woolf, who had been most intrigued by her daring, suddenly found her horrifying (Luckhurst 1998: 21–22). Woolf reacted to Todd's efforts to start a new publication to rival *Vogue* by complaining, "The whole of London does nothing but talk about bringing out magazines" and now found Todd's makeup repellant: "She is like a slug with a bleeding gash for a mouth—She paints badly" (1977: 478–9). There is a strong element of self-reproach in this remark: Todd represented the risks associated with Woolf's own semi-revelation of attraction to glamorous lesbianism in *Orlando*, the draft of which she finished just days before making this comment. In the following decades, Todd eked out a living translating and writing occasional articles. In her grandson's perception, the anecdotes Todd told, over bowls of chocolate, about people from her *Vogue* era—"The more homosexual they were, the more formidable they sounded"—contrasted with her current reality, in which, "In the Kings Road we would meet…faded lesbians who kissed Dody on the cheeks as if she were a baby," making vague invitations to dinners that never took place (Todd 1975: 133, 41; Todd 1981: 73). "Dody had a passion for the figure of the Author, of whatever kind. She ranked nothing above it," her grandson recalled (Todd 1981: 73 [my translation]). And why not? With the other writers for British *Vogue* in the 1920s, she created a magazine that continues to offer attentive readers the queer pleasures of androgynous fashion, campy wit, and visual extravagance that are some of the pleasures of sexual subculture.

Notes

1. See also Woolf (1977: 295). Madge Garland confirmed Sackville-West's report a half-century later, recalling that "in the days when homosexuality was a criminal offence [Condé Nast] was not above using the threat of disclosure to avoid paying up for a broken contract" (1982). Stein's novel, although unpublished until 1958, was written around 1926.
2. Madge Garland recalled that Chase required all *Vogue* staffers to wear hats and clean white gloves, and forced one London *Vogue* editor to move so that she would be seen taking the Tube to work (1982). For Chase's perspective on Crowninshield's disruptions of *Vogue*'s Editor and staff, see Chase 1954: 95–99.
3. So closely did aspects of *Vanity Fair* anticipate the camp aesthetic, that "camp" was said to have been first defined in English by Jean Cocteau in *Vanity Fair* in 1922 (Core 1984: 81); although several of Cocteau's aphorisms express camp ideas—"Genius, in art, consists in knowing how far we may go too far" and "The bad music, which superior folk despise, is agreeable enough. What is really intolerable is what they think *good* music"—he does not use the term (Cocteau 1922: 61).
4. Todd's often-cited focus on figures like Jean Cocteau and Gertrude Stein was anticipated by *Vanity Fair*, which frequently published these and other French authors. Despite such overlaps, most of British *Vogue* was unique and original to its London writers, and Todd adapted some of *Vanity Fair*'s models to her purposes. British *Vogue*'s version of *Vanity Fair*'s "We Nominate for the Hall of Fame"

photo-spreads mingling celebrities from diverse fields, for instance, always included women. A 1920 publication by Condé Nast's staff lists, along with British *Vogue*, another magzine, *The Patrician*, described as "the English edition of *Vanity Fair*" (Parker, Chappell, and Crowninshield, n.p.), but there is no record in Condé Nast's London archive of this publication. During Todd's time as editor, Nast also folded the British edition of *House and Garden* into British *Vogue* (Early April 1924: 69).

5. Garrity mischaracterizes *Vogue*'s presentation of sexuality and gender to buttress her claim that "Bloomsbury, in particular the male members of the Group," championed "English high culture" in *Vogue* in a way that "intersects" with "the dual ideologies of nationalism and imperialism" (1999: 29). To sustain this argument, Garrity rips quotations from contexts, and draws her examples of nationalist rhetoric heavily from travel features that ran before and after Todd's period as Editor, though she names Todd as "the impetus behind the specific marketing and publicity structures employed by British *Vogue*" during the 1920s (1999: 33).

In fact, *Vogue*, during Todd's era, regularly presented antinationalist, anti-imperialist, antiracist attitudes as modern. A far from comprehensive set of examples includes Allan Walton's claim, in an article on Baroque antiques, that "Today in England we can be amused by... the more elaborate of these foreign styles" precisely because there is no English identification with their "exotic flavour" (Early August 1923: 69); Osbert Sitwell's attack on the Empire Exhibition for reveling in the "grotesque romance" of the Empire and "the people and customs that it smothers" (Late June 1924: 90); Raymond Mortimer's critique of the "subtle snobbishness" of British anti-Semitism (Late May 1924: 77); Aldous Huxley's "The Importance of Being Nordic," a contemptuous review of the racist anthropology that grounded imperialism ideologically (Late March 1925: 57, 94), and his "Other People's Prejudices," an argument for liberal cultural relativism that compares Christianity to Hinduism and phallus worship (Early February 1926: 49).

Garrity's misrepresentation of the evidence plainly available on the pages of *Vogue* marks an extreme instance of a phenomenon I have criticized elsewhere (Reed 2000), though I apparently erred in identifying this as a peculiarly British phenomenon. Factually unfounded and illogical attacks on Bloomsbury are widespread enough to suggest that they perform welcome ideological work in the academy: the rhetoric of outraged critique of what Garrity calls the "contaminants of capitalism, imperialism, and privileged consumption" in Bloomsbury (1999: 48) indulges the implication that academia, and individual academics, are somehow pure of such ideological investments. John Walter de Gruchy also notes this hypocrisy in relation to Garrity (2003: 180, n. 6).

6. The present essay was written before the publication of Cohen's equally insightful article on Madge Garland (2005), and I am pleased that my arguments reinforce her discussion of the relationship between "camp" and "discretion" in Garland's long career.

7. Antagonism toward feminine decorum in both behavior and fashion is suggested by the echo of a traditional nursery rhyme: "Little Polly Flinders/ Sat among the cinders/ Warming her pretty little toes./ Her mother came and caught her,/ And whipped her little daughter/ For spoiling her nice new clothes." Flinders wrote again, mocking the staid theatrical revivals of the Renaissance Society, whose actors seem to have "forgotten how to kiss, laugh, and flirt" (Late April 1925: 65), and Clive Bell coyly chided "Mam'zelle" Flinders in the same issue (66). Condé Nast's editorial staff often used pseudonyms, even when also publishing under their own names. Dorothy Parker contributed approximately eighty pieces to *Vanity Fair* under the byline Helène Rousseau, chosen to evoke the free-thinking eighteenth-century philosopher (Crowninshield 1944: 201). That the emphasis on Laurencin's all-female world came from the editorial staff of *Vogue*'s London office is clear from a comparison with the far more generic captions—"The delectable pictorial fantasies of Marie Laurencin have completely captivated a public hitherto habituated to realism"—when the same illustrations appeared in *Vanity Fair* (February 1924: 25).

8. Pictures of other women in drag include Jeanne de Casalis in the title role of *The Man of Destiny* (Late July 1924: 24), Phyllis Monkman in "her imitation of Laddie Cliff in one of his famous Co-Optimist songs" (Late October 1924: 39), Mrs. John Barrymore, a.k.a. Michael Strange, "under which name she has published several plays and books of poems" (Early November 1924: 42), Gertrude Lawrence as Pierrot (Early May 1925: 69), sisters Iris and Viola Tree attired as "London urchins" for a costume party (Late July 1926: 46), and, arguably, Josephine Baker in more revealing urchin attire (Late January 1926: 56). Laura Doan's very useful overview of masculine fashions for women in the 1920s cautions that such attire "did not always signify 'lesbianism'" in the 1920s (2001: 96), which is true to the extent that "lesbianism," a term rarely used at the period, implies a fixed and exclusive identity at odds with the queer life-experience of the "sapphists" involved with *Vogue*. Garland was briefly married and Dorothy Todd bore a daughter out of wedlock by a man whose identity she never revealed—her grandson speculated, "Maman and I think Dody made love with a man once and once only" (Todd 1975: 23). Doan somewhat exaggerates the extent to which "in England in the 1920s, fashion-conscious women of all sexual persuasions were obliged to 'cross-dress' by donning boyish or mannish attire" (2001: 97); many of the fashionable outfits illustrated in the magazines of the period are indisputably womenswear. Given the consistent focus

of British fashion magazines on Paris, Doan may also too sharply distinguish Britain from France, where, she allows, cross-dressing more clearly signified challenges to heteronormativity; certainly the francophile staff of British *Vogue* understood these connotations.

9. The "Fashions for Spinsters" column Cohen offers as an example of Todd's sensibility was shared with *Vogue* (e.g. February 15, 1925: 67).

10. That Nijinsky's prewar roles were on the minds of *Vogue* writers is suggested by a casual allusion to "Nijinsky in Debussy's *Jeu*" [the actual title was *Jeux*] to describe a linen pattern depicting tennis players (Late March 1924: 59).

11. Dukelsky (who went on to fame on Broadway as the composer Vernon Duke) and Kochno (he and Cole Porter were later lovers) were also sketched together by Christopher Wood in 1926 (drawing sold at Sotheby's London, June 14, 2001).

12. Mortimer's writing also appeared unsigned in other departments of British *Vogue*. An anonymous editorial, "Fashions of the Mind," for instance (Early February 1924: 49), is an abridged version of an essay that appeared under his name in *Vanity Fair* (September 1923: 41).

13. It was left to the indubitably heterosexual Aldous Huxley and Leonard Woolf to address homosexuality explicitlyin *Vogue*. Huxley's "A History of Some Fashions in Love" extrapolates from fashion to argue that sex is a matter of social construction, taking as his example Greek men, for whom "it was natural—and fashionable—to turn to romantic and passionate friendships with the youth of one's own sex" (Late August 1924: 49, 72). Woolf, substituting for Mortimer in the "New Books for the Morning Room Table" column, reviewed a translation of Plato by *Vogue* contributor Francis Birrell. Describing the *Symposium* as "the finest thing which has ever been written about that now rather hackneyed subject, Love," he acknowledges that "Many modern readers... will be shocked" because "much of the 'Platonic love' which is discussed in it is now a criminal offence in twentieth-century England" (Late January 1925: 55).

14. On Todd (Todd 1975: 132–3). On Mortimer (Yoss 1998: 5), as well as photographs in the Department of Rare Books and Special Collections, Princeton University Library.

15. Many of Mortimer's letters to Rylands, including one expressing his hope of keeping the original of the Beaton photograph (April 4, 1924) are preserved in the Modern Archive, King's College Cambridge.

16. Woolf's letter to Vanessa Bell says, "I have asked her to write her life, but I gather that there are passages of an inconceivable squalor" (Woolf 1977: 270); the connotations of "squalor" are suggested in a contemporary letter from Vita Sackville-West

describing a Bloomsbury party in Gordon Square that she attended with Woolf after a performance of the Sitwells' *Facade*: "The conversation became personal and squalid. I was amused" (in Nicolson 1992:152).

17. "The Camp sensibility is one that is alive to a double sense in which some things can be taken. But this is not the familiar split-level construction of literal meaning, on the one hand, and a symbolic meaning, on the other. It is the difference, rather, between the thing as meaning something, anything, and the thing as pure artifice" (Sontag 1964: 57).

18. "When nothing shocks, there is a danger that soon nothing will interest" Mortimer wrote in one of his literature columns (Late February 1925: 41). Compare Jean Cocteau in *Vanity Fair*: "We have in our keeping an angel whom we are continually shocking. We must be that angel's guardian" (1922: 61).

19. Roderick's explanatory comment, that "he was not cut out for the part of Horner," only replicates the ambiguity of the blush. The allusion—which Constance admits is lost on her anyway—is to a character in William Wycherley's *Country Wife* who cuckolds the other men by pretending to be impotent. The nature of Horner's sexuality, therefore, is to be dissembled. Even if we accept an authentic male heterosexuality behind Horner's dissembling, however, Roderick's comment that he was not "cut out for the part" is ambiguous.

20. This survey was both limited and flawed (D. Reed 1997: 15–16, 171–2), and women's magazines were especially secretive about their circulation (White 1970: 117). Nevertheless, if Nast's biographer is right that wartime circulation of British *Vogue* was around 14,000, it had fallen substantially, to under 9,000, by the time Todd took over (Seebohm 1982 124–5). Although still around 9,000 in 1924, a "circulation rise" interrupted by the 1926 General Strike is recalled by Yoxall (1966: 124). This rise is only vaguely quantified by his recollection of stockpiling 7,000 copies of the magazine to deliver to London newsagents during the strike in contrast to "the bulk of our mid-May issue" that was stuck on the idled railroads (Yoxall 1966: 125–26). British *Vogue*'s circulation by 1929 was 20,000 (Yoxall 1966: 130). One indication of the difficulties faced by fashion magazines at this period is that *Eve*, the women's weekly that was *Vogue*'s nearest competitor in circulation and style, was absorbed by *Britannia* in 1929.

21. Not only does the percentage of advertising seem to remain steady as the size of the magazine increased during Todd's era, but many advertisers adopted the jazzy modern graphics and youthful slang of *Vogue*'s copy. In the same issue where the "Notes from Paris" column reported that, at a party to which only young people were asked, "Mah Jong proved a greater attraction than dancing!"

Harrod's ran an ad for the "Mahjong model" dress "that will be
'Punged' at sight" (Early March 1924: xvi, 51). Murphy notes a
similar phenomenon at *Vanity Fair* (1996: 69–70).

22. Although *Vogue*'s readers were middle class, it is wrong to accept
too credulously Condé Nast's often-repeated claims, aimed at
advertisers, that his publications not only limited their "appeal to
men and women of known means, and inferred high breeding and
high taste" (in G. Douglas 1991: 101), but also worked "rigorously
to exclude all others" (in Seebohm 1982: 80); see also (Chase1954:
66–67). Similar claims are regularly made for the fashion products
advertised in *Vogue*. Elizabeth Arden's biography claims that, after
a brief period around 1918, her cosmetics were not sold in common
drugstores, but became "a status line by concentrating only on
prestigious outlets," naming several prestigious department stores
(Lewis and Woodworth 1972: 105). Although Arden may have
made a spectacle of canceling accounts with Manhattan stores not
on Fifth Avenue, my own grandmother, as documented in family
letters of 1927, that year sold $3,000-worth of Arden's products
from behind the counter of the Gilbert-Bishop drugstore in Greeley,
Colorado, where she was a devoted reader of *Vogue*.

    That the range of readership for British *Vogue* included those
whose middle-class identity was more aspirational than actual
is suggested by advertisements and editorial copy promoting
"Vogue's School Service" "for women who desire a career of their
own, we can put you in touch with the best vocational schools—
of Art, Dress, Design, Business Training, Journalism, Dancing,
etc." (Early September 1924: n.p.). *Vogue* used aspirations to
class mobility to interpellate readers into queer culture, opposing
"tyrannous" American middle-class conformity that leads people
to "bitterly…hate those who are different" to the "proverbially
eccentric English aristocrat," "the apostle of personal liberty, the
sworn enemy to popular prejudice," who is "generally prepared to
protect the eccentrics of other classes (Early November 1922: 69).
However optimistic this may be, it does not "enforce 'the habit of
tidiness on the nation'" through the "acquisition of English *things*
such as servants" as Garrity claims *Vogue* did during Todd's era
(1999: 42).

23. The film followed a production by the Greenwich Village Follies
designed by Robert Locher, the companion of painter Charles
Demuth, an illustrator whose work appeared in *Vogue* and *Vanity
Fair*; the movie was costumed by Valentino's wife, who was reputed
to be Nazimova's lover (Russo 1981: 27). Both the play and the film
were covered in illustrated features in *Vanity Fair* (October 1921:
47; September 1922: 46).

24. Lyrics from the piano roll (www.queermusicheritage.com, accessed
August 24, 2004). This song by Edgar Leslie and James V. Monaco

was recorded around 1926 by bands as diverse as Chicago's "Merritt Brunies and His Friar's Inn Orchestra" and London's "Reg Batten and The Savoy Havana Band" (www.queermusicheritage.com and the Museum of London, *Music from the Roaring Twenties*, compact disc, River Records, 2003).

Acknowledgments

I had—in 1920s fashion—a simply marvelous time preparing this article. Profound thanks for that go to Becky Conekin, who suggested it, facilitated the research, encouraged the writing, and laughed along with me. Thanks too to Janine Button of Condé Nast, to Rebecca Miller and Cory Stevens at Lake Forest College, and to Alison Matthews David, Clare Rogan, and Andrew Stephenson for suggestions and help with the research. Thanks always to Chris Castiglia.

References

Numerous references to British *Vogue*, in which material often appeared in anonymous untitled features, or as regular columns carrying the same title from issue to issue, are given in the text, following the magazine's designation of its biweekly issues as simply "Early" and "Late" and with the month.

Amory, Cleveland and Frederic Bradlee (eds). 1960. *Vanity Fair: Sections from America's Most Memorable Magazine*. New York: Viking.
Beaton, Cecil. 1951. *Photobiography*. Garden City, NY: Doubleday.
Benstock, Shari. 1986. *Women of the Left Bank: Paris, 1900–1940*. Austin: University of Texas.
Castiglia, Christopher and Christopher Reed. 2004. "Ah Yes, I Remember It Well: Gay Memory in *Will & Grace*" *Cultural Critique* 56 (Winter): 158–88.
Chase, Edna Woolman and Ilka Chase. 1954. *Always in Vogue*. Garden City, NY: Doubleday.
Chauncey, George. 1994. *Gay New York: Gender, Urban Culture, and the Making of the Gay Male World, 1890–1940*. New York: Basic.
Cocteau, Jean. 1922. "The Public and the Artist," *Vanity Fair*, October: 61.
Cohen, Lisa. 1999 "Frock Consciousness: Virginia Woolf, the Open Secret, and the Language of Fashion," *Fashion Theory* 3.2: 149–74.
Cohen, Lisa. 2005. "Velvet Is Very Important: Madge Garland and the Work of Fashion," *GLQ* 11.3: 371–90.
Core, Philip. [1984] 1999. *Camp: The Lie that Tells the Truth*, repr. *Camp: Queer Aesthetics and the Performing Subject*, (ed.) Fabio

Cleto, pp. 80–86. Ann Arbor: University of Michigan Press, 1999: 80–86.

Crowninshield, Frank. 1944. "Crowninshield in the Cubs' Den," *Vogue* [New York], September 15: 162–63, 197–201.

de Gruchy, John Walter. 2003. *Orienting Arthur Waley: Japonism, Orientalism, and the Creation of Japanese Literature in English.* Honolulu: University of Hawaii Press.

Doan, Laura. 2001. *Fashioning Sapphism: The Origins of a Modern English Lesbian Culture.* New York: Columbia University Press.

Douglas, Ann. 1995. *Terrible Honesty: Mongrel Manhattan in the 1920s.* New York: Farrar, Straus and Giroux.

Douglas, George H. 1991. *The Smart Magazines: 50 years of Literary Revelry and High Jinks at Vanity Fair, The New Yorker, Life, Esquire, and The Smart Set.* Hamden, CT: Archon.

Garland, Madge. 1982. "Condé Charm" [review of Seebohm]," *Financial Times* [London], September 11, section 1, page 10.

Garrity, Jane. 1999. "Selling Culture to the 'Civilized': Bloomsbury, British *Vogue*, and the Marketing of National Identity," *Modernism modernity* 6.2: 29–58.

Geraldy, Paul. 1922. "Quelques observations sur l'antagonisme entre l'amour et le mariage," *Vanity Fair,* January: 64.

Hankins, Leslie Kathleen. 2004. "Iris Barry, Writer and *Cinéaste,* Forming Film Culture in London 1924–1926: the *Adelphi,* the *Spectator,* the Film Society, and the British *Vogue*," *Modernism modernity* 11.3: 488–515.

Kavanagh, Julie. 1996. *Secret Muses: The Life of Frederick Ashton.* London: Faber and Faber.

Kerth, Peter. 1995. "Dorothy Parker, 1893–1993" www.peterkerth.com (accessed September 24, 2004).

Latimer, Tirza True. 1999. "Balletomania," *GLQ* 5.2, 173–97.

Lewis, Alfred Allan & Constance Woodworth. 1972. *Miss Elizabeth Arden: An Unretouched Portrait.* New York: Coward, McCann & Geoghegan.

Luckhurst, Nicola. 1998. *Bloomsbury in Vogue.* London: Cecil Woolf.

Mahood, Aurelea. 2002. "Fashioning Readers: The Avant Garde and British *Vogue*, 1920–9," *Women: A Cultural Review* 13(1), 37–47.

Meade, Marion. 1988. *Dorothy Parker: What Fresh Hell is This?* New York: Villard.

Murphy, Michael. 1996 "'One Hundred Percent Bohemia': Pop Decadence and the Aestheticization of Commodity in the Rise of the Slicks," in *Marketing Modernisms: Self- Promotion, Canonization, Rereading,* (eds) Kevin J. H. Ditmar and Stephen Watt. Ann Arbor: University of Michigan Press.

Nicolson, Nigel (ed.). 1992. *Vita and Harold: The Letters of Vita Sackville-West and Harold Nicolson.* London: Weidenfeld and Nicolson.

Noble, Joan Russell (ed.). 1972. *Recollections of Virginia Woolf*. New York: William Morrow.

Parker, Dorothy, George S. Chappell, and Frank Crowninshield. 1920. *High Society*. New York: G. P. Putnam's Sons.

Pénet, Martin. 2003. "Des années vraiment folles," in *ParisObs*, May, obsdeparis.nouvelobs./com/articles/p121/a198800 (accessed August 15, 2004).

Quennell, Peter. 1976. *The Marble Foot: An Autobiography*. New York: Viking.

Reed, Christopher. 2000. "A Tale of Two Countries," in *Charleston Magazine* 22 (Autumn/Winter): 35–39.

—— 2004. *Bloomsbury Rooms: Modernism, Subculture, and Domesticity*. London: Yale University Press.

Reed, David. 1997. *The Popular Magazine in Britain and the United States, 1880–1960*. Toronto. University of Toronto Press.

Russo, Vito. 1981. *The Celluloid Closet: Homosexuality in the Movies*. New York: Harper and Row.

Seebohm, Caroline. 1982. *The Man who was VOGUE: The Life and Times of Condé Nast*. New York: Viking.

Sontag, Susan. [1964] 1999. "Notes on Camp." repr. *Camp: Queer Aesthetics and the Performing Subject*, Fabio Cleto (ed.) Ann Arbor: University of Michigan Press, pp. 53–65.

Stein, Gertrude. 1958. *A Novel of Thank You*. New Haven: Yale University Press.

Todd, Olivier. [1972] 1975. *The Year of the Crab* , trans. Oliver Coburn. Henley-on-Thames, Oxon: Aiden Ellis.

—— 1981. *Un Fils rebelle*. Paris: Bernard Grasset.

White, Cynthia L. 1970. *Women's Magazines, 1693–1968*. London: Michael Joseph.

Wilson, Edmund. 1975. *The Twenties: From Notebooks and Diaries of the Period*. New York: Farrar, Straus and Giroux.

Woolf, Virginia. 1977. *The Letters of Virginia Woolf, Volume Three, 1923–1928*, (eds) Nigel Nicolson and Joanne Trautman. New York: Harcourt Brace Jovanovich.

—— 1978. *The Diary of Virginia Woolf, Volume Two, 1920–1924*, (eds) Anne Olivier Bell and Andrew McNeillie. New York: Harcourt Brace Jovanovich.

—— 1980. *The Diary of Virginia Woolf, Volume Three, 1925–1930*, Anne Olivier Bell and Andrew McNeillie. New York: Harcourt Brace Jovanovich.

Yoxall, H. W. 1966. *A Fashion of Life*. New York: Taplinger.

Yoss, Michael. 1998. *Raymond Mortimer: A Bloomsbury Voice*. London: Cecil Woolf.

Fashion Theory, Volume 10, Issue 1/2, pp. 73–96
Reprints available directly from the Publishers.
Photocopying permitted by licence only.

"We Are Fatally Influenced by Goods Bought in Bond Street"

London, Shopping, and the Fashionable Geographies of 1930s *Vogue*

Bronwen Edwards

Bronwen Edwards is a Research
Fellow in the Geography Department
at Royal Holloway, University of
London, UK. She is part of the
ESRC/AHRC-funded "Shopping
Routes" project, conducting
research on postwar urban planning
and retail architecture, the 1953
Coronation celebrations, and West
End tourism. She recently completed
a PhD at the London College of
Fashion, on the West End shopping
cultures of the 1930s.
BronwenEdwards@aol.com

In 1936, *Vogue*'s photographers captured a moment in Oxford Street in the West End of London (Figure 1).[1] On the sheltered sidewalk in front of a striking new shoe shop, a woman turned to face the camera as if surprised while engaging with this modern monument to consumption. She was dressed smartly and fashionably in a tailor-made suit, hat and furs, a child by her side. Around her, the life of the streets continued: purposeful feet pounded the sidewalks and shoppers carefully examined the contents of the display windows. This photograph appeared in the article "A New London" (British *Vogue* 1936, August 5: 8–13). It spoke of both the cultural importance and the distinctive modernity of the West End's shopping district at this time. It also typified British *Vogue*'s

Figure 1
"The covered pavements of this
new London" photographed
in the article "A New London".
(British *Vogue*. 1936. August 5:
8.) Costa and Spender/British
Vogue.

habitual evocation of London's West End, spinning its fashionable
geographies out from this hub of fashionable living. It used shopping
cultures as a means of defining the city, as an indicator of the modernity
of society, in the tradition of Zola's epic department store novel, *The
Ladies' Paradise* (Zola 1998). This woman, the street she inhabited,
the buildings and displays that preoccupied her, encapsulated the self-
consciously modern and fashionable consumption cultures of the 1930s
West End. "Shopping is... made enticing for all, in this new London"
(British *Vogue* 1936, August 5: 13).

Vogue provides an account of vibrant and highly fashionable consumption cultures based in the 1930s West End, inviting a reassessment
of this as a rather drab, depressed era for the shopper, sandwiched
between the Victorian and Edwardian heyday of department stores such

as Selfridges on Oxford Street (Rappaport 2000), and the emergence
of the "swinging" postwar cultures of Carnaby Street and the Kings
Road (Breward 2004: 150–176). It also contributes to a more textured
narrative of the broader 1930s retail landscape, which has hitherto
prioritized the study of lower-middle-class experience, often suburban
or provincial in focus, making links with the rise of cheap ready-to-wear
and the chain store (Alexander 1994, Winship 2000). Certainly, the
growth of these kinds of retail outlets was considerable in the interwar
period: the records of Marks and Spencer reveal that 167 new stores
opened during the 1930s, compared to 23 in the 1910s and 27 in the
1920s.[2] Humble has even suggested that, in response to the perception of
consumer culture as a lower-middle-class phenomenon, the established
middle class withdrew from public engagement with consumption and
developed instead a culture of "thrift" at this time (Humble 2001: 88).
The evidence of Vogue firmly refutes the dominance of such a culture,
and is one of many sources (including retail records, tourist guides,
and accounts in the popular press) which point to the existence of a
flourishing and broad middle class, a group which lavished its prosperity
on leisure and consumption, concentrated numerically and culturally in
London and the Southeast. These sources also show that alongside the
undoubted expansion of lower-middle-class consumption described by
Alexander et al., the luxury end of the retail market based in the West
End enjoyed continued popularity and potency as a symbol of bourgeois
consumption. There was a marked but not homogenous engagement
with consumer culture right across the middle class: subtle distinctions
were made between the different groups invested in this new consumer
society; the discourses surrounding the West End enabling the place to
retain associations of luxury and specialness.

In British Vogue, the dominant ideal of femininity within the magazine
was clearly metropolitan, and the associated models of consumption
were highly fashionable, expensive and West End based. However, a
broader territory is suggested by the existence of an extensive national,
and indeed considerable expatriate, readership. It is also significant that
the affluent world found on the pages of the magazine had a complex
national and international geography of fashionable living, of which
its shopping geography was only one part: country house weekends,
shooting parties, days at the races, foreign holidays, and so on. While
Vogue fashion was bound together with the geographies of its social
calendar, clothes were still infused with "London." For 1930s Vogue,
the West End was the specified place for shopping, a place where a
woman was kitted out for the broader territory of her fashionable
lifestyle so that, as a Vauxhall car advertisement in Vogue suggested,
"on the quaintest country lane or in fashionable Bond Street, she will
never feel out of place" (British Vogue 1938, June 8). The magazine
thus constituted a guide for the West End, but was also a manual for
metropolitan shopping identities. For example, fashion features regu-

larly recommended outfits sourced from the West End for wearing on shopping trips, so that place was the destination of the trip and also literally cloaked the consumer. A typical article, "For Town," included garments from Digby Morton, Palace Gate; Miss Ware, Bond Street; Asprey, Bond Street, and Fortnum and Mason in Piccadilly (British *Vogue* 1935, March 20: 69).

The story of twentieth-century advertising has been told in terms of brands, and therefore dislocated representations of commodities. Winship writes, "'widened, scythed through' encapsulates the undercutting of place by market and the changing landscape of chain stores (chain cinemas, chain pubs, chain teashops) which dramatically pushed their way into British high streets in the 1930s" (Winship 2000: 18). However, advertising in *Vogue* definitely located consumption within the West End. The magazine *did* reflect a trend toward national brands within British shopping habits: many of the goods advertised in *Vogue* were nationally available and fashion features were sometimes appended by lists of garment stockists based across the country, for the benefit of its national readership. But it is apparent that the capital still had a focal pull within this network. Indeed, the geographical nature of brand advertising has been overplayed in existing studies: chain stores and brands were often both firmly located within 1930s advertisements through the prominent provision of a street address, and many chains had a prominent West End flagship store such as Jaeger and Austin Reed in Regent Street. Through the centralization of these networks into radials from a London base, chains in local high streets were infused with a certain measure of West End shopping cultures.

The West End nature of *Vogue*'s shopping geography could be straightforwardly ascribed to the fact that its advertisers were predominantly West End shops, department stores, or designers with a West End address. By the 1930s, advertisers had well-established leverage within the world of women's magazines, accounting for a significant proportion of a magazine's contents and revenue (Leiss, Klein and Jhally 1986). During the 1930s, the boundaries between the voices of the internal editorial departments and those of substantial external advertising material were certainly collapsing in terms of approach, text, and visual style, lending the powerful advertisers the authority of the editorial voice. Shopping columns and features on trips to town frequently read like advertorials, and have been interpreted by several historians as such (Scanlon 1995: 47, Rappaport 2000: 127).

However, the success with which magazines attracted advertising revenue can also be read as a testament to advertisers' belief in women's power as consumers, and the vibrancy of feminine consumption cultures. It is clear that women had responsibility for the consumption not just of fashion and domestic items, but also for commodities such as cars and gas, which were extensively advertised within women's magazines like *Vogue* in this period. It is suggested here that a reading of the West End map as advertiser-prescribed overly privileges the power of advertisers and indeed editorial to dictate its geography. There were other factors at play within consumer cultures, not least the consumers and the cultures of the city itself. The relationship between editorial and advertisers might be better seen as symbiotic: the importance of the West End as a fashion and shopping center for the target audience of *Vogue* needed to be meaningful for readers. This draws on Gilbert's reading of the urban branding of late twentieth-century fashion goods, in which he argues that "the continued cachet of the name 'Paris' depends not just on the sustained intensity of the virtual city of promotional campaigns and the fashion press, but also on the credibility of the city as a center of fashion and consumption and particularly as an embodied experience of fashion" (Gilbert 2000: 9). Consumption practices and their textual representations were mutually constitutive.

However, claims made in this article about the West End focus of fashionable consumption in *Vogue* might be seen to be undercut by the prominence of the department store within the magazine's shopping news and retail advertisements. The shopping columnist confided, "There is something very soothing about department stores, something reassuring in the proximity of every comfort for body and soul" (British *Vogue* 1936, October 28: 96). William Whiteley's declaration that everything from a pin to an elephant could be purchased in his store has become an oft-quoted element of department store mythology. It is certainly true that the large London department stores had a well-established, highly evolved retail system by 1930, housing a large number of departments, and offering an extensive range of commodities and services. The department store system would potentially allow a single store to operate independently from its location, providing a convenient shopping environment. The single-store trip provided the structure for some shopping articles. For example, in "8-Hour Day in Town," *Vogue* advised:

> At last you've booked your day – for a trip to town. You simply had to. You want a spring suit. Your skin looks alarmingly post-winter. It's Leslie's birthday in a week. Emma is murmuring about the glass cloths. The sun parlour wants redecorating. Your husband's pullovers are a sight. Old Crabtree says don't blame *him* if you have no cut flowers from the garden this summer. "A day!" you think, "I need a month. It'll take me half a day just travelling from one place to another, from dress shop to beauty salon, on to a toy shop, a decorator's, a man's shop, a seedsman's and so on." Yes, but need you? Probably you've no idea of the versatility of the modern "department store" where you can cash cheques, have beauty treatments, choose from the latest Paris models, attend an auction, watch a television programme, read and write letters, buy anything on earth from a candle to a cockatoo (British *Vogue* 1938, 16 March: 92–3).

This was a discourse that spoke of the anxiety of negotiating city shopping routes to the extent that journeys *within* a store might also prove excessively fatiguing. One *Vogue* shopping column reported a new service:

> If you have been discouraged from store shopping because of the multitude of the departments and the time taken journeying up and down the floors in search of accessories, know that your troubles are over. Mrs. Ralph Lambton has come to Peter Jones. She has simply made a big fitting room into a sanctum where you can discuss what you want and have everything assembled before your eyes in one quiet and comfortable corner (British *Vogue* 1936, November 26: 106).

Historians have been captivated by the idea of the store as panacea to consumer desire, and have ascribed too much weight to "universal providing," failing to sufficiently interrogate the claims of department store owners and the conventions of magazine journalism. There has been an assumption that convenience was not only desirable, but was a shopping priority. While this might have been true for the kind of everyday provisioning which has been the subject of many retail studies, particularly of those on the postwar period, it fundamentally misunderstands the complexity and spatiality of West End consumption.

Vogue makes it clear that concepts of "place" were at the very center of 1930s shopping cultures: infusing shopping practices, retail strategies, and narratives of consumption. A lot of useful work has already been done on the location of consumption, for example highlighting the essentially urban, even metropolitan, nature of emerging modern consumer society in the late nineteenth century, singling out the importance of particular sites (Bowlby 1985, Domosh 1996). The importance of the West End of London has already been established within this story (Breward 1999, Nava 1996, Rappaport 2000).

A close examination of the contents of *Vogue* suggests that the single department store shopping trip was largely an editorial conceit and a department store advertising strategy, as the shopping trip was neither easily nor desirably contained within one site. The overwhelmingly dominant message of a fashionable women's magazine like *Vogue* was that not only was the West End the location of London's most important shops, but that this place had a particular meaning within metropolitan cultures. While one shopper *might* shop exclusively at Peter Jones, another might do so at Harrods, Dickens and Jones, and several little shops in Bond Street, a third at a myriad of different stores. It was in this variety and multiplicity that the value of the West End lay: in the pleasurable practices of browsing and choosing through which shopping cultures were examined and identity constructed. West End stores exploited connections with the street through their careful positioning in relation to other businesses, their design, their window displays, and other use of spectacle. They advertised extensively in *Vogue*, and thus positioned themselves within the collective of shops comprising the magazine's urban narrative. Indeed, the fact that location was so very crucial for a shop meant that the shopping trip could not be "dislocated" in a real sense, whether or not it took place within a single store.

Vogue's West End was the area of London associated with entertainment, shopping, and fashionable living. It has never been easily physically defined, cutting across boundaries of local government and landowning, and encompassing parts of several smaller London districts: Soho, Mayfair, Bloomsbury, St James's, Kensington's and so on. This was a place that existed most coherently and meaningfully not as a precise territory, but as an imagined or represented place. Its map was drawn most clearly in the urban commentaries of London guidebooks, newspapers, and women's magazines such as *Vogue*, which often assembled the place from key clusters of activity, filtering out elements that did not cohere.

Vogue was of course a stage for the parading of the latest garments, a tool for their acquisition, and a textual evocation of a lifestyle in which shopping held a key role. But it also provided one of the most important narratives of the 1930s West End, one which was concerned primarily with luxury, the exclusive, the feminine and, above all, the fashionable. It was a patchwork of streets, shops, restaurants, and services, but was greater than the sum of its parts. It had a clear center: the tight cluster of streets around and between Oxford Street, Regent Street, Bond Street, and Piccadilly that was universally acknowledged as "London's most fashionable shopping district" (*London: What to See and Where to Stay*, 1930: 48).

Vogue's West End was structured by the main shopping thoroughfares, along which were London's most famous stores. Although certainly no longer novel, the department store was still an absolutely necessary component of the shopping map, *Vogue*'s shopping columnist claiming it "unthinkable to visit the Brompton Road and not Harrods" (British *Vogue* 1930, September 16: 90). Particular favorites of *Vogue* were Selfridges in Oxford Street; Dickins and Jones, and Liberty in Regent Street; and Simpsons and Fortnums in Piccadilly. The network of conspicuously positioned department stores was extended to the fringes of the West End, including Derry and Toms in Kensington High Street, Peter Jones in Sloane Square, Harrods and Harvey Nichols in Knightsbridge, telescoping the real distances between them in a manner that echoed Hadlaw's description of Beck's 1933 London Underground map: "Its magic is such that it... 'consumed' the spatial relations which existed before its creation" (Hadlaw, 2003: 25).

But it was the exclusivity of smaller streets in the heart of the West End, like Grosvenor Street, Wigmore Street, Bruton Street and, above all, Bond Street, that *Vogue* loved the most: "However one looks at the snobbish question of district, address and reputations, it is no good blinking at the fact that we are fatally influenced by goods bought in 'Bond Street', 'in Mayfair' or its purlieus" (British *Vogue* 1936, August 19). The shopping columns reveled in the designer salons, chic gown shops, milliners, jewelers, and florists, as well as the more upmarket dressmakers to be found there. The appeal of these shops was dual, and contradictory. On one hand they were positioned within a long tradition of elite West End consumption, their marketing strategies emphasizing qualities such as "timelessness" and "pedigree" in order to distinguish themselves from the more *arriviste*, showy stores of Oxford Street. On the other hand, the very exclusivity of the goods, and the highly fashionable elite cultures with which they were associated, suggested limited runs and availability. *Vogue*'s very *raison d'être* was to report and celebrate a model of consumption whose status was assured by an established history, but whose specific fashions were fleeting.

Vogue also promoted an additional community of businesses in the classified section of the back pages: the dressmakers, fur-cleaners, manicurists and dress agencies which were hidden in the real street scene: located in the upper storeys and less salubrious back streets. These elements were less glamorous, but essential for the maintenance of fashionable urban femininity,

> All together, girls – Shop-hound would like to give three loud barks and have you join in the cheering for "the little people"... those chaps you and I and all good shoppers have a passion for collecting. You know them – the "little" man who does such wonders with slip covers "at a price" – the "little woman" who runs you up a frock in no time. Hound, after spending the last fortnight tracking down a few of these treasures, now spills the beans and tells you where to find them. (British *Vogue* 1938, August 3: 48).

The magazine positioned itself as an essential mediator between London and its occupants, filtering and taming the city within its pages. The resulting urban account functioned straightforwardly as a navigational aid to the complex material city and its position within broader fashionable networks: *Vogue*'s message was very clear that the *precise* location where shopping took place was as important as what was bought, because the item's meaning was colored by the location of purchase. Yet, the magazine was also *constructing* the West End for its audience through the processes of writing about it, listing and advertising it, and photographing it.

The exclusion of particular elements was as significant as what was included. As Cosgrove writes, "All maps are thematic, selecting and highlighting particular phenomena, consciously removing others, ignoring yet more, rendering some choices incapable of adoption by virtue of prior decisions about scale and frame. Such choices and the presences and absences they create are profoundly significant both in the making and meaning of maps" (Cosgrove 1999: 11). In *Vogue*'s West End there was no hint of J. B. Priestley's downmarket London of the bypass and arterial road: "Filling stations and factories that look like exhibition buildings, of giant cinemas and dance halls and cafés, bungalows with tiny garages, cocktail bars, Woolworth's, motor coaches, wireless, hiking, factory girls looking like actresses, greyhound racing and dirt tracks, swimming pools, and everything given away for cigarette coupons" (Priestley 1934: 401). The national clothing chains such as Marks and Spencer and Dolcis, which flourished on Oxford Street as much as on the suburban high street, were also nowhere to be seen. Class was clearly an important filter within interwar shopping maps.

While the place of the West End might be expected to have a powerful "aspirational" pull for those ostensibly excluded by the geography, prices, and "exclusive" atmosphere, on the whole *Vogue*'s implicit message about class-segregated shopping geography was echoed in magazines aimed at lower-middle-class and working-class women. In two such titles, *Home Chat* and *Woman*, the West End was ostensibly absent as a shopping location, replaced by the local high street. When the different agendas of these two magazines are examined, the significance of this shopping geography becomes more apparent. Of the two, *Home Chat* was much more domestically orientated, and so its rejection of metropolitan consumption is perhaps not surprising. But *Woman* was a brand new magazine, launched in 1937. Although aimed at a similar income bracket as *Home Chat*, it had a rather different profile, seeking to represent a younger, more modern version of womanhood. It had a territory extending beyond the confines of the home: in addition to housewives, it addressed working women, often depicted as secretaries and sales assistants of the sort that peopled the West End's flourishing retail and office districts.[3] This group, positioned by historians such as Alexander at the very heart of the thriving interwar consumer society, enjoyed increased levels of disposable income, ripe for expenditure on cheap ready-to-wear dresses, which drew on Hollywood-inspired models of fashionability (Alexander 1994). However, whereas in *Vogue* femininity was largely constructed through the consumption of fashion, in *Woman*, as in *Home Chat*, it was done primarily through women's domestic role, whether or not this role was juggled with waged work. Furthermore, in both magazines, the very practice of shopping for fashionable goods held a distinctly ambiguous position, in conflict with more family-centered housekeeping knowledges and other, more creative, methods of engaging with fashionable cultures.

It would appear that the consumers represented in *Home Chat* and *Woman* did not simply *prefer* to shop locally: they actually felt excluded from the fashionable West End shopping map. This experience of ostracism was articulated through comments about provincial isolation and insufficient income. A typical correspondent complained, "I live in the country and the nearest town doesn't possess any very smart women's shops so that when I see exciting frocks and accessories in *Woman* I long to send for them… " (*Woman* 1939, July 22: 4). Another wrote, "Alas a modest country bumpkin, I rarely visit London, I find it simply eats up money" (*Woman* 1939, September 23: 4). While the doors of the famous West End stores were theoretically open to anyone, not all women felt in a position to take up the invitation.

Vogue's processes of urban "editing" echo the strategies for controlling and redefining the chaotic, irrational city to create order, legibility, rationality, and modernity are described in Nead, Rappaport and Walkowitz's accounts of Victorian and Edwardian London (Nead 2000, Rappaport 2000, Walkowitz 1992). Shifting the focus from the writing to the reading of *Vogue*, there is also a substantial and multidisciplinary body of work that explores the nature of the relationship between text and city, which suggests ways in which *Vogue*'s blueprints for shopping trips, contained in shopping columns, could constitute mental maps for urban imaginings (Crang, Crang and May 1999, Donald 1999, Gilbert 2002, Schlör 1998, Vasudevan 2003). Donald talks of a city "which, snail-like, I carry around with me… It has been learned as much from novels, pictures and half-remembered films as from diligent walks round the capital cities of Europe." This is an "imagined environment [that] embraces not just the cities created by the 'wagging tongues' of architects, planners and builders, sociologists and novelists, poets and politicians, but also the translation of the places they have made into the imaginary reality of our mental life" (Donald 1999: 7–8). *Vogue*'s West End narratives shaped the West End into a map, a "modern" system of routes, which blurred with another lived and imagined city that was less easily deciphered, but was more obviously infused with the ephemerality, kineticism, and chaos that were the lifeblood of West End shopping cultures.

Narratives of London within *Vogue* often constructed the city, for outsiders, as the destination of an expedition. Indeed, that the West End's shopping crowds were largely formed of those who lived somewhere else was a common theme of contemporary accounts of the city. One author commented, "The passenger traffic is tidal, flowing in the morning and ebbing at night. The centre of London is depopulating steadily whilst the suburbs, its dormitories, are filling" (*Round and About London by Tram* 1930). The "trip" was a particularly important mechanism with which *Vogue* discussed shopping, and constructed its shopping geographies. This trip was shown to involve a sense of occasion, whether the shopper traveled the short distance from Hampstead for an afternoon, from suburban Surbiton for a day, or from Yorkshire for a precious week. Indeed such explicit distinctions between categories of reader were often collapsed by the magazine; all ascribed the same adhesion to metropolitan cultures. This reflected a deliberate attempt to broaden the appeal of the magazine's contents, but also provided a comment on the London-centric nature of the cultures of England's affluent middle classes.

One discernable response to the "otherness" of central London was that of "marveling," as expressed in one guide book:

> The train spins smoothly over the points, and whether your terminus is Charing Cross, Victoria, Paddington, Waterloo or Holborn, you feel the spell of the greatest Metropolis of the world enthralling you every moment as you approach it… Already, perhaps, London has cast her spell over you. How vast she is; how enigmatic; how difficult to know; how fiercely life flows through the labyrinth of her ways; how exciting the smell of her; the steady throb of the abounding life in her as her million wheels go pounding past (*The Magic of London* 1931: 7).

However, this seduction of strangers did not capture the essence of *Vogue*'s depiction of London. Paris or Rome might be featured as tourist cities where the reader could meander, wondering at the curiousness of the city, but London, for the *Vogue* reader, was meant to be; "home" turf she was a habitué, even if she did not actually live there. Neither was she represented as a *flâneuse,* her senses overstimulated by the exhibition of London streets: her visit was altogether more purposeful, if still pleasurable. While women illustrated in *Vogue*'s society profiles, fashion features, and advertisements were often experienced urbanites, other parts of the text acknowledged an additional readership of partial "strangers" to the city who didn't want to appear as such. Advice columns and articles thus recurrently presented the West End as the destination of a journey, or "expedition":

> We can't advise you too strongly to plan your day several days ahead… with as much care and cunning as if it were a trip to the tropics. List what you want to buy. If you are shopping for your family and house, make a note of all the necessary data. (Your husband's collar size, your children's measurements, the area of the lawn.) Collect swatches of all your existing clothes, so that the things you buy will fit into your colour schemes (British *Vogue* 1938, March 16: 92).

The magazine clearly styled itself as the source of urban knowledge to enable a confident and nonchalant navigation of the West End's shopping streets without rhapsodising inappropriately about its wonders.

Vogue represented London as a world city, constructing a map of consumption which extended way beyond the boundaries of the British Isles to far-flung corners of the globe. This network existed alongside,

Figure 2
The front cover of the
Coronation Issue of *Vogue*.
(British *Vogue*. 1937. April 28.)
Pierre Roy/British *Vogue*.

and intersected with, still potent concepts of Empire, and also the
fraught international political relations which formed the content of
1930s news bulletins. *Vogue*'s fashionable social whirl was lived out on
an international stage, of which a shopping geography was one part,
but a pivotal one. In this context, the West End was portrayed as a
storecupboard to provide the goods to equip people for international
living. In addition to the British-based social calendar, *Vogue* also painted
an atlas of travel destinations. For instance, one single issue contained
articles entitled: "Fashions from the Riviera," "Cruising: What Clothes
to Take," "When You Go to Egypt," "Pleasures of India," "The School
of Skiing," and "Golf in Southern France" (British, *Vogue* 1930.

January). All of these environments required a dedicated wardrobe, and *Vogue* structured its fashion features so as to provide them.

This image of London as a world city was echoed by Yardley, a frequent advertiser in British, American, and French editions of *Vogue*. Yardley frequently promoted the West End as internationally important due to a potent connection of goods and place, selling its products to a British audience with the phrase, "Complexion born in Bond Street, now known around the world" (British *Vogue,* 1936, September 16: 1). Similarly, it advertised the English Lavender range in American *Vogue* with a letter purportedly from an Englishman in Calcutta, who described his wife, "Each morning when she starts off from the terrace, her obviously West End tussor, her sure horsemanship... and most of all her fresh, clear complexion make you know that a real bit of England is driving through the compound" (American *Vogue* 1930, April 12: 135). Furthermore, West End shopping was presented by Yardley as a means of reconciling the demands of operating within complex national and international circuits: "Into London these days come flocking hundreds of lovely, sun-saturated women from their holiday hideaways bent upon turning themselves immediately from careless summer beauties into creatures of radiant, formal loveliness... hurrying to one famous House in Bond Street as first step in the transformation" (British *Vogue* 1936, September 16: 1).

Vogue's broader networks of fashionability also came into play. These networks did not straightforwardly replicate the shopping map, presenting an imagined geography of fashion references, of high-fashion culture, rather than tracing the routes of shopping and shops. In this map, Paris and London were positioned as key hubs. The preoccupation with the Parisian followed a well-established tradition within British feminine fashion, mediated through women's magazines. The relationship was described in an article entitled "How They Brought the Good News from Paris to London"

> Our fashion editors have been in Paris since the Openings began, but then, theirs is no simple, straightforward task of mere reporting. From hundreds of new styles *Vogue* sets out to separate the successes from the sensation... And this goes on till the very last 'plane has rushed the last scrap of information to *Vogue*'s London office, in the nick of time for the Paris Fashions issue. But since nowadays London itself is so important – even at Paris Collections time! – *Vogue* plans to show, too, pages of fashion from our own famous houses... (British *Vogue* 1936, February 19).

By setting up this binary fashion system, British *Vogue* turned its back on the rise in importance of the US as a fashion influence.

Figure 3

Graphically illustrating the tensions between Paris and London in "*Vogue*'s-Eye View of the Mode." (British *Vogue*. 1935. September 18: 57.) British *Vogue*.

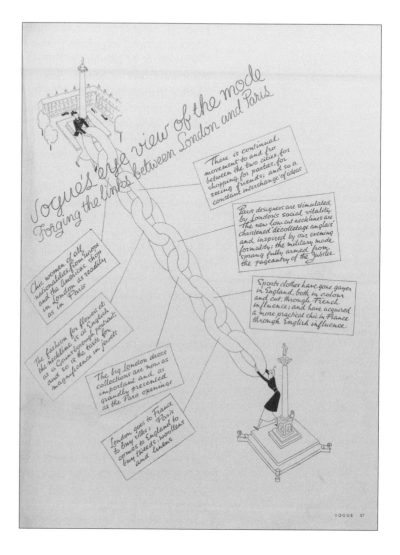

An image of West End shopping cultures extending tendrils of influence across the globe was clearly attractive for a British audience, and probably resonated particularly strongly with the expatriate community, on whose consumption practices and cultures more work would be extremely useful. British *Vogue* publicized its availability from any bookseller in the British Dominions and Dependencies, and the limited evidence available from oral histories and directories of *Vogue* dress pattern availability both suggest an important *Vogue*-reading expatriate community from Rome to Delhi, with a shared investment in London's metropolitan consumption cultures, despite their physical distance from the place.[4]

But *Vogue*'s map did not just imply that the West End was a world player, it claimed it was pivotal within an international network of fashionable consumption for those who were *not* British. It is relevant that the 1930s was a period of growth in the British tourist industry, reaching a peak in the coronation year of 1937. London became increasingly a self-consciously "tourist" city: within the flurry of tourist literature, the West End was consistently included as a key element of London's special nature. Shopping itself had a key role within tourism: shopping was portrayed as a leisure activity for tourists and West End shops were positioned as tourist "sights," with their iconic architecture and spectacular displays. As *Art and Industry* claimed, "London's shops are part of London's attractions. Almost every visitor makes a point of seeing what London offers the shopper" ("Come to Britain!" 1936: 86).

British *Vogue*'s positioning of the West End as a crucial node within an international network of fashionable consumption is significantly complicated when compared with American and French versions of the same network. *Vogue* was a American-owned tripartite business during the 1930s, with editions published in London, New York, and Paris. Some content was shared between editions, and each painted an atlas of fashionable life that privileged the other two nations above other places, habitually using them as points of comparison with their own cultures. However, each version of *Vogue* had its own staff, distinctive style, editorial slant, and advertisers. Most importantly, the city of publication infused each edition: New York and Paris were portrayed as the focus of fashionable life and consumption in the American and French editions respectively, just as London was the pivot for British *Vogue*. Each sketched out its own shopping geography, with fashion features, directories, and shopping columns. Links were also made by each to differently structured national and international networks.

Importantly, within American and French *Vogue*'s international networks, London was not primarily presented as a modern center of fashion or fashionable consumption, although very occasionally guides to London shopping did appear.[5] These editions usually characterized the city in terms of tradition rather than modernity, of heritage rather than of consumption. Coverage highlighted country-based elite pursuits, for example Nancy Mitford's article, "The English Shooting Party" (American *Vogue* 1930, March 29: 58–9, 84), or accounts of more metropolitan society etiquette. Fashion features and advertisements for British fashions focused on English tweeds and Scottish tartans: "Hear the word 'tweeds' and all that is indigenous to British life—mist-shrouded moors, heather, gorse, grouse-shooting—comes immediately to mind" (American *Vogue* 1934, October 15: 72). Additionally, and connectedly, they painted a view of the West End which celebrated traditional, masculine shops rather than the modern departures that might be valued by the British shoppers: "'What can I buy that is typically

English?' asks the visitor to London. 'What clothes can I get here that are better than anything of the sort anywhere else?'... Look in the men's shops. Not for nothing is London famed as the highest authority on men's fashions" (American *Vogue* 1930, June 21: 54). Similarly, French *Vogue* highlighted the essential tradition and masculinity of the West End's shopping cultures: "Mayfair is not just an area of London, it is first and foremost a grand way of living... It's the shop windows that make you realize that London is the most civilized city in the world... London chic is masculine: women's fashion is considered an optional extra, a lesser art that should not be allowed to take center stage" (French *Vogue* 1938: July: 42).

American *Vogue*'s territory of international consumption gave Paris a much more important position than London, lauding French fashions and designers and explicitly acknowledging their influence on American fashions, with frequent "Paris fashion" editions. The relative merits of each country were clearly set out in the article "London after Dark":

> The American craze for England is growing in leaps and bounds. All the American "social head-liners" now include England in their yearly rounds, as regularly as clockwork. Their routine is apt to be this: a fortnight's hard work in Paris with dressmakers; a month or six weeks' fun in England, with a return visit to Paris; a fast crossing to America; a fortnight or so of the New York season around Christmas, and then points south (American *Vogue* 1935 January 1: 84).

Advertisements in the American edition displayed a marked francophilia, for example the New York based Lily of France corset company and Mello-glo cosmetic powder, recommended as "C'est Paris... as smart as Paris itself" (American *Vogue* 1935, February 15: 97). In addition, Paris was presented as a city to shop in. Readers were provided a fashionable navigation of city's shops through articles such as "A Guide to the Seeker for Gifts in the Turmoil of Paris Shopping" (American *Vogue* 1930, May 10: 158) and "Highways and Buyways of Paris" which advised, "To reach Gabry's smart little handkerchief shop, at 18 Rue Godot-de-Mauroy, you must pass through the Galerie des Quatre Chemins, which often has exhibits of very good modern paintings and invariably has interesting French editions of modern books" (American *Vogue* 1930, March 29: 20). Occasionally, *Vogue* even carried a directory of advertisements for Parisian shops and designers, collected together in pages titled "The Shops of *Vogue* in Paris."

American *Vogue*, of course, commodified and constructed Paris specifically for its American readers, an approach echoed by the Service Aimcee, which advertised in *Vogue*. It was a "centrally located, intelligently planned, helpfully staffed information and guidance office, with the American point of view, for American visitors in Paris"

(American *Vogue* 1930, January 4: 5). It structured a map of Paris by answering questions such as: "What shall I take home to Cousin Amanda? Where can my husband get ham and eggs? Where can I read American magazines? What 'little' dressmaker in Paris combines real style with moderate prices? Where shall I have my mail sent? Where can I make reservations for theater tickets... wagon-lits... steamer accommodations... airplane flights... sightseeing tours... automobile jaunts?" Marshall Field department store boasted in a *Vogue* advertisement that it was "Transplanting Paris" to the US, depicting a "typical" Paris scene delivered direct to Americans by liner and train:

> At a famous numero of the Rue de la Paix, appraising eyes review passing creations... Somewhere on the Rue St. Honoré a man who has bought millions of gloves for us selects several of the better new styles... These are some of Marshall Field and Company's large staff of resident representatives in Paris. In addition, scores of men and women from Field's in Chicago visit Paris periodically. Alert, fashion-wise, their purchases reflect an intimate knowledge of Continental correctness. You are cordially invited to come to Field's for almost anything you might like from Paris (American *Vogue* 1930. May 24: 5).

Yet, Paris remained conceptualized as somewhere "other." The perceived stylistic and conceptual extremes of Parisian haute couture, for example the Indian-inspired fashions of spring 1935, were felt to be not quite acceptable for American audience who dressed more practically:

> Had a string of sacred elephants been led into the Spring Collections, the shock could not have been greater than when Schiaparelli and Alix ushered in their astonishing Hindu evening dresses. Seductive saris. Ihram headscarves. Mysterious, gauzy drapery. Nautsch-girl sandals. The press scribbled wildly. The buyers gaped. Only the private French clients seemed unaghast... Among the American contingent, questions flew thick and fast. Would New York wear these robes? (American *Vogue* 1935, March 15: 51).

Such a response was particularly invited by the surrealist work of Schiaparelli, but it was also a broader undercurrent within American commentary on the French collections. Parisian haute couture seemed happy enough to play along given the business at stake, self-consciously designing differently for the home and foreign markets. Yet the French edition of *Vogue* was much more insular than either the British or American editions. Furthermore, in French *Vogue*, Paris was largely conceptualized and mapped as a fashion city rather than as a shopping city, as one 1935 article captured:

Paris is too alive to not reinvent itself along with the seasons. A hidden but powerful force is pulling it westward. This migration has accelerated during recent months, and the Champs Élysées traffic circle will soon be known in the hearts of all women as the "traffic circle of couture." More than anywhere else in the city it represents the gateway controlling access to the couturier and milliner. The Avenue Matignon is the principal artery where the pulse of elegance beats furiously. Agnès, Reboux, Talbot, Lelong, Rochas, Alix, Fourrures Max, next to each other, on top of each other, fight over each square meter of this precious location. Even Worth has deserted the stuffy Rue de la Paix to move closer to this enchanted circle. Basking in its shadow, l'Avenue Montaigne draws faithful visitors to Mainbocher, and the Champs Élysées houses Maggy Rouff and Heim, as well as *Vogue*, positioned conveniently to oversee proceedings. It's in this rich terrain that fashions are born and take their first steps before flying the nest to live out their fleeting existence (French *Vogue* 1935, December: 29).

Importantly, these international networks of shopping, fashion, and tourism were not altogether static. Whilst French *Vogue* remained largely concerned with Paris, during the 1930s American *Vogue* reflected a homegrown fashion industry increasingly confident in homegrown designs, a movement accelerated but not instigated by difficulties in accessing Paris during the Second World War. In 1938, the magazine had established an annual "Americana Issue" with an entirely new fashionable geography, complementing the continued feature on Paris collections. The 1940 Americana issue revealed an American fashion industry with a newfound self-confidence, which was shifting its relationship with international networks:

It is no news that American clothes today have a definite and recognizable quality of their own. Sometimes, they have achieved this by purely American design; sometimes by the intelligent adaptation, evolution, or naturalization of French designs. But however it is accomplished, the fact is that in their own field they have a quality recognized all over the world of fashion; and in their best expression, they are delightful not only to American women of sophisticated taste, but to smart internationals as well. What *is* news is the stirring life in the creative field of American clothes… we are newly eager to stamp every expression of our lives "American" (American *Vogue* 1940, February 1: 86).

The issue included an extensive directory of the rising stars of American fashion design (American *Vogue* 1940, February 1: 147–9). By this time, Marshall Field had stopped "transplanting Paris" and advertised clothes expressing "American affinity."

There was, then, a dissonance between the British, French, and American geographies of consumption and narratives of the West End. Yet British constructions of international shopping networks, in which the West End held an important place for foreigners, were nonetheless meaningful for a British audience, pointing to the usefulness of exploring perceptions of international relationships within concepts of Britishness. *This* was the audience for whom the suggestion that "the feminine world of fashion, from China to Peru, has heard of Bond Street" attached value to shopping in the West End (*London: A Combined Guidebook and Atla*s. 1937: p. xiii). Shopping practices and goods accrued meaning through wrapping them with this imagined international context within the pages of *Vogue.*

To return, then, to the central issue of how British *Vogue* worked as a narrative of London, drawing its maps and positioning it at the center of complex fashionable networks: it was in the very nature of fashionable consumption to resist the precise "fixing" that this might suggest. The constantly shifting nature of the modern city has preoccupied historians of modernity, and is usefully described by Wilson: "Continual flux and change is one of the most disquieting aspects of the modern city… That which we thought was most permanent dissolves as rapidly as the kaleidoscopic spectacle of the crowds and vehicles that pass through its streets" (Wilson 1991: 3). Nead has argued that the fear of this flux created an urge to repeatedly re-narrate Victorian London (Nead 2000:8), in ways that draw parallels with 1930s *Vogue.* The 1930s was an era with a heightened awareness of the shifting national geographies of shopping, not least because of the transformations occasioned by expansions of suburban centers and the impact of chains. Lawrence Neal lamented the very instability of these geographies: "The thoroughfares in and out of London are littered with derelict shopping areas that have fortuitously risen and then fallen with the popularity and decline of their surrounding neighbourhoods" (Neal 1932: 67). *Vogue* can be interpreted as a medium especially suited to documenting the ever-changing real and imagined geographies of fashionable shopping described in this article, due to its own inherently ephemeral nature.

Vogue was issued fortnightly and, even more than its competitors, was intricately connected with the world of fashion and fashionable metropolitan consumption, whose preoccupation with novelty drove the editorial framework and content. Associations with this world dictated an especially heightened importance given to nuanced change. The purchase of successive date-stamped issues was portrayed by publishers as essential to updating shopping knowledge:

> If you should pick up a *Vogue* of spring 1929, and compare it with the present issue, you would realize very forcibly the great change that fashion has undergone in a year. The year 1929 seems definitely *démodé.* The 1930 woman has a new silhouette, a new

Figure 4
Mapping the shifting city in "London Town is Moving Round." (British *Vogue*. 1938. June 8: 72.) Seymour Leslie/ British *Vogue*.

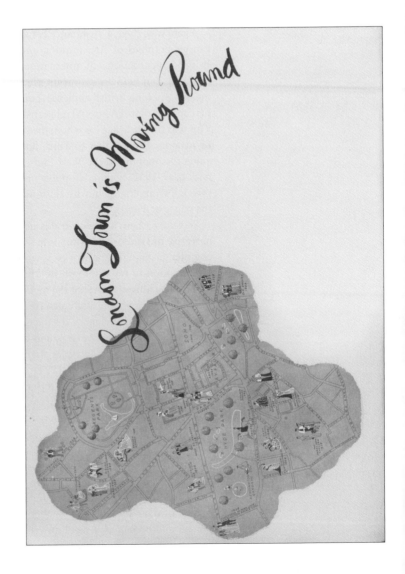

spirit, and an entirely new feeling for clothes. There are new intricacies and shadings—all of which make life more interesting for women in general, for shops, and for *Vogue* (American *Vogue* 1930, March 15: 66).

The message about the fleeting nature of fashion was echoed in *Vogue*'s mapping of the city. The article, "London Town is Moving Round" charted the shifting geographies of fashionable living in the West End: "All London is on the move as it has been for centuries, though the tempo is faster today. Old sections become déclassé, others are renewed, transformed" (British *Vogue* 1938, June 8: 72). Belgravia was plotted on the map as the locus for "stuffy dowagers" in 1888, but was "very smart" in 1938; Baker Street was deemed "smart" in 1788, "dowdy" in 1888, and "smart but sick" in 1938.

However, women's magazines had what Beetham terms a "double relationship with time": "Each number of a periodical is both of its moment and of a series, different from and yet the same as those which have gone before" (Beetham 1996: 12). The evidence of oral histories suggests that women's magazines were often not treated as "throwaway," but were rather collected and shared.[6] This lasting value was especially likely to be ascribed to the expensive, glossy issues of *Vogue*. The impression of inbuilt obsolescence masked a certain continuity in the editorial message about matters such as the class and geography of fashionable consumption. A "cumulative" reading constructed a shopping map that might sometimes dabble in French style, and might meander in places from the beaten track, but was consistently rooted in the West End of London.

This article has argued that an important kind of interwar modernity is evidenced by the fashionable metropolitan shopping cultures of a magazine like *Vogue*, which must be allowed to sit alongside received understandings of 1930s Britain. Far from being a period of decline and of preparation for the exodus of customers and businesses from the city center, the 1930s West End was still an important hub of fashionable consumption in Britain, with ripples sent farther out to other places where the West End held meaning. In the 1930s, the question of the future of British shopping geographies was far from settled. Indeed, invocation of the West End as a place was one of the most important tools in the hands of West End businesses and the metropolitan fashion industry, enabling them to stand their ground. *Vogue* maintained that shopping which occurred in the West End was special and specific to that place, conferring value, status, and meaning on both the activity and items bought, suggesting that within 1930s consumption cultures, this spatial performance was as important as the purchase of particular commodities. The argument is that location and networks are a crucial means of understanding historical retail and shopping cultures. While the importance of the West End of London has already been established within this story (Breward 1999, Nava 1996, Rappaport 2000), the backdrop has largely been a Victorian and Edwardian London viewed through a framework of polarities specific to that historical moment: pleasure and anxiety, safety and danger, respectability and immorality (Nava 1996: 42, Walkowitz 1992), whereas the London of 1930s *Vogue* was a very different kind of place: a territory of more confident and plentiful fashionable feminine consumers, occupied with navigating their way through its complexities.

Notes

1. This article discusses the British edition of *Vogue*, unless otherwise stated.
2. Statistics from the Marks and Spencer Archive.
3. See, for example, articles such as "Women Must Work," *Woman*, 1937: June 12.
4. Oral history collection, "Home Dressmaking Reassessed," Hampshire Record Office, AV550.
5. See, for example, the "London Address Book" published in American *Vogue*, 1934, June 15 and October 15.
6. This pattern of usage is reflected in the discussion of magazines in "Home Dressmaking Reassessed," Hampshire Record Office, AV550.

The research and writing of this paper was generously supported by the ESRC/AHRC Cultures of Consumption Programme as part of the "Shopping Routes Project" (No. RES-143-25-0038).

References

Anonymous. 1938. "8-Hour Day in Town." 1938. British *Vogue*, March 16.
Anonymous. 1930. "A Guide to the Seeker for Gifts in the Turmoil of Paris Shopping." 1930. American *Vogue*, May 10.
Anonymous. 1936. "A New London". 1936. British *Vogue*, August 5.
Alexander, Sally. 1994. "Becoming a Woman in London in the 1920s and 30s," in *Becoming a Woman and Other Essays in 19th and 20th Century Feminist History* London: Virago.
American *Vogue*. 1930. January 4.
American *Vogue*. 1930. March 29.
American *Vogue*. 1930. April 12.
American *Vogue*. 1930. May 24.
American *Vogue*. 1930. June 21.
American *Vogue*. 1935. February 15.
American *Vogue*. 1935. March 15.
American *Vogue*. 1940. February 1: 147–9.
Beetham, Margaret. 1996. *A Magazine of Her Own? Domesticity and Desire in the Woman's Magazine 1800–1914*. London: Routledge.
Bowlby, Rachel. 1985. *Just Looking: Consumer Culture in Dreiser, Gissing and Zola*. London: Methuen.
Breward, Christopher. 1999. *The Hidden Consumer: Masculinities, Fashion and City Life, 1860–1914*. Manchester: Manchester University Press.

—— 2004. *Fashioning London: Clothing and the Modern Metropolis.* Oxford: Berg.

British *Vogue.* 1930. January.

British *Vogue.* 1936. September 16.

British *Vogue.* 1938. June 8.

"Come to Britain!" 1936. *Art and Industry*, September.

Cosgrove, Denis (ed.). 1999. *Mappings.* London: Reaktion.

Crang, Mike, Phil Crang and Jon May (eds). 1999. *Virtual Geographies: Bodies, Space and Relations.* London: Routledge.

Domosh, Mona. 1996. "The Feminised Retail Landscape: Gender Ideology and Consumer Culture in Nineteenth-Century New York City," in *Retailing, Consumption and Capital: Towards the New Retail Geography*, (eds) Neil Wrigley and Michelle Lowe. Harlow: Longman.

Donald, James. 1999. *Imagining the Modern City.* London: Athlone Press.

"For Town." 1935. British *Vogue*, March 20.

Gilbert, David. 2000. "Urban Outfitting: the City and the Spaces of Fashion Culture," in *Fashion Cultures: Theories, Explorations and Analysis*, (eds) Stella Bruzzi and Pamela Church Gibson. London: Routledge.

Gilbert, Pamela (ed.). 2002. *Imagined Londons.* Albany: State University of New York Press.

Hadlaw, Janin. 2003. "The London Underground Map: Imagining Modern Time and Space," in *Design Issues*, 19: 1, 25–35.

"Highways and Buyways of Paris." 1930. American *Vogue*, March 29.

"How They Brought the Good News from Paris to London." 1936. *Vogue*, February 19.

Humble, Nicola. 2001. *The Feminine Middlebrow Novel, 1920s to 1950s: Class, Domesticity and Bohemianism.* Oxford: Oxford University Press.

"La Symphonie de Londres." 1938. French *Vogue*, July.

"Le Rond-Point de la Couture." 1935. French *Vogue*, December.

Leiss, William, Stephen Kline and Sut Jhally. 1986. *Social Communication in Advertising: Persons, Products and Images of Well-Being.* London: Methuen.

London: A Combined Guidebook and Atlas. 1937. London: Thomas Cook and Son.

"London After Dark." 1935. American *Vogue*, January 1.

"London Town is Moving Round." 1938. British *Vogue*, June 8.

London: What to See and Where to Stay 1930. London: Residential Hotels' and Caterers' Association.

The Magic of London: Guide to London and Round About. 1931. The Southern Railway of England and Great Western Railway of England.

Nava, Mica. 1996. "Modernity's Disavowal: Women, the City and the Department Store," in *Modern Times: Reflections on a Century of English Modernity*, (eds) Mica Nava and Alan O'Shea. London: Routledge.

Nead, Lynda. 2000. *Victorian Babylon: People, Streets and Images in Nineteenth-Century London*. New Haven: Yale University Press.

Neal, Lawrence E. 1932. *Retailing and the Public*. London: George Allen and Unwin.

Priestley, J. B. 1934. *English Journey*. London: Heinemann.

Rappaport, Erika. 2000. *Shopping for Pleasure: Women and the Making of London's West End*. Princeton: Princeton University Press.

Round and About London by Tram: North of the Thames. c.1930.

Scanlon, Jennifer. 1995. *Inarticulate Longings: The Ladies' Home Journal, Gender and the Promises of Consumer Culture*. New York and London: Routledge.

Schlör, Joachim. 1998. *Nights in the Big City*. London: Reaktion Books.

"Shop-hound." 1930. British *Vogue*, September 16.

"Shop-hound." 1936. British *Vogue*, August 19.

"Shop-hound." 1936. British *Vogue*, October 28.

"Shop-hound." 1936. British *Vogue*, November 26.

"Shop-hound." 1938. British *Vogue*, August 3.

Vasudevan, Alexander. 2003. "Writing the Asphalt Jungle: Berlin and the Performance of Classical Modernity," *Environment and Planning D: Society and Space*, 21, 169–194.

"*Vogue*'s-Eye View of the Mode: Forging the Links Between London and Paris." 1935. British *Vogue*, September 18.

Walkowitz, Judith. 1992. *City of Dreadful Delight: Narratives of Sexual Danger in Late Victorian London*. London: Virago.

Wilson, Elizabeth. 1991. *The Sphinx in the City: Urban Life, the Control of Disorder, and Women*. California: University of California Press.

Winship, Janice. 2000. "Culture of Restraint: The British Chain Store 1920–1939," in *Commercial Cultures: Economies, Practices, Spaces*, (eds) Peter Jackson et al. Oxford: Berg.

Woman. 1939. July 22.

Woman. 1939. September 23.

"Women Must Work." 1937. *Woman*, June 12.

Zola, Emile. 1998. *The Ladies' Paradise*. Oxford: Oxford University Press.

Fashion Theory, Volume 10, Issue 1/2, pp. 97–126
Reprints available directly from the Publishers.
Photocopying permitted by licence only.
© 2006 Berg.

Lee Miller: Model, Photographer, and War Correspondent in *Vogue*, 1927–1953

Becky E. Conekin

Dr. Becky E. Conekin is Senior
Research Fellow and Principal
Lecturer in Historical and Cultural
Studies at the London College
of Fashion, the University of the
Arts. She is the author of *The
Autobiography of a Nation: The
1951 Festival of Britain* (Manchester
Studies in Design: 2003) and
the co-editor of *The Englishness
of English Dress* (Berg: 2002)
and *Moments of Modernity:
Reconstructing Britain 1945–1964*
(Rivers Oram: 1999).
b.conekin@fashion.arts.ac.uk

Although the constant queues outside the exhibition of her portraits in the National Portrait Gallery, London, surely mean that Lee Miller is finally a well-known photographer, at least in her adopted country, what has not always been recognized is the importance of *Vogue* magazine to her career. Perhaps it is not an accident that as she has come to be recognized as a true artist, her association with a fashion magazine has been downplayed. But, in fact, Miller was employed by *Vogue* for almost the entirety of her career, beginning in 1927 as a model, then from 1930 as a photographer, and by 1944, she had added a baby Hermes typewriter to her tools of the trade. Lee Miller moved seemingly effortlessly from one side of the camera to the other and then on into the role of war

Figure 1
Lee Miller on the cover of
American *Vogue*, age twenty,
by Georges Lepape, March 15,
1927. Georges Lepape/Vogue
© Condé Nast Publications Inc.

correspondent and writer. In 1953 she wrote and photographed her
last substantive piece for British *Vogue*, ending an affiliation that had
spanned over twenty-five years and three countries.[1]

Born in Poughkeepsie, New York, to a middle-class family, Lee Miller
ended up as what her dear friend, *Life* photographer Dave Scherman, has
called "the nearest thing I knew to a mid-twentieth-century renaissance
woman" (Scherman, foreword to Penrose ([1992] 2005: 13). Miller's
relationship with *Vogue* magazine began when she was twenty years old
and studying lighting and theater design at the Art Students' League in
New York City. Born Elizabeth Miller in 1907, she was called Liz, then
Li-Li, and finally Lee (Scherman, foreword to Penrose 2005). Thanks
to an "accidental" meeting with Condé Nast (the publisher saved her
from being run over on a Manhattan street), she was the cover girl

for American *Vogue*'s March 1927 issue (Figure 1).[2] From then on Edward Steichen and Arnold Genthe often photographed her before she moved to Paris two years later and became the favorite model of French *Vogue*'s George Hoyningen-Huene, as well as Man Ray's model, muse, lover, and apprentice. By the winter of 1930 she had her own apartment and studio in Montparnasse and was regularly landing assignments as a photographer for leading Paris designers, including Patou, Schiaparelli, and Chanel (Penrose [1985] 2002: 32–7). She was subject and object, photographer and model, artist and muse simultaneously. Her look was perfect for the time—tall and blonde, with an athletic body and large, intense eyes. A glass manufacturer designed a champagne goblet inspired by the shape of her breast, and when *Time* magazine ran an article about Man Ray, which included a photograph of him accompanied by Miller, the text asserted that she was "widely celebrated for having the most beautiful navel in Paris" (Penrose [1985] 2002: 32 and "Rayograms," *Time*, April 18, 1932, as quoted by Penrose [1985] 2002: 32).

Lee Miller was young, female, cosmopolitan, fashionable, sexually liberated, and involved in one of modernism's most important art movements—surrealism. Unlike the formalist, modernist movements—Postimpressionism and cubism—that preceded it, surrealism was very interested and involved in the world of fashion. In his book *Fashion and Surrealism*, Richard Martin argues that "Fashion became surrealism's most compelling friction between the ordinary and extraordinary..." (Martin [1988] 1996: 9). Martin reports that by the 1930s, surrealists had "entered the realms of fashion, fashion advertising, and window display" and that the surrealist style was "pervasive" "among the major fashion publications, most especially *Vogue* and *Harper's Bazaar*" (Martin [1987] 1996: 217). Jean Cocteau, Leonor Fini, George Hoyningen-Huene, and Man Ray, among others, according to Martin, "were recruited as the unlikely missionaries for the stylistic revolution" (ibid.). Lee Miller positioned herself at this intersection of art and fashion when in August 1930, French *Vogue* covered the white-themed "Bal Blanc" thrown by Count and Countess Pecci-Blunt. Man Ray's photograph of a group dressed as classical statues in white accompanied the French text. Man Ray's autobiography (1963) explains that the count and countess had installed a white dancefloor in their garden, with the orchestra hidden behind the bushes, and that he had been "asked to think up some added attraction." He had set up a film projector in an upper-floor room and projected an "old hand-colored film by the pioneer French filmmaker, Melies" onto the white couples "revolving on the white floor"; "the effect was eerie." He remembered that he had taken "as assistant a pupil who studied photography" with him and that they both dressed in tennis whites; hers were "very smart" and "especially designed" by the Paris designer, Madame Vionnet. This "assistant" was Lee Miller: "A slim figure with blonde hair and lovely legs, she was continually being taken away to dance, leaving me to concentrate alone on my photography. I was pleased with her success, but annoyed at the same time, not because of the added work, but out of jealousy; I was in love with her" (Man Ray, 1963: 168 and Penrose [1985] 2002: 24–5).

Two months later, French *Vogue* readers were informed that "Miss Lee Miller" was playing the lead female role as a statue in Cocteau's first film, *Blood of a Poet*. Miller appeared in another canonic surrealist image, Man Ray's *Object of Destruction*, a photograph of her eye attached to a metronome, created as a kind of angry memento of their relationship after she returned to New York in the fall of 1932 (French *Vogue*, Octobre 1930: 90–91 and Penrose [1985] 2002: 28–42).

Miller said of herself more than once later in her life that at this time she "looked like an angel, but was a demon inside"[3] (Reid 2004). Perhaps it was this combination that was so compelling: her look matched the ideal of interwar cosmopolitanism. She was among the first generation of professional fashion models, as the fashion magazines moved away from their earlier reliance on portraits of society women (Chadwick 2003: 211–12). Hoyningen-Huene photographed her for French *Vogue* in toile and flannel pants by Helene Yrande and Schiaparelli, respectively, for the July 1930 issue, picturing Miller as the epitome of the relaxed, sporty, modern woman. Other Hoyningen-Huene photographs show her looking aloof and elegant in evening dresses by, for example, Jeanne Lanvin from October 1930, Mainbocher from February 1931, and Jean Patou from May 1931.

Miller's own photographs for French *Vogue* at this time often focused on objects, rather than women. Yet her surrealist eye for shadows is apparent, even when she was only shooting backgammon boards, as was the case in April 1931 (French *Vogue*: 61). Miller said in an interview in 1975 that Man Ray had "taught her everything in her first year [with him]: "... fashion pictures... portraits... the whole technique of what he did.'" (Miller, as quoted by Amaya 1975: 55). And, in turn, she studied studio lighting with Hoyningen-Huene, as he photographed her for *Vogue*. According to her son and biographer, Tony Penrose, "these modelling sessions with Hoyningen-Huene were rather like a privileged tutorial, allowing Lee to experience the work on both sides of the camera at the same time" (Penrose [1985] 2002: 29).

Bringing her work as a model and a photographer together, Miller also photographed fashion layouts for *Vogue*. The most interesting of these, for the historian, are from 1930 and 1931. In each case, Miller appears on the same page as the model in the upper image and the photographer in the lower (British *Vogue*, September 15, 1930 and June 10, 1931; and Penrose [1985] 2002: 38) (Figure 2). These spreads clearly assert Miller's status as a professional photographer at a time when this sort of work required equipment that was bulky and demanding. More remarkably, Miller here (alone among models) claims authorship of her image and her look—the look that captivated many people and influenced even more.

Figure 2
On this page of 1931
American *Vogue*, Lee Miller
is the photographer and the
model. British *Vogue*, 10 June
1931, page 50 © Condé Nast
Publications/courtesy of Lee
Miller Archives, England 2006.
All rights reserved.

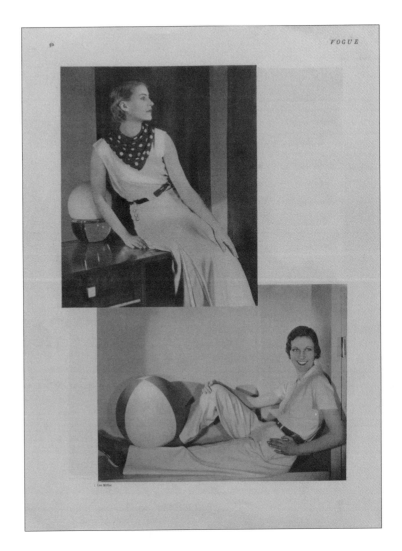

Miller's identity as a photographer was solidified when, in 1932, she returned to Manhattan and opened her own studio on East 48th street with her brother, Erik, as her assistant (Penrose 2002: 245). They specialized in high-end advertising photographs and portraits of society figures, as well as of performers, for commercial publications. As the Depression in the US worsened, portraits became the mainstay of her business, and she used self-portraits to experiment with innovative lighting and angles.[4] Acknowledging the roles Miller played as both model and photographer in creating these images (this in addition to continuing to work as a fashion model for others in the interwar period) suggests her centrality to the process by which she was constructed as a symbol of modern femininity.[5]

Lee Miller also developed her identity as an artist during this period in New York. Between February and March of 1932, Julien Levy, one of the few collectors and gallery owners to take surrealist photography seriously at the time, featured Miller's work in a show of twenty artists in New York City, entitled "Modern European Photographers," which included Man Ray, Peter Hans, and Moholy-Nagy. Early in 1933, Julien Levy gave Miller the only solo show of her life (Penrose [1985] 2002: 45). And in May of 1934, *Vanity Fair* listed her with Cecil Beaton and others as among "the most distinguished living photographers" (*Vanity Fair*, May 1934: 51). Just as she was achieving success in the US, however, Miller married (in July 1934) Aziz Eloui Bey, a wealthy Egyptian businessman, with whom she had been involved in Paris, and moved to Cairo. In the desert near Cairo, she shot some of her most arresting photographs. *Portrait of Space*, taken near Siwa in 1937, is generally considered one of her best 'surrealist photographs" and it is said to have inspired Magritte's painting, *Le Baiser*[6] (Penrose [1985] 2002: 45–96).

Although Miller made stunning photographs of the Egyptian desert, she found her husband's "black satin and pearls set," with whom she was expected to socialize, stultifying (Miller, as quoted by Penrose [1985] 2002: 78). In 1939 she and Eloui parted amicably. She left to be with Roland Penrose, British surrealist painter, collagist, and collector. At first they traveled, but when Hitler invaded Poland and it became clear war was imminent, they settled in Hampstead, North London (Penrose [1985] 2002: 93–98). By 1940, Miller was a staff photographer for British *Vogue*. The November 1940 issue of that magazine includes six small photos by Miller, to illustrate the bomb damage sustained by its headquarters, under the caption "Here is *Vogue* in spite of it all." The text read:

> **Outside** – on several nights, bombs have spattered within twenty yards. This street below our window now holds a new crater, and another length of the arcade has crashed. We were turned out temporarily for a time bomb.

> **Inside** – our offices have been strewn with broken glass. (See the freakishness of blast, that leaves a tumbler of water, uncracked, unspilled.) Though five storeys up, our floors have been deep in soil and debris flung through the roof.

> **Beneath** – we work on when our roof-watcher sends us down. Our editorial staff plan, lay-out, write. Our studio photograph in their wine-cellar-basement. Our fashion staff continue to comb the shops. Congestedly, unceremoniously but cheerfully, *Vogue*, like its fellow Londoners, is put to bed in a shelter (British *Vogue*, November 1940: 19).

Also in 1940, Miller published photos of the home front, as *Grim Glory: Pictures of Britain Under Fire*. By illustrating the resolve of the British people, it was Miller's aim in that book to encourage the US to enter the war. The book was edited by Ernestine Carter, then fashion editor for *The Times*, and carried a preface by the prominent American broadcaster, Ed Murrow; it was simultaneously published in New York by Scribners and it met with positive reviews on both sides of the Atlantic (Penrose [1985] 2002: 102–104).

Miller became increasingly frustrated with covering the European theater of war from London and Vogue House. At the end of 1942, thanks to her US citizenship, and at the suggestion of her friend, *Life* photographer Dave Scherman, Miller became an accredited US Forces War Correspondent. Breaking down boundaries between fashion and news journalism, just as she had earlier ignored the presumed barriers between artist and model, and fine art and commercial fashion photography, Miller submitted extraordinary photojournalism to *Vogue* in London. Her work was often reproduced in the New York edition as well. Miller's *Vogue* reporting covered topics from Henry Moore working as an official war artist in Underground air-raid shelters to the liberation of the concentration camps at Dachau and Buchenwald.

Peter Palmquist, founder and curator of the Women in Photography International Archive, has noted that many photographers during World War II began as print journalists and moved into photography (Palmquist 1994: 248). Lee Miller did the opposite. She was a photographer who was often frustrated by what she deemed to be the ineffectual text that publishers put next to her photographs. So, in 1944, in the words of Tony Penrose, she "badgered" British *Vogue*'s Editor, Audrey Withers, into allowing her to write stories as well as photograph them (Penrose [1985] 2002: 114). The resulting articles were direct, often shocking, and frequently witty. But, although Miller's wartime photography has been the subject of an exhibition and book, her writing has gone virtually undiscussed.[7]

The first of Miller's articles as *Vogue*'s European war correspondent appeared in the summer of 1944, when instead of fulfilling her assignment to produce a small picture story on nurses working in Normandy's US Army field hospitals, Miller filed a hard-hitting piece, along with fourteen photographs of two tent hospitals and a front-line casualty clearing station (Figure 3). Second Lieutenant Herbert "Bud" Myers, the medical liaison staffer on the regimental commander's staff, recently recalled Miller's visit to the Normandy clearing station. He described how Miller had arrived in a jeep with a one-star general, when Company B's collecting station was "within earshot" of the battle at Falais Gap. Myers reported that many journalists and photographers came through their three battalion aid stations, but that they were "all male" and they "showed very little interest in our end of it, most of them. They wanted to be in the combat like Ernie Pyle...they wanted to be a part

Figure 3
Operating Theatre, by Lee
Miller. Captain Dick Eisenberg,
combat medic, US Army, 44th
Evac. Hospital, Normandy,
assisted by an unknown nurse.
From "Unarmed Warriors",
British Vogue, September
1944. © Lee Miller Archives,
England 2006. All rights
reserved.
Second Lieutenant Herbert
"Bud" Myers, who served
with him, says: "He was
marvelous… the men just
worshiped him because all the
men in Company B knew that
if they got hurt, no one was to
look at them except Captain
Dick, period. He was the guy.
He was wonderful. But he was
really funny when it came to
militarization. I mean he flunked
everything."

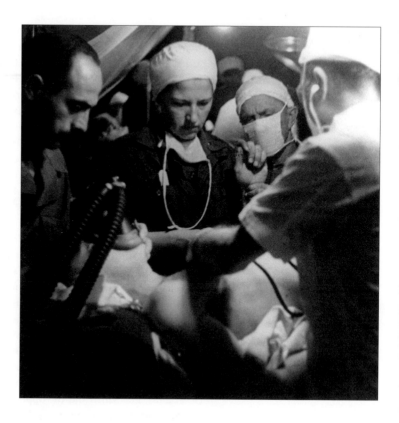

and be able to explain what it was like to be a GI Joe under fire, in a
firefight, you know. That was where they were playing." But, Miller
was "unusual" and conducted herself with "real class," as she moved
respectfully among the wounded men, asking intelligent questions
(Myers 2003).

British *Vogue* published the resulting article in full, in two double-
page spreads under the title "Unarmed Warriors," in their September
1944 issue, with US *Vogue* publishing it as a four-page piece in their
September 15 edition. Miller opened the British version:

> As we flew into sight of France I swallowed hard on what were
> trying to be tears and remembered a movie actress kissing a hand-
> ful of earth. My self-conscious analysis was forgotten in greedily
> studying the soft, grey-skied panorama of nearly a thousand
> square miles of France… of freed France.
>
> The sea and sky joined in a careless watercolour wash…
> below, two convoys speckled the fragile smooth surface of the
> Channel. Cherbourg was a misty bend far to the right, and ahead
> three planes were returning from dropping bombs which made
> towering columns of smoke. This was the Front (Miller, British
> *Vogue*, September 1944: 35).

Here Miller saw herself, as she approached the front from the air, as a sort of Hollywood actress, but also as an artist thinking of "watercolor washes." It is worth commenting on the way Miller's prose exemplifies John Berger's contention, in his widely influential book, *Ways of Seeing*, that women see themselves seeing—that is that unlike men, women are taught to think of themselves as always being on view. Or, in Berger's words, "Women watch themselves being looked at" (Berger 1972: 45, 47). Miller's writing here serves as a reminder of her multifaceted career with *Vogue*, both in her imaginings of herself and in the way the text fuses aesthetic and news journalism.

At an evacuation hospital, Major Esther McCafferty, Chief Nurse of the First Army and "an old acquaintance" of Miller's, showed her the operation. There since "D-Day plus 5," for the previous month forty doctors and forty nurses had averaged 100 operations a day on six operating tables, as well as caring for their 400 transient patients (Miller, British *Vogue*, September 1944: 35). Then Miller went to a collecting station, where she found that:

> ...The wounded were not "knights in shining armour" but dirty, dishevelled stricken figures...uncomprehending. They arrived from the frontline Battalion Aid Station in lightly laid-on field dressings, tourniquets, blood-soaked slings...some exhausted and lifeless. The doctor with his Raphael-like face turned to a man on a litter which had been placed on upended trunks. Plasma had already been attached to the man's outstretched left arm...his face was shrunken and pallid under dirt...by the time his pierced elbow was in its sling, his opaque eyes were clearing and he was aware enough to grimace as his splint was bandaged into place (Miller, British *Vogue*, September 1944: 85).

Here the doctor is positioned as an artist, while the ordinary soldiers are rendered passive and grubby. Miller's imagining of herself as an artist, earlier in the article, allied her with the doctor, the professional, who could oversee and ameliorate the situation of the common men. Her denial of the soldier as a "knight in shining armour" and her reference to Raphael make Miller's work very different from the vast majority of contemporary coverage of World War II, committed as it was to stories of heroism.[8] Her articles overflowed with rich descriptions of her sensual impressions of the scene of war before he—sounds, smells, and especially sights, which she frequently described in terms of high art, and the details of clothing, bodies, and hair. These references speak to Miller's extraordinary eye, honed by her experiences of the previous two decades where she often had been at the center of the fashion and art worlds, first as a model and then as a photographer.

Perhaps unsurprisingly, given the circumstances and her background, Miller's wartime writing for *Vogue* seems influenced by surrealism. Her piece for the October 1944 issue, for example, includes a scene that

could have been lifted from a Buñuel film. She had been at the siege of
St. Malo, where she later claimed that she had "believed the newspapers
when they said that St. Malo had fallen on August 5," "captured not
occupied" by the Germans. But the war was not over there and she was
in the midst of the B26 bombings. She wrote:

> Gunfire brought more stones down into the street. I sheltered in a
> Kraut dugout, squatting under the ramparts. My heel ground into
> a dead, detached hand and I cursed the Germans for the sordid
> ugly destruction they had conjured on this once beautiful town. I
> wondered where my friends that I had known here before the war
> were; how many had been forced into disloyalty and degradation
> – how many had been shot, starved or what. I picked up the hand
> and hurled it across the street, and ran back the way I'd come
> bruising my feet and crashing in the unsteady piles of stone and
> slipping in blood. Christ it was awful! (Miller, British *Vogue*,
> October 1944: 51).

In the summer of 1944, after spending a couple of days under house
arrest for violating the terms of her accreditation by entering that
combat zone, Miller headed to Paris, where it was rumored that the
city was on the brink of liberation. Her resulting *Vogue* article appeared
in the October 1944 issue and combined analysis of quotidian Parisian
women's style with stories of her reunions with famous writers and
artists, such as Paul Eluard and Pablo Picasso (Figure 4). She wrote:

> Paris had gone mad... The long, graceful, dignified avenues were
> crowded with flags and filled with screaming, cheering, pretty
> people. Girls, bicycles, kisses and wine and around the corner
> sniping, a bursting grenade and a burning tank. The bullet
> holes in the windows were like jewels, the barbed wire in the
> boulevards a new decoration... Everywhere in the streets were the
> dazzling girls, cycling, crawling up tank turrets. Their silhouette
> was very queer and fascinating to me after utility and austerity
> England. Full floating skirts, tiny waistlines. They were top-heavy
> with built-up, pompadour-front hairdos and waving tresses;
> weighted to the ground with clumsy, fancy, thick-soled wedge
> shoes... They all look incredibly young: mostly because make-
> up style has changed to fresh healthy naturalness or an imitation
> thereof... They deliberately organized this style of dressing and
> living as a taunt to the Huns, whose clumsy and serious women,
> dressed in grey uniforms, were known as the "souris gris". If
> the Germans wore cropped hair, the French grew theirs long. If
> three yards of material were specified for a dress – they found
> fifteen for a skirt alone. Saving material and labour meant help to
> the Germans – and it was their duty to waste instead of to save
> (Miller, British *Vogue*, October 1944: 27 and 78).

Here Miller wove together strands of war and fashion reporting, pointing out the political importance of French fashion during the war. Miller's explanation that the many yards of fabric in their skirts was an act of resistance by women in occupied France should really be a central part of the story of Chanel's New Look.

Audrey Withers described Miller's articles as "the most exciting journalistic experience of my war. We were the last people one could conceive having this type of article, it seemed so incongruous in our pages of glossy fashion" (Withers, as quoted by Penrose [1985] 2002: 118). Not that *Vogue* or other fashion magazines ignored the war. As early as 1940, *Vogue* had published photos by Therese Bonney, of refugee women and children fleeing the fighting in France, and *Ladies' Home Journal* had its own war correspondent, Cecelia Jackie Martin[9] (Hall 1985 and Palmquist 1994: 247–55). But British *Vogue*'s coverage of the war, before Miller became their European war correspondent, focused primarily on the domestic scene in England. There were articles on how to "make good meals" from "simple foods" with "imagination" and spices (British *Vogue*, 1940). And there was *Vogue*'s own, more elegant version of "make do and mend."[10] Of course, there were also numerous pieces on women's war work—be they wives of foreign ambassadors, professional British women in the forces, or US Army nurses and Red Cross workers (British *Vogue*, March 1942; March 1944; May 1943; June 1943). Miller recalled in a 1974 article in *American Vogue* on her as a "surrealist cook" that:

> [I] knew all the American war correspondents. There were men but no women in the European Theater of War and I wanted to

do something so I invented the job. They asked me what the rules should be and I said, "Just treat me like one of the boys," which they did. That was long before Women's Lib and I felt like a one-woman brigade."[11]

You had to be calm and non-squeamish—go to the latrine with the men. You paid no attention to them and they paid no attention to you. Sometimes we'd go for weeks without a bath or clean clothes. Then you'd get somewhere where they'd set up portable shower baths. We'd all strip and they would hand me a sheet or a towel. You'd go through the line with the men and you'd ask for clothes by size. You'd get other people's clothes all nicely cleaned and deloused…I was with the first American troops in the liberation of Paris and the first thing I did was to go to see my old friend Picasso. Picasso always said I was the first American soldier he saw (Miller as quoted by Gold and Fizdale, U.S. *Vogue*, April 1974: 162).

After the liberation of France, Miller's next big assignments for *Vogue* were to help Michel de Brunhoff get French *Vogue* going again and to cover the first major fashion shows of liberated Paris. (De Brunhoff had voluntarily closed down all his papers and magazines in 1940.) Miller photographed most of the post-liberation fashion collections under extremely difficult conditions. She was furious when she received a telegram from her British editor stating that the editor of American *Vogue*, Edna Woolman Chase, was: "CRITICAL OF SNAPSHOT FASHION REPORTAGE AND ESPECIALLY CHEAP MANNEQUINS URGES MORE ELEGANCE BY STUDIO PHOTOGRAPHS + WELLBRED WOMEN AND EXCELLENT DRAWINGS STOP…EDNA SAYS QUOTE CANT BELIEVE PICTURES TYPICAL OF HIGHCLASS FRENCH FASHION…CANT SOLANGE GET LADIES TO POSE UNQUOTE…" Miller's indignant reply asserted her immediate experience of wartime conditions that New Yorkers were privileged to ignore:

I find Edna very unfair – these snapshots have been taken under the most difficult and depressing conditions in the twenty minutes a model was willing to give of her lunch hour, most of which was being taken up with further fittings for unfinished dresses or after five o'clock with no electricity…Any suggestion that *dames du monde* could and should have been used is strictly out of this world. Edna should be told that there is a war on—that maybe Solange hasn't the heart to concentrate with the knowledge of the horrors her husband and family are going through in German prison camps (as quoted by Penrose [1992] 2005: 80, 84).

It is as if Miller served as a sort of conscience for *Vogue* magazine at times during World War II.

For the January 1945 issue of British *Vogue*, Miller finally filed an article that Withers had been asking her to write for months, under the title "Pattern of Liberation." But, it was far from the piece her editor had imagined. Instead of an article on the fashion mood of 1945 France, Miller wrote a dreamlike, intimate piece on the lives of people who were returning to their homes for the first time in years. She wrote: "The pattern of liberation is not decorative. There are the gay squiggles of wine and song. There is the beautiful overall colour of freedom, but there is ruin and destruction. There are problems and mistakes, disappointed hopes and broken promises… There is grogginess as after a siesta, a 'sleeping beauty' lethargy" (Miller, British *Vogue*, January 1945: 80). The fairytale allusions and the somnolent quality of this piece are striking and somewhat in opposition to the tone of the text, as well as Miller's accompanying photographs of refugees.

Max Ernst had explained in 1934 that the surrealist "procedure" was "the exploitation of the fortuitous meeting of two distant realities on an inappropriate plane." (Ernst 1934). Miller's June 1945 piece, "Germany – the war that is won," relied on startling juxtapositions to make her descriptions as discomfiting as possible. Miller had been one of the first people to enter Dachau concentration camp outside Munich, photographing it on April 30, 1945. Hard-hitting from the first line, she wrote:

> Germany is a beautiful landscape dotted with jewel-like villages, blotched with ruined cities, and inhabited by schizophrenics. There are blossoms and vistas; every hill is crowned with a castle. The vineyards of the Moselle and the newly ploughed plains are fertile. Immaculate birches and tender willows flank the streams and the tiny towns are pastel plaster like a modern watercolour of a medieval memory. Little girls in white dresses and garlands promenade after their first communion. The children have stilts and marbles and tops and hoops, and they play with dolls. Mothers sew and sweep and bake, and farmers plough and harrow; all just like real people. But they aren't; they are the enemy. This is Germany and it is spring.

Evoking travel writing frequently found in *Vogue* at the time, Miller continued:

> My fine Baedecker tour of Germany includes many such places as Buchenwald which were not mentioned in my 1913 edition, and if there is a later one I doubt if they were mentioned there, either, because no one in Germany has ever heard of a concentration camp, and I guess they didn't want any tourist business either.

> Visitors took one-way tickets only, in any case, and if they
> lived long enough they had plenty of time to learn the places of
> interest, both historic and modern, by personal and practical
> experimentation.

She went on to recount the horrors of the concentration camps, and
slave labor, as well as her incredulity at the "slimy invitations to dine in
German underground homes." "How dare they?" she wrote.

> Who do they think we'd been braving flesh and eyesight against,
> all these years in England? Who did they think were my friends
> and compatriots but the blitzed citizens of London and the ill-
> treated French prisoners of war? Who did they think were my flesh
> and blood but the American pilots and infantrymen? What kind
> of idiocy and stupidity blinds them to my feelings? What kind of
> detachment are they able to find, from what kind of escape zones
> in the unventilated alleys of their brains are they able to conjure
> up the idea that they are liberated instead of conquered people?
> (Miller, British *Vogue*, "Germany...," June 1945: 40–42, 84, 86,
> 89).

Miller's reference to travel articles interpellates her female readers into
a text where the righteous anger of the Allied victors is cast in terms of
surrealist disdain for repression and emphasis on what is visible to the
eye.

Lee Miller employed a similarly eerie juxtaposition, once again
utilizing the language of an upmarket women's magazine, in her quirkily
titled "Hitleriania," published in British *Vogue* in July, 1945. It begins
with a vivid account of Hitler's mountain retreat going up in smoke and
ends with a detailed description of the interior of the Munich villa of Eva
Braun, Hitler's mistress. This is the article that included the now famous
photo of Miller in Hitler's Munich bathtub, taken by her friend and
colleague, *Life* photographer Dave Scherman. In the piece, Miller told
of how portraits of "Hitler tenderly autographed to Eva and her sister
Gretl, who lived with her, were in plain view." She went on to catalog
the apartment's furnishings: "Part of the china was modern peasant and
part was white porcelain dotted with pale blue flowers. The furniture
and decorations were strictly department store like everything in the
Nazi regime: impersonal and in good, average, slightly artistic taste..."
(Miller, "Hitleriania," British *Vogue*, July 1945: 74).

When Miller goes on to report: "I took a nap on her bed and tried
the telephones, which were marked Berlin, Berchtesgaden, Wachenfeld,
the name of Hitler's house on the mountain above Berchtesgaden", the
effect is to destabilize her text, bringing out the surreal qualities of this
account of the domestic fashions of a dictator. The idea of sleeping in
Eva Braun's bed, with its connotations of making love to Hitler, is truly

chilling. Miller ends the article by describing "the large brass globe of the world" on "Eva's living room table", designed to hold "glasses and bottles for toasting... 'Morgen Die Ganze Welt'... 'Tomorrow, the Whole World'" (ibid.). Miller's strange combination of the sort of detailed descriptive writing you could expect to find in an article on domestic interiors elsewhere in *Vogue*'s pages, along with the staggering reminder of Hitler's plan of world domination, exemplifies her surrealist use of juxtaposition.

But, even more importantly, the juxtapositions gesture toward the rather gruesome nature of any sort of reporting on fashion or decorating in the face of Auschwitz, Buchenwald, and Dachau. How could we ever again blithely drink liquors after learning of Hitler's globe-shaped holder? How was life to return to normal for Miller or anyone after she had reported on the Nazi atrocities? As we shall see, not long after the war in Europe ended, British *Vogue* wished to return to normality, as far as possible under postwar conditions. But it is clear that Lee Miller found such attempts far from easy, if not impossible.

For Miller, covering the war in Europe had been exhausting but invigorating. Her son asserts that from the first article in the summer of 1944, "her former hypochondria vanished without a trace... Gone was the *soigné* appearance and the refined taste in food and wine; now she wore crumpled battle dress and ate K rations or worse... foreign travel, insatiable desire for excitement, social mutability, iron-hard resolution, and natural ebullience coalesced into one huge creative output" (Penrose [1985] 2002: 118). An article for the April 1, 1945 issue of American *Vogue* reflects both Miller's identification with the US soldiers she was following and the sense of fun she was experiencing. In "G.I. Lingo in Europe," she wrote: "Now we 'liberate' a bottle of brandy when we beat down a mercenary publican, we 'liberate' a girl when we detach her from her chaperone" (Miller, American *Vogue*, April 1, 1945: 131).

But once the European war ended, Miller was expected to go back to London and resume her fashion photography for British *Vogue*. A rather rare extant letter to Roland Penrose in late August, 1945 indicates the depths of Miller's depression and disillusionment. Following a burst of anger, significantly on the occasion of a London luncheon thrown by *Vogue* to honor her, Miller returned to Paris. Existing on a cocktail of Benzedrine, alcohol, and sleeping pills, she wrote to Penrose:

> Dear Roland,
>   I haven't forgotten you. Every evening when I could take the time and certainly have the interest to write you I think that tomorrow I'll know the ultimate answer or that my depression will have lifted or my exaltation ebbed or whatever – so that I'll be able to write you a more coherent impression containing some sort of decision – whether it be that I'm staying or coming home,

licked. That moment never comes. You've known that for years
already. Either I have had diarrhoea of words or constipation.

When the invasion occurred – the impact of the decision itself
was a tremendous release – all my energy and all my pre-fabricated
opinions were unleashed together; I worked well and consistently
and I hope convincingly as well as honestly.... This is a new and
disillusioning world. Peace with a world of crooks who have no
honour, no integrity and no shame is not what anyone fought
for... I knew that we weren't fighting for anything any of us
wanted anyway and it didn't matter, we were just stuck with it
like always. Then I saw the guys who were grey or bloody or
black. The boys were white with anger or green with fatigue and
sometimes shook because they were afraid, I was awfully sorry
that the war wasn't for anything at all – and I was very angry.

Really great groups of humans are suffering the same shock
symptoms caused by peace that I'm combatting – and I don't in
the least mean the boys going back home to find that they've
become dependent upon a benevolent maternal army – that they
have outgrown their wives or become socially unfit or drunks or
misanthropes. Its just an impatience with the sordid dirt which
is being slung around now compared with the comparative
cleanliness and the real nobility of the men in the lines, or men
and women in the lousy little jobs they thought were helping to
win the war – and the people who bought bonds so that their
disreputable government could continue after the war loan had
been paid off – the families who are still short of rations so that a
lot of grasping bastards with greedy gloating appetites should have
enough schlag on their coffee. A more disorganised, dissolute and
dishonest population has never existed in the history books...

I'm leaving for this Austrian trip tomorrow morning, Saturday,
at dawn with a great deal of dread and boredom. Davie [Scherman]
is hanging round waiting for me to get off because he knows that
if he doesn't I'll never leave.
Love,
Lee
(Miller, as quoted by Penrose [1985] 2002: 147–8).

Miller's identification with the US soldiers she had followed across the
battlefields of Europe for the past year seems complete here. She felt
she was "suffering the same shock symptoms caused by peace" and
the same disdain for "benevolent maternal" civilian life.[12] In addition,
although we have no other evidence of her political leanings, it seems
in the mess that was Paris at the end of the war, thanks to occupation,
collaboration, and profiteering, Miller felt much as the European Left
did. Like them (including the surrealists around Breton), Miller had a
profound sense of betrayal and frustration with politics.

As is presaged at the end of that letter, Miller spent the rest of 1945 and 1946 primarily in Eastern Europe, because, as she explained to Dave Scherman, she had "damned itchy feet" that kept her moving (Penrose [1985] 2002: 168). Those feet took her to "destinations as inhospitable as possible," including Vienna, Bucharest, and Budapest, where she photographed the execution of Laszlo Bardossy, the fascist, collaborator, and ex-prime minister (Livingston 1989: 89–95 and Penrose [1985] 2002: 145–76). But by the winter of 1946, with Roland Penrose drifting towards a permanent relationship with another woman, after arguments and then months of silence from Miller, her friend, Dave Scherman, cabled her two words from New York: "GO HOME." And a week or so later, she did (Penrose 1985).

Miller married Penrose and had a son with him at the age of forty in 1947 (Penrose [1985] 2002). Her fashion work for British *Vogue* in the post-war period is elegant, lively, and appropriate. [13] It frequently uses outdoor settings and resembles the work of Norman Parkinson, Erwin Blumenfeld, or Irving Penn in the same period. [14] Like Parkinson, Miller took many of her fashion photographs around her homes, either in London, or at Farley Farm in Sussex, or the nearby town of Lewes. Yet a return to fashion photography could never rival the journalistic work Miller did between 1944 and 1946.

Miller's son and biographer now says she had postnatal depression after he was born in 1947, as well as posttraumatic stress syndrome, both of which seem like reasonable diagnoses (Penrose, as quoted, WWD.com in "Snapshots in Time: Lee Miller," 2003). We know that Margaret Bourke-White, for example, felt compelled to write a book on Germany in 1946, after her experience of photographing Buchenwald for *Life* magazine, and that the British photographer George Rodger decided to abandon photojournalism after he took photos of Belsen (Zelizer 1998: 87–8). For Rodger, as Stephen Brooke has explained, utilizing Sontag's term for Holocaust photography in general, "this was a negative epiphany." [15] Rodger later said of the experience:

> It wasn't even a matter of what I was photographing as what had happened to me in the process. When I discovered that I could look at the horror of Belsen and think only of a nice photographic composition, I knew something had happened to me and I had to stop... I said this is where I quit (Rodger, as quoted by Zelizer 1998: 88–89). [16]

His response was to flee from Europe, questioning whether what remained could be considered "civilization" and seeking its apparent opposite among the Nuba in southern Sudan: "I had to get rid of the filth of war, the screams of the wounded, the groans of the dying. I sought some spot in the world that was clean and untrammelled – tribal Africa" (Rodger, as quoted by Stephen Brooke 2004: 23). And so he left Europe for Africa in early 1948.

We have no such direct statement from Miller as to how the spectacle of Nazi torture and extermination affected her subsequent life and work. At Dachau, Miller wrote: "Soldiers were encouraged to 'sightsee' around the place, they were abetted to photograph it and tell the folks back home" (Penrose [1992] 2005: 187; see also Struk 2004: 131). But, according to recent work by Janina Struk, the photographer and writer, such soldiers encountered difficulties when they attempted to show the images at home: "Many found that they were either dismissed as fabrications or seemed too shocking to show. As a result many remained silent about their experiences in the camps and kept their photographs hidden" (Struk 2004: 131).[17] Perhaps Lee Miller's response to the scenes she had photographed was, in the end, similar.

Miller's state of mind in late 1947 is revealed by a special British *Vogue* piece for the Christmas edition. In it "*Vogue* photographers interpret Christmas," as the title read. The magazine explained:

> *Vogue* invented a game – you try it, too. Close your eyes, and think of Christmas, conjure up its essence and make a mental picture. We played it on our photographers, who went one stage further; they took the pictures, wrote the words, borrowed priceless props from famous houses – and asked several well-known people to join in the fun. Turn over and see the results for yourselves… (British *Vogue*, December 1947: 53).

In stark contrast to Cecil Beaton, who chose Nellie Wallace, who Beaton claimed "epitomized" "traditional pantomime" as "the ageless spirit, half sprite, quarter cockatoo, quarter human, of harlequinade" (British *Vogue*, December 1947: 54), John Deakin, who photographed "the epitome of the Christmas theatre spirit" as "vermilion satin, diamond encrusted – in short, Mae West" (59) or Anthony Denney, who created a still-life collage of jewels, lace, and evening gloves to evoke winter's "icy fronds" (56), Miller photographed her six-week-old son, Antony Penrose. But this is not in and of itself the most remarkable aspect of her choice, since Norman Parkinson also photographed a child—a sceptical, perhaps unhappy, little girl of about seven in a party dress and fur capelet, descending outdoor stairs, carrying a present, watched by her uniformed nanny. He named his work *Better a Picnic in July* and his caption read: "Childhood doubts and fears are with you always – the panic before a party – the let-down of Christmas, too eagerly looked-for. Better a spontaneous bubble of happiness. Better a picnic in July" (55).

What is both most revealing and distinct about Miller's answer to the game *Vogue* invented is her text. She titled her photograph *First Baby, First Christmas* and she wrote: "Gay tinsel and a brand new baby is my formula for a Merry Christmas this year. Maybe by the time he finds there isn't a Santa Claus this not so shiny world won't need one as badly as it does now" (58). Looking at the feature today, if Miller's contribution were excluded, you could be forgiven for forgetting how recently World War II had ended or how very difficult the circumstances of postwar recovery were in Britain.

After this rather gloomy contribution, along with a witty piece on how to make the most of your fortnight's stay in the maternity hospital, Withers seems to have tried to get *Vogue*'s star war reporter back on the fashion photography track. Among other articles, in May of 1949 British *Vogue* published ten pages of travel and vacation clothes from Sicily "photographed by Lee Miller"; in the first issue of 1950 there appeared her surrealistic spread on "Boutiques—in London," featuring a woman rifling through a drawer of gloves at Molyneaux, and in October of that year there was Miller's fashion piece, "Slim Suits," shot on the site of the 1951 Festival of Britain, then under construction (British *Vogue*, "Boutiques," January 1950: 68–9 and "Looking to 1951: Slim Suits," October 1950: 110–113).

But, according to Margot Collingbourn-Beevers, who was a junior at London's *Vogue* photographic studio in 1949, that year saw Miller officially leave the photographic staff of the magazine. Collingbourn-Beevers recalled that Miller's official "departure from *Vogue*" was "abrupt and tearful." She explained that Miller "had frequently been asked to economise on film and work to a budget" and that this was "probably an impossible task for one so creative and impetuous." Collingbourn-Beevers remembered Miller more clearly than Beaton or Parkinson: "Whenever she flung herself into the studio with the latest batch of negatives to be printed, the atmosphere surged with the sense that something new and different was about to happen…" (Collingbourn-Beevers, 2001: 9).

After this, Miller was only rarely afforded the opportunity to photograph and write for British *Vogue*. Yet, when the chance arose, the insightfulness and feistiness of her wartime work were still evident, even if the focus was more frivolous. The prime example appeared in the July 1953 issue of British *Vogue*. It was a piece, illustrated by her photographs, entitled "Working Guests" (Figure 5). The subjects of the photographs, pictured at Farley Farm, included Alfred Barr, director of the Museum of Modern Art in New York, feeding the pigs, the Victoria and Albert's keeper of sculpture, H. D. Molesworth, re-covering living-room chairs, and Henry Moore adjusting or "hugging his sculpture" on the lawn[18]. Having "devoted four years of research and practice to getting all my friends to do all the work," Miller asserted that: "The visitors' book is flanked by a photo album of grim significance: in it are no 'happy hols' snaps of leisured groups wearing sunglasses and sniffing Pimm's Cup. It could easily be taken for a set of stills from a Soviet workers' propaganda film. Everyone busy doing a job: Joy Through Work." She continued, "This catalogue of 'merry workers' is designed to instil confidence in newcomers and manual morons who can herein see

Figure 5
Dorothea Tanning (Mrs. Max Ernst), Painter, Operates as Master-Electrician by Lee Miller, from "Working Guests," British *Vogue*, July 1953.

some butter-fingered acquaintance doing highly skilled work, to show the variety and scope of the projects, and to suggest social ostracism of drones and sit-down strikers" (Miller, British *Vogue*, July 1953: 55 and Penrose [1985] 2002: 191–3). The final photograph of the article is of the author/photographer asleep on the couch.

Despite the lighthearted tone, by this time, according to Tony Penrose, "the process of writing had become so traumatic that the turmoil it caused threatened to engulf Roland [Penrose]. He wrote secretly to Audrey Withers—'I implore you, please do not ask Lee to write again. The suffering it causes her and those around her is unbearable.'" Miller had always had trouble with deadlines, often not meeting them, and Withers found her work so "distinctive" that it had to be "accommodated" in *Vogue*, rather than merely included (Penrose [1985] 2002: 193). Miller thus ended her more than twenty-five-year relationship with *Vogue* magazine. She ceased responding to requests for her photographs and negatives. Her answer to inquiries was along the lines of: "Oh, I did take a few pictures—but that was a long time ago." And she was so persuasive that "everyone was convinced that she had done little or no work of significance," in her son's words (Penrose [1985] 2002: 209). Miller turned all of her creative energies to gourmet cooking, classical music, and competitions. Although she did contribute to the London Institute of Contemporary Art's 1956 exhibition and book on her old friend Picasso, called "Picasso Himself", by 1966, when her husband was knighted for his contributions to contemporary British art, Miller was represented in the resulting assorted articles as "Lady Lee," the cook and hostess.

Conclusion

It is significant that only in the 1950s did Lee Miller and British *Vogue* seem mutually unable to adapt to the odd, peacetime world around them. Miller's unique voice and vision (not to mention her erratic work habits) became impossible for the magazine to incorporate, as it tried its best to represent life as back to normal. Yet, of course, life in postwar Britain was far from normal. Rationing continued until 1954. Carolyn Steedman, who was born in 1948, has written that: "The war was so palpable a presence in the first five years of my life that I still find it hard to believe that I did not live through it. There were bomb sites everywhere, prefabs on waste land, most things still on points" (Steedman 1987: 27). At the same time "homemaking" was being constructed by various sources, including women's magazines and radio programmes, as "the new art" (P. L. Garbutt 1954, as quoted by Jeremiah 2000: 166). Just as it had adapted to World War II, British *Vogue* reflected the cultural and social changes of the postwar era. An article published by novelist Joyce Carey in the October 1952 issue, for instance, juxtaposed the 1920s period of "decadence, neurosis, and futility," in which woman had "denied her nature, cut her hair like a boy, [and] dressed like an immature child," avoiding husband, home, and children—with the early 1950s: a time witnessing a "renaissance of the family and family conscience," with fashions never more feminine (Cary, British *Vogue*, October 1952: 126). Thus, perhaps Lee Miller was, by this period, not just a bit "difficult," but perhaps even dated, representing not only the frightening and depressing wartime, but also interwar decadence, frivolity, and wrong-headedness.[19]

The April 1974 issue of American *Vogue* carried a piece on Lee Miller that managed to combine many of the diverse parts of her rich life. Arthur Gold and Robert Fizdale's "How Famous People Cook: Lady Penrose, The Most Unusual Recipes You Have Ever Seen" described Miller as the inventor of "surrealist cuisine." It recounted her stories—of her time as a *Vogue* model, as the lover and student of Man Ray, of her marriage to the Egyptian Assiz [sic] and their "Arab chef with French training," as an American war correspondent, as well as as a postwar student at the Cordon Bleu school (which she "didn't like much," due to the lack of cleanliness and the deafening noise). Perhaps it was her special relationship with *Vogue* for over a quarter of a century that encouraged Miller to tell so much of her story to Gold and Fizdale, duo pianists, partners, and food writers, who "knew everyone," as Miller had (Aspler 2003). But, whatever the reason, that *Vogue* article clearly captured her wit, her audacity, and her talents. In the end, it was a fitting last tribute. Miller died of cancer at her home in the English countryside, Farley Farm, Chiddingly, East Sussex in 1977.

Acknowledgements

Thanks to Tony Penrose, Arabella Hayes, and Carole Callow of the Lee
Miller Archive; and to Janine Button, librarian at Vogue House, London;
and to Harriet Wilson of Condé Nast. I would like to acknowledge
the support of the London College of Fashion in the form of a Senior
Research Fellowship. More friends and colleagues than I can remember
have commented on versions of this article, but in particular I would
like to thank: Christopher Reed, J. Adam Tooze, Carolyn Steedman,
Laura Downs, Christopher Breward, Caroline Evans, Sonia Ashmore,
Stephen Brooke, Deborah Cohen, Craig Koslofsky, Antoinette Burton,
and Marilyn Booth. Thanks also to Zephyrine Craster for excellent
research assistance at a critical moment.

Notes

1. Miller's very last article for *Vogue* appeared in the early 1970s and
   concerned surrealist cinema.
2. Some people would argue that events before the age of twenty were
   key to shaping who Lee Miller was. For example, we will probably
   never know the truth of what happened to her at the age of seven,
   but she was sexually assaulted and contracted venereal disease, which
   necessitated (in the days before penicillin) an excruciating medical
   treatment. The official story is that she had been staying briefly with
   some family friends in Brooklyn while her mother recuperated from
   an illness and that the family's son was home on leave from the US
   Navy and sexually assaulted her. The story continues that Miller's
   parents were so forward-thinking that they enlisted the help of a
   psychiatrist, who advised that she be told that sex and love were not
   related and that sex was merely a physical act, in the hope that she
   would not suffer from guilt, as well as the physical pain precipitated
   by this dreadful occurrence (Penrose [1985] 2002: 12). Whether
   this can explain why Miller was especially sexually liberated, yet
   prone to bouts of depression and, as some claim, unable to be truly
   close to people she loved, we can never know, of course. But it did
   mean that her parents were exceedingly indulgent; she was forever
   playing practical jokes and rebelling against her teachers and so,
   inevitably, she was expelled from numerous schools. By the spring
   of 1925 there were no more schools close to Poughkeepsie for
   Miller to attend. The solution to finishing her education came when
   Madame Kockashinski, a Polish woman who had taught French at
   one of the private schools Miller briefly attended, suggested that
   she and a companion take her to Paris to study classical arts and
   culture. They sailed from New York on May 30, 1925. Miller soon
   escaped entirely from her chaperones and announced that she was

going to be an artist. Her parents "grudgingly" paid her fees at the new L'Ecole Medgyes pour la Technique du Theatre, run by stage designer Ladislas Medgyes, and the architect Erno Goldfinger. But in the winter of 1926, her father went to Paris and took her back home to Poughkeepsie (Penrose [1985] 2002: 13–15; Calvocoressi 2002: 7) She was studying at the Art Students' League when Nast saved her and "discovered" her in Manhattan.

3. Thank you to Sonia Ashmore for introducing me to Katherine Reid. Thanks also to Katherine for sharing her memories of Lee Miller with me, as well as a fascinating postcard Miller sent her in Paris in the summer of 1966 or 1967. In a slightly different version of this quote, Penrose states in his *The Lives of Lee Miller* (16) that "Thinking back on this period many years later, Lee said, 'I was terribly, terribly pretty. I looked like an angel, but I was a fiend inside.'" (He does not provide a reference for this quote.)

4. There are examples of two portrait sittings taken in 1932, where Miller used herself as the subject, which no one has ever commented upon before. I would like to thank Carole Callow, Archivist and Photographic Fine Printer of the Lee Miller Archives, for bringing these self-portraits to my attention.

5. Tellingly, in addition, curator, Jane Livingston, has written of how many of Man Ray's photographs of Miller "seem created through a process in which the model and photographer have collaborated fully as artists" (Livingston 1989: 35). Livingston cites Man Ray's photograph of Miller, *Neck* (1929), and a solarized image of her entitled *La Dormeuse* (undated), as examples of this collaboration between the two artists. Please see pages 8 and 15 of Livingston (1989) for reproductions of these two photographs by Man Ray.

6. Magritte saw Miller's Egyptian photograph in London in 1938 (Livingston [1989]: 48).

7. Antony Penrose is clearly impressed with her wartime articles and says that "her ability as a writer was now poised, fully primed and ready to go," but he doesn't actually analyze the texts, separate from the photographs (Penrose [1985] 2002: 116). He also edited *Lee Miller's War* (1992), which contains a foreword by Miller's old friend and fellow war correspondent, Dave Scherman. There Scherman puts Miller's World War II stories in specific contexts and dubs her "Patterns of Liberation" as "as eloquent and telling an account as you'll find anywhere," and the "Alsace story" as "one of the best examples of front-line reporting ever filed" (Penrose 1992: 11). The scholar who has written on some of Miller's wartime articles is Jane Gallagher. (1998: 68–96).

8. On World War II reporting, see Paul Fussell, *Wartime: Understanding Behaviour in the Second World War* (1989). Fussell argues that "There was no room in this war-culture for individual opinions or personalities, no freedom of dissent or approval; the culture was

homogenous, shallow and boring" (Eileen M. Sullivan, "Refraction and Fantasy: A Study of Magazine Advertisements During World War II," Senior Thesis, University of Pennsylvania, May 1986, as quoted by Fussell).

9. American *Vogue*'s staff photographer from 1931–1942, Toni Frissell, became an American Red Cross photographer in 1943 (Palmquist 1994: 247–55).

10. "Make Do and Mend" was a government slogan during World War II in Britain.

11. Dave Scherman calls Miller "the only woman combat photographer to follow the Allied advance across Western Europe in World War II" (Penrose 1992: 7). This is perhaps true. But we know she was not the only female war correspondent. For instance, American photographer Margaret Bourke-White had covered the war on the Russian front for *Life* magazine. Martha Gelhorn (who, at the time was incidentally married to Hemingway) had gone to Paris in 1930 to become a foreign correspondent and in 1937 she began working as a war correspondent, covering the wars in Spain, Finland, China, Java, and then World War II in Europe. During World War II she primarily worked for *Collier's* magazine in New York. Gelhorn and Miller's writings on the end of the war and the concentration camps share a frankness in their incredulity and shock at both the camps and the reactions of "ordinary" Germans to their defeat. Miller photographed Gelhorn for British *Vogue* and Antony Penrose believes that the two of them were on "friendly terms" and "hung out in the same places." (See Miller photo *News Breakers*, British *Vogue*, March 1944: 43; interview between the author and Arabella Hayes, Registrar and Picture Librarian of the Lee Miller Archives, July 22, 2004 and August 26, 2004.) For fine examples of Gelhorn's World War II writing, see her collection, *The Face of War* (London: Granta [1959] 1998), especially pages 176–204. Additionally, Scherman relates that Marguerite Higgins of the *New York Herald Tribune* once complained to him: "How is it that every time I arrive somewhere to cover a story you and Lee Miller are just leaving?" (Penrose 1992: 12), thus providing us with another example of an American female war correspondent in the European Theater.

12. On GI's problems with readjusting to civilian life postwar, see for example D. Gerber 1994: 551–2. For similar problems in Britain, see Bendit and Bendit (1946). Robert Murphy argues in his chapter "Tigers and Smoke" (Murphy 2001) that anxieties about readjusting to peacetime after the war lurk behind the popularity of film noir and murder plots in late 1940s British cinema. For another take on these themes see Martin Francis's "A Flight from Commitment?". I would like to thank Martin Francis for his very helpful suggestions on this topic.

13. Looking at the contact sheets, one can find more interesting, imaginative, and even what might be called more "surrealist" photographs taken by Miller for *Vogue* assignments, which did not make it into the magazine. Yet the "Unseen *Vogue*" exhibition at the Design Museum in London in 2002 showed us that this is not unique to Miller.
14. For an accessible way to make these comparisons, see their work reproduced in *Vogue Book of Fashion Photography*: 80, 81, 85–6, 88, 89, 92, 93, 96, 97, 101–3.
15. Brooke (2004: 23); Sontag (1977: 19).
16. Zelizer cites Jorge Lewinski, (1978), *The Camera at War: A History of War Photography from 1848 to the Present Day*, page 14, and an interview with George Rodger, in Paul Hill and Thomas Cooper (eds) (1979), *Dialogue with Photography*, pages 59–60.
17. Struk cites here as evidence, R. H. Abzug, (1985) *Inside the Vicious Heart*, page 138.
18. Following exhibitions of Miller's portraits, two books which include some of the photos in "Working Guests" appeared (Calvocoressi, 2002; 2005).
19. All sorts of "difficult" women were hard to accommodate in the postwar period. Sonia Orwell, once a key member of the editorial staff of the London literary magazine, *Horizon*, and briefly George Orwell's second wife, comes to mind. Her intelligence, strength, beauty, life between Paris and London, love affairs, drinking, smoking, and intensity all resonate with tales of Lee Miller (Spurling 2002). According to her biographer, Hilary Spurling, in the immediate postwar period Sonia Orwell was "blamed, mocked and derided" (Spurling 2002: 64). Miller and Sonia Orwell may have been friends. There is a photo by Miller from 1953 of Sonia Orwell taken at Farley Farm. (See Calvocoressi 2002: 156.)

References

Primary sources

Interviews

Anonymous, telephone interview with the author, London, August 2002.
Hayes, Arabella, interview with the author, July 22, 2004.
McNulty, Bettina, interview with the author, London, August 13, 2002.
Myers, Herbert "Bud," interview with the author at his home, Collinsville, North Carolina, USA, June 21, 2003.
Reid, Katherine, interview with the author, London, May 12, 2004.

Articles and photographs

"Bal Blanc," French *Vogue*, Août 1930: 50–51.

"Doing things By Halves," British *Vogue*, August 1944: 76.

Gold, Arthur and Robert Fitzdale, "How Famous People Cook: Lady Penrose, The Most Unusual Recipes You Have Ever Seen," American *Vogue*, April 1974: 160–61 and 186–67.

"La vie d'un poete… premier film de Jean Cocteau," French *Vogue*, Octobre 1930: 90–91.

McNulty, Bettina, "How to Make an Art of the Happy Weekend: The Personal Strategy and Beautiful Food of Lee Penrose," American *House and Garden*, June 1973, 68–73.

Miller, Lee, "'Believe It': Lee Miller Cables from Germany," American *Vogue*, June 1945: 104–8.

—— "Boutiques – in London" (photos), British *Vogue*, January 1950: 68–69.

—— "First Baby, First Christmas," British *Vogue*, December 1947: 58.

—— "Germans Are Like This," American *Vogue*, June 1945: 101–3, 192, 193.

—— "Germany – the War that is Won," British *Vogue*, June 1945: 40–42, 84, 86, 89.

—— "G.I. Lingo in Europe," American *Vogue*, April 1, 1945: 102, 131.

—— "The High Bed," British *Vogue*, April 1948: 83, 111.

—— "Hitleriania," British *Vogue*, July 1945: 36–7, 74.

—— "Loire Bridges/How the Germans Surrender," British *Vogue*, November 1944: 50–51, 82, 90.

—— "Looking to 1951: Slim Suits," British *Vogue*, October 1950: 110–113.

—— "Paris… Its Joys… Its Spirit… Its Privations," British *Vogue*, October 1944: 26–29 and *passim*.

—— "The Pattern of Liberation," British *Vogue*, January 1945: 80.

—— Photographs and contact Sheets, Lee Miller Archives, Farley Farm House, Chiddingly, East Sussex, England.

—— "Picasso," British *Vogue*, November 1951: 113, 160, 165.

—— "St. Malo," British *Vogue*, October 1944: 51.

—— "Unarmed Warriors," British *Vogue*, September 1944: 35 and American *Vogue*: 135.

—— "Working Guests," British *Vogue*, July 1953: 54–7, 90, 92.

—— "News Breakers," British *Vogue*, March 1944: 43.

—— "*Vogue* Photographers Interpret Christmas," British *Vogue*, December 1947: 53–58.

Secondary sources

Amaya, M. 1975 "My Man Ray," in *Art in America*, May–June 1975: 55.

Aspler, Tony, Tony Aspler the Wine Guy, "Spice up your Kitchen, posted May 22, 2003, Tony Aspler.com

Abzug, R. H. 1985. *Inside the Vicious Heart*. New York: Oxford University Press Inc.

Bendit, P. D. and L. J. Bendit. 1946. *Living Together Again*. London: Gramol.

Berger, John. [1972] 1990. *Ways of Seeing*. London: Penguin.

Brooke, Stephen. 2004. "Framing the Body in War and Peace: The Photography of George Rodger and Bill Brandt in the 1940s," unpublished paper for the semi-plenary at the North American Conference of British Studies, Philadelphia, October 2004.

Burke, C. 2001. "Framing a life: Lee Miller," in *Roland Penrose, Lee Miller: The Surrealist and the Photographer* Edinburgh: Scottish National Gallery of Modern Art, exhibition catalog.

Calvocoressi, R. 2002 *Lee Miller: Portraits from a Life*. London: Thames and Hudson.

—— and David Hare. 2005. *Lee Miller Portraits*. London: National Portrait Gallery.

Caws, M. A. 1991. "Seeing the Surrealist Woman: We are a Problem," introduction to *Surrealism and Women*, M. A. Caws, R. Kuenzli and G. Raaberg (eds). Cambridge, MA: MIT Press.

Chadwick, W. 2003. "Lee Miller's Two Bodies," in Chadwick and Tirza True Latimer (eds), *The Modern Woman Revisited: Paris Between the Wars*, pp. 199–221. New Brunswick, NJ and London: Rutgers University Press.

Collingbourn-Beevers, Margot. 2001. Letter to editor, partially reprinted in "Letter from the Editor: Lee's Way," by Judith Hall, BBC *Homes & Antiques*, November 2001: 9.

Conekin, B. 2005. "Lee Miller and the Limits of Post-war British Modernity: Femininity, Fashion, and the Problem of Biography," in *Fashion and Modernity*, Christopher Breward and Caroline Evans Oxford: Berg.

Ernst, Max. 1934. *Une Semaine de Bonte, ou les sept elements capitaux*. Paris: Jeanne Bucher.

Foster, S. C. et al., (eds) (1989) *Perpetual Motif: The Art of Man Ray*. New York: Abbeville Press.

Francis, Martin. "A Flight from Commitment?: Domesticity, Adventure, and the Masculine Imaginary in Postwar Britain," in *Gender and History* (forthcoming).

Fussell, Paul. 1989. *Wartime: Understanding Behaviour in the Second World War*. New York and Oxford: Oxford University Press.

Gallagher, J. 1998. "Vision, Violence and *Vogue*: War and Correspondence in Lee Miller's Photography," in *The World Wars: Through the Female Gaze*, pp. 68–96. Carbondale, Illinois: Southern Illinois University Press.

Gelhorn, M. [1959] 1998. *The Face of War*. London: Granta.

Gerber, D. 1994. "Heroes and Misfits: The Troubled Social Reintegration of Disabled Veterans in *The Best Years of Our Lives*," *American Quarterly*, Vol. 46, No. 4 (1994): 551–2.

Hall, C. 1985 *The Forties in Vogue*. London: Octopus Books.

Hare, D. 2002. "The Real Surrealist," in *The Guardian Weekend*, October 26: 14–24.

Harrison, M. 1991. *Appearances: Fashion Photography Since 1945*. London: Jonathan Cape.

Hill, Paul and Thomas Cooper. 1979. *Dialogue with Photography*. Manchester: Cornerstone Publishing.

Jeremiah, D. 2000. *Architecture and Design for the Family in Britain, 1900–70*. Manchester: Manchester University Press.

Keenan, B. 1977. *The Women We Wanted to Look Like*. London: Macmillan.

Kerr, J. and K. Ware. 1994. "Women Photographers in Europe 1919–1939," *History of Photography*, Vol. 18, No. 3, Autumn, 1994: 219.

Lewinski, Jorge. 1978. *The Camera at War: A History of War Photography from 1848 to the Present Day*. London: Hamlyn Press.

Livingstone, J. 1989. *Lee Miller: Photographer*. London: Thames and Hudson.

Lyford, A. 1994. "Lee Miller's Photographic Impersonations, 1930–1945," in *History of Photography*, Vol. 18, No. 3, Autumn 1994: 230–41.

Man Ray. 1963. *Self-portrait*. Boston: Little Brown/Atlantic Monthly Press.

McEuan, M. A. 2000. *Seeing America: Women Photographers Between the Wars*. Lexington: University of Kentucky Press.

Martin, Richard. [1988] 1996. *Fashion and Surrealism*. London: Thames and Hudson.

Murphy, Robert. 2001. *British Cinema and the Second World War*. London: Continuum International Publishing Group—Academi.

Palmquist, P. E. 1994. "Resources for Second World War Women Photographers," in *History of Photography*, Vol. 18, No. 3, Autumn, 1994: 247–55.

Penrose, A. *The Lives of Lee Miller* London: Thames and Hudson.

—— (ed.) [1992] 2005. *Lee Miller's War*. London: Thames and Hudson.

Penrose, R. 1981. *Scrap Book*. London: Thames and Hudson.

Prose, Francine. 2002. *The Lives of the Muses: Nine Women and the Artists They Inspired*. New York: Harper Collins.

Roberts, M. L. 2002. *Disruptive Acts: The New Woman in Fin-de-Siècle France*. Chicago: University of Chicago Press.

"Snapshots in Time: Lee Miller." Report on an exhibition at the Bermuda National Gallery and Ace Gallery, 2003, from August 18, 2003. WWD.com.

Sontag, Susan. 1977. *On Photography*. New York: Dell.

Spurling, Hilary. 2002. *The Girl from the Fiction Department: A Portrait of Sonia Orwell*. London: Hamish Hamilton.

Steedman, C. K. 1987. *Landscape for a Good Woman: A Story of Two Lives*. New Brunswick, NJ: Rutgers University Press.

Struk, Janina. 2004. *Photographing the Holocaust: Interpretations of Evidence*. London: I. B. Tauris and Co. Ltd.

Vogue Book of Fashion Photography. 1979. Introduction by Alexander Liberman, text by Polly Devlin, design by Bea Feitler, and creative research by Diana Edkins. London: Thames and Hudson.

Zelizer, Barbie. 1998. *Remembering to Forget: Holocaust Memory Through the Camera's Eye*. Chicago and London: University of Chicago Press.

Fashion Theory, Volume 10, Issue 1/2, pp. 127–152
Reprints available directly from the Publishers.
Photocopying permitted by licence only.
© 2006 Berg.

Vogue and the V&A Vitrine

An exploration of how British *Vogue* has responded to fashion exhibitions at the Victoria and Albert Museum from 1971 to 2004, with specific reference to the exhibition "Fashion: An Anthology by Cecil Beaton" and garments that have been imprinted with wear

Amy de la Haye

Amy de la Haye is a Senior Research Fellow at the London College of Fashion (0.4), an independent fashion curator, and creative consultant. She is co-curator of the exhibition "Fashion and Fancy Dress: Six Generations of the Messel Family Dress Collection 1865–2005," which opened at Brighton Museum, Brighton, UK in October 2005, and co-author of the accompanying publication (with Philip Wilson). From 1991 to 1999 she was Curator of Twentieth-Century Dress at the Victoria and Albert Museum, London. amy.delahaye@btinternet.com

Vogue always did stand for people's lives. I mean a new dress doesn't get you anywhere; it's the life you're living in the dress, and the sort of life you had lived before, and what you will do in it later.

Diana Vreeland, former *Vogue* Fashion Editor and Curator

Introduction

Pristine new garments selected from the international catwalks, and on occasion period pieces and items from the high street, are styled by

Vogue to entice, inspire, and assist their readers' own fashion and style choices. Fashionable dress for the forthcoming season is presented in the context of consumption. To fuel our desire for the new, past fashions are dismissed as "out"—to be erased from our memories, in order to make way for the latest styles that are "in." But, when the occasion calls, how does *Vogue* convey, textually and visually, the history and museological interpretations of its subject to the reader? In recent years, reportage of the outfits worn by celebrity guests at the private-view parties of fashion exhibitions has sometimes taken precedence over descriptions of the dress displayed in the exhibition gallery; so how does the magazine engage with dress that has been worn and possesses biography, and that is presented for contextual interpretation rather than for wear?

Vogue works with images; the Victoria and Albert Museum, on the other hand, tells its story through material garments. The social, economic, and aesthetic implications of the fashion photograph and its relationship with text in *Vogue* has been analyzed elsewhere (Jobling 1999), as have the links between consumption and museum collecting (Belk 1995). This article focuses upon the museological significance of the images and text that have appeared in British *Vogue* in relation to fashion exhibitions staged at the V&A since 1971, and in particular upon "Fashion: An Anthology by Cecil Beaton," because this exhibition was a turning point in fashion museology. A Chanel suit dating from 1937–38, originally worn by *Vogue*'s one-time Fashion Editor Diana Vreeland and subsequently photographed for the magazine's 1971 preview article on Beaton's exhibition, is case-studied to explore the implications of re-presenting worn dress that possesses biography within the context of *Vogue*. Briefer reference is made to more recent exhibitions which have focused upon "worn" clothes, or where *Vogue* has engaged with the clothes they have photographed in a museological context. This includes reportage of the dress worn by celebrity guests attending the private-view parties for the magazine's "People" page or commissioned still-life photography of "empty" garments, to illustrate fashion exhibition previews.

In the years up to 1971, *Vogue*'s editorial policy and the V&A's policy for acquiring fashionable dress were both unashamedly elitist, with their emphasis upon luxurious garments created by international designers. And both prioritized women's dress. Where they differed was that *Vogue* placed great emphasis upon the socially exclusive lives of the women who wore elite fashion, whereas the V&A regarded the garments themselves as exemplars of design. *Vogue*'s former Editor-in-Chief, Edna Woolman Chase, quotes the magazine's founder, Arthur Baldwin Turnure, who in 1892 declared that the definite object of the magazine (personified as his "débutante") was to establish a "dignified, authentic journal of society, fashion and the ceremonial side of life" (Chase 1954: 23). The V&A (founded in 1852 as the Museum of Manufactures) was, in contrast, a public institution dedicated to the applied arts with a mission to educate and inspire the public, designers, and manufacturers. By 1971 their differing objectives remained intact.

Fashion: An Anthology by Cecil Beaton (1971)

The Evolution of the Exhibition

"Fashion: An Anthology by Cecil Beaton" was the first major exhibition of modern fashion staged at the V&A. It attracted a large audience of more than 90,000 visitors, making it one of the most highly attended shows the museum had ever staged.[1] In addition to its popularity, the exhibition set the stage for a revolution in terms of the collection and exhibition of modern fashion, both in Britain and abroad.

Philippe de Montebello, Director of New York's Metropolitan Museum of Art (the Met), wrote in his preface to the 1993 exhibition catalog for "Diana Vreeland: Immoderate Style":

> Until the spring of 1973, it could be said that the field of costume had been a sleepy and rarified one, at least in the context of museums. An aura of antiquarianism seemed to enshroud every costume display, and they had, for all intents and purposes, no audience beyond a few specialists (Martin and Koda 1993: 3).

Montebello credits the appointment of Diana Vreeland to the Met's Costume Institute in spring 1973 with "creating a large and enthusiastic audience [for costume] ... not only in New York but around the world as well" (Martin and Koda 1993: 3). Yet the Beaton show had already fulfilled these criteria more than a year prior to Vreeland's arrival at the Met.

Socialite, fashion editor for both *Harper's Bazaar* and *Vogue*, and later curator, Diana Vreeland went on to stage exhibitions which attracted large audiences and engaged with modern fashion, but while she was still Editor-in-Chief at American *Vogue* (a position she held from 1963 until her appointment at the Met), Vreeland presented Beaton with one of her own outfits for the V&A's 1971 exhibition. An evening ensemble designed by Chanel and dating from 1937–38, it comprises a black, sequined, bolero-style jacket with matching pants and a cream-colored silk blouse with lace, pin-tucks, and pearl buttons. This was the outfit that *Vogue* featured in the main photograph of its 1971 exhibition preview.

An investigation into the preparatory stages of this exhibition reveals that in 1969–71 the V&A was only just beginning to engage seriously with fashion as a museological medium. However, in keeping with the museum's collection policy, the emphasis was firmly upon design and making. Unlike *Vogue*, it did not concern itself with the lives of those women who wore elite fashion.

The 1971 exhibition was instigated by a letter written by Sir Cecil Beaton to V&A Director Sir John Pope-Hennessy on October 14, 1969, in which Beaton outlined his desire to collect "[the] best of women's fashions of today."[2] He declared that, while most museum collections were indiscriminately comprised of items that had been offered, "I would hope to flatter the donors by only asking for specific garments that I had seen and admired; and would be very selective in anything that was merely 'offered.'"[3] He suggested that, once formed, this collection would form an exhibition at the V&A. Three days later the Director replied—with perhaps surprising enthusiasm, given the prevailing academic and museological status of fashion. Following a discussion with George Wingfield Digby, Keeper of the V&A's Textiles Department, the Director wrote to Beaton: "My only surprise is that no one till now has ever thought of the idea of forming a collection of dresses based on the same criteria of taste and quality as collections of paintings and other artefacts. It would be a marvellous thing to form and would be a great enrichment of this museum. Please go ahead."[4]

It is well known that Sir Roy Strong, Pope-Hennessy's successor, did much to support fashion at the V&A, but this correspondence provides evidence that the previous Director was at least receptive to the subject. That said, Pope-Hennessy did qualify his approval to Beaton: "I think the focus of the exhibition should not be fashion (which is a pretty generic thing) but dresses chosen as works of art by you."[5] And, in a further letter to update Wingfield Digby, the Director emphasized that it was important to keep haute couture as the central theme of the show, noting that this was something the public would not normally see at the V&A. He advised: "If we accept this we shall have to be careful to avoid including costumes which belonged to celebrities or the Royal Family, with one or two possible exceptions."[6] Here the Director makes explicit his wish that fashionable garments be presented as exemplars of art and design—as the finest items of their kind in terms of quality, workmanship, and innovative design—over and above the celebrity of the men and women who wore them (there was a small menswear component in the show).

This approach was entirely in keeping with the museum's design-led collection policy. Where it differed from *Vogue*'s emphasis on elite fashion was that *Vogue* had always highlighted the lives of the well-known women who wore the clothes featured on its fashion pages. Famous and aristocratic women were invited to model the latest collections, and there were regular features about their lives and personal fashion choices.[7]

In 1969, Avril Hart was employed as a Museum Assistant in the V&A's Department of Textiles, and she worked closely with the V&A's costume specialist Madeleine Ginsburg during the preparation and presentation of the Beaton exhibition. Hart, who became a historical and menswear dress specialist and remained in the department until she retired in 1997, states emphatically that: "Fashion exhibitions were not at the time the V&A's *thing*."[8] The collection policy of the Department of Textiles—as the name implies—privileged textiles: dress was collected for its textile significance rather than for its cut, style, and fashionability. Thus, Hart states that in 1969 the museum's collection of fashionable dress was "poor and not representative."[9] Clearly, Beaton's proposal was foresighted and destined to chart new territory in fashion museology.

Selecting and collecting the exhibits

At first Beaton collected luxurious and fashionable dress belonging to the wealthy and stylish women whom he knew through his professional and social life, clients of the world's most exclusive fashion houses, who were regularly featured in *Vogue*. As Vreeland recalled:

> Cecil really could call up anyone in the world. He couldn't call up royalty—they don't take telephone calls—but *they'd* call *him*. *Everyone* wanted to meet this extraordinary character and be photographed by him (Vreeland 1984: 116–17).

Although he was to prove highly successful as a collector in this field, Beaton rued the fact that he was already too late to acquire dress worn by such style leaders as Margot Asquith and Daisy Fellowes. In his introduction to the exhibition catalog, Beaton reflected on his selection criteria and intentions.

> An original idea is born, lies dormant; then suddenly it comes to flower because the time is right. It is to those who are responsible for this creation that, in making this anthology, I wish to pay homage. Who would these originals be? Ideally I would like to collect something that belonged to Queen Alexandra. She was ineffably chic. Her silhouette was that of a figurine from Knossos with her hourglass corset and high, tightly packed hair, and her late-in-life use of spangled and black sequin daytime coatees was certainly original. And Lily Elsie's huge black "Merry Widow" hat, worn with a gossamer evening dress, was a landmark. Mrs Lydig's first "backless" ballroom gown caused a sensation, as did her fantastic shoes with long tongues of medieval brocade. Certainly of this eclectic company is Lady Ottoline Morrell, who wore picturesque Velasquez Infanta skirts in the 'twenties and Edith Sitwell, whose Pre-Raphaelite silks were embroidered with vivid flowers (Beaton 1971: 8).

Here Beaton makes explicit that, in common with *Vogue*'s editors, he was as inspired by the stylish women who wore the clothes as by the design of the garments they chose.

The exhibition catalog (Beaton 1971) reveals that some 160 people provided Beaton with clothes for the show, and of these about twenty-five were designers, shoemakers, and milliners. Starting with a wish-list of about 150 outfits, Beaton went on to acquire 405, and forty accessories—around 800 individual items. Many of these were shown in the exhibition, which—to gain maximum impact—was staged on the first- and second-floor levels of the V&A's main entrance.

Fashion and Memory

Most of the fashionable clothes that Beaton collected for his exhibition were luxurious haute couture garments which had been cut and stitched to fit the individual clients' bodies perfectly. As worn clothes, each garment bore imprints and possessed its own biography; many were poignant holders of personal memory. In turn, as Beaton's official biographer Hugo Vickers notes, once brought together as a collection the exhibition "[i]n a sense ... represented Cecil's own life in the clothes that were shown. These included the Hartnell presentation dress worn by Cecil's sister Nancy, and the Charles James wedding dress for Baba, a Beaton black and a white Ascot number..." (Vickers 1993: 552).

Vickers describes how Beaton looked on in wonder as Valentina Schlee, the New York couturière, packed a dress for the exhibition and was utterly absorbed in the process, "preparing a work of art for posterity. As she manoeuvred the final gesture with the baby-like sleeves folded into a little roll, she leant down and kissed it. 'Goodbye,' she said. It was really very touching because absolutely genuine" (Vickers 1993: 552).

Just as Beaton was struck by the poignant ability of precious clothes to trigger memories, so too Avril Hart was overcome when she unpacked the parcels Beaton sent to the V&A. She recalls, as she unwrapped the forty-two items of worn dress presented by Mrs. Loel Guinness: "It was a magic moment when her collection was unpacked and these wonderful clothes were taken out one by one ... they still retained the aroma of expensive perfume which wafted out as the clothes were disturbed. We were all entranced..."[10]

The significance of memory within material culture studies has been documented (Kwint et al. 1999; Kavanagh 2000), but these studies have not engaged explicitly with fashionable dress. Later in this article, one of the ensembles photographed for *Vogue*'s exhibition preview has been case-studied to examine the implications of memory and "worn" dress when re-presented on the glossy pages of a fashion magazine. But first it is necessary to examine *Vogue*'s reportage of the Beaton exhibition, to place this in context.

***Vogue*'s Exhibition Preview**

"Each dress is a milestone in fashion," announced *Vogue*'s preview of the exhibition ("Cecil Beaton's Own Gallery of Fashion: A Preview of an Exhibition at the Victoria and Albert Museum beginning on October 13," *Vogue*, October 1971: 93). The short text (unattributed, but written by either Georgina Boosey, Georgina Howell, or Antonia Williams) noted that there were twenty outfits by Balenciaga, nine by Schiaparelli, eight Poirets, two Vionnets, a Fortuny, and "masses of Chanels" (p. 123).

Vogue could—but chose not to—have reviewed the exhibition in the context of its own historiography or of Beaton's almost fifty-year-long relationship with the magazine. The preview was picture-led. As the exhibits did not at the time belong to the museum (at this point they had loan status) they were not subject to the same rigorous conservation and display conditions that would be imposed upon accessioned objects. As a result, five ensembles including the Vreeland Chanel suit, each previously worn, were selected and borrowed for *Vogue*'s photo shoot, to be worn by a living model—a process that would never have been permitted with garments belonging to the V&A.

Vogue chose Norman Parkinson to photograph the preview. Like Beaton, Parkinson had worked with *Vogue* for many years. Robin Muir (curator of the Parkinson retrospective exhibition at London's National Portrait Gallery in 2004) states that: "In the 1970s, commissions [for Parkinson] from *Vogue* did not prove elusive but became sparser, treated as 'special assignments' for a grand old man" (Muir 2004: 24). *Vogue* thus, in selecting Parkinson, chose a photographer who was a contemporary of the later 1930s fashions to be photographed. The modernistic photographic set comprised an array of circular white stools in the foreground against a white backdrop (the piece was photographed in black and white, as were many of *Vogue*'s fashion shoots at this time).

Instead of employing an anonymous professional model to wear the clothes for the prelude piece and the preview, *Vogue* invited Marisa Berenson, the twenty-five-year-old actress, to model the exhibits. During the 1960s Berenson (granddaughter of the Parisian couturière Elsa Schiaparelli, whose designs were represented within the exhibition) had worked as a professional model, often employed by *Vogue* and one of Vreeland's favorites. Berenson's break into acting came when Luchino Visconti cast her in his film *Death in Venice* (also in 1971). At the time of the *Vogue* photo shoot, the film *Cabaret* was about to be released, starring Liza Minelli, in which Berenson had a supporting role. For this carefully styled photo shoot, Berenson was thus presented as a sophisticated actress who had a special relationship with the clothes she was photographed wearing.

Berenson modeled five garments, all previously worn—including two from Schiaparelli's Spring/Summer 1938 "Circus" collection: a pink jacket with brocaded horses and acrobat buttons, and the "Tear" dress with a decorative *trompe l'oeil* print depicting torn flesh, designed in collaboration with Salvador Dali. Both garments were presented to Beaton by the actress Ruth Ford (who became Mrs. Zachary Scott),

Figure 1
Marisa Berenson modeling a Chanel evening suit from 1937–38, originally worn by Diana Vreeland. She is seated next to Cecil Beaton, who wears his own clothes, British *Vogue*, October 1, 1971. Photograph: Norman Parkinson. © Norman Parkinson Ltd/Fiona Cowan.

sister of the surrealist poet Charles Henri Ford. The "Tear" dress had been worn by Miss Ford and the jacket by her mother.

The main picture in *Vogue*'s preview, illustrated here (Figure 1), is of Berenson, seated with Beaton. She is wearing the Chanel evening suit of 1937–38 that belonged to Diana Vreeland. The *Vogue* stylists accessorized this ensemble with Chanel's signature camellia corsage and satin shoes from Rayne, masses of pearls, "glitter rings," and a bracelet comprising four rows of rhinestones (which, according to the editorial, were available from Adrien Mann at the London department store Marshall & Snelgrove). Vreeland herself had worn the outfit with a black ribbon tied around the neck, into which a red rose was placed (Wilcox and Mendes 1991:58). The hairstylist, Christopher of Vidal Sassoon, provided Berenson with a cropped white wig to wear, which curiously suggests neither Chanel, the late 1930s, nor 1971 hair fashions.

Worn Clothes and Recreated Photographic Images in *Vogue*

In *The Study of Dress History*, Professor Lou Taylor discusses the problematics of "recreated images" for the dress historian. With reference to a Christian Dior New Look cocktail dress from 1947, which appears in Beaton's (1971) exhibition catalog, she points out that "[t]he sleek

Figure 2
Diana Vreeland wearing her
Chanel pantsuit, c.1938.
Courtesy of The Metropolitan
Museum of Art, New York.

blonde chignon of the model, her style of make-up and the very large pearl beads of her necklace are not at all redolent of 1947" (Taylor 2002: 161). Taylor also emphasizes that this dissociation is not confined to the 1970s, citing the Imperial War Museum's justly acclaimed exhibition "Forties Fashion and the New Look" staged in 1997, which was successfully marketed with a photograph of ballerina Darcy Bussell wearing another seminal New Look ensemble (Taylor 2002: 161). Over twenty-five years on, a period costume was modeled by an up-to-date personality and photographed to market a fashion exhibition. Taylor concludes that the value of such an image "[t]o dress historians rests only in its history as recreated image" (Taylor 2002: 161). This comment, of course, could equally apply to the *Vogue* preview photographs which juxtapose historical and modern dress and a modern actress whose personal styling is entirely "1971."

It could further be suggested that the significance of such recreated images lies not only in the fact that they are "false" in terms of chronological representation, but that to re-present worn, historical clothing on a modern model is to deny the biography of the consumer who originally chose the garment, and, in the case of haute couture, who commissioned it to fit her body perfectly, and who wore it.

Perhaps more than any other medium, worn clothing offers tangible evidence of lives lived, partly because its very materiality is altered by, and bears imprints of, its original owner. A garment's shaping can become distorted in an echo of personal body contours. It can become imbued with personal scent, and bear marks of wear—from fabric erosion at hem, cuffs, and neck, to stains that are absorbed or linger on the surface of the cloth. When worn clothes enter a museum they embark upon a new "life" and serve new functions. In the process, what was once intimate can become impersonal—although often the very reason worn clothes are presented to a museum is to prevent them becoming part of the anonymous detritus of our material culture, and thus to retain their meaning.

The cultural biography of "things" has been highlighted by Igor Kopytoff (in Appadurai 1986), and a number of artists have also exploited the significance of worn dress, notably Christian Boltanski, who places piles of worn clothing in an art gallery context as poignant symbols of lives lost. As Boltanski says, "[W]hat is beautiful about working with used clothes is that these really have come from somebody. Somebody has actually chosen them, loved them, but the life in them is now dead. Exhibiting them in a show is like giving the clothes a new life—like resurrecting them" (Semin et al. 1997: 19).

The memory held within worn clothing has also been a theme that has inspired many designers and artists of conceptual dress, and curators to exhibit their work, such as in "Empty Dress" (Independent Curators New York, 1994) and "Doublures" (Québec, 2003). However, the cultural meanings of the imprints we leave upon the clothes we wear are barely explored within fashion history or curation.

Vogue's photo-shoot preview of the 1971 Beaton exhibition success-fully presented the images of the forthcoming exhibition in an accessible, glamorous, and contemporary style for its readership. However, it could be argued that this approach drained the garments of their contextual meaning and the specific memories of their owners. This angle will be explored in specific relation to the Chanel suit that Diana Vreeland gave Cecil Beaton for the exhibition.

A Case Study: Diana Vreeland's Chanel Suit

Diana Vreeland clearly cherished her Chanel evening suit. She had pre-served it for over thirty years as an exemplar of 1930s Parisian haute couture (a period in fashion she especially adored), and it had been designed by a couturière whom she also considered a friend. She may also have retained it as a holder of precious memories. In her autobiography, Vreeland makes explicit her own association between dress, biography, and memory. She recalls her last afternoon in Paris, on the eve of the German occupation in 1940. She had just been for a fitting at Chanel:

> I can remember exactly what I had on: a little black *moiré tailleur* from Chanel, a little piece of black lace wrapped around my head,

and beautiful, absolutely exquisite black slippers like kid gloves
... it's curious to visualize yourself like this, isn't it? But I always
have to think about what I had on. Just today, I thought of those
slippers and I remembered everything (Vreeland 1984: 97).

The styling and materiality of the ensemble was presumably also very
special to her. A pantsuit, it is entirely covered in overlapping sequins so
that the surface of the suit resembles gleaming metal. When tempered
with soft lace, it presents a juxtaposition of materials that she revered.

I have a passion for armor. To me a gauntlet is the most beautiful
thing ... I always have armor in my Metropolitan shows ... In
"Vanity Fair" I had a very beautiful lace room, and in the middle
of it I had a gold breastplate. It was swollen gold ... and out
of the neck poured *point de Bruxelles*, the most beautiful lace
in the world. The combination of gold and steel and lace!—no
combination is as beautiful (Vreeland 1984: 101–2).

These associations, personal to Vreeland, were entirely lost in the
recreated *Vogue* image of 1971. If the exhibits selected for the *Vogue*
preview were not to be photographed on the original wearers (Vreeland
was sixty-five years old in 1971), it might seem incongruous to invite an
actress, a known figure, to pose in them, rather than a socially anonymous professional model. But on reflection, the magazine's reasons for
this choice become more clear. Throughout her adult life Vreeland was
noted for her extraordinary appearance, demeanor, and sense of personal
style, which would possibly have made this photograph unsettling for
the *Vogue* viewer. Beaton devoted four pages of *The Glass of Fashion*
(1954) to describe his friend, including this passage:

Above her small-boned, beautiful body, with its feet like the bound
feet of Chinese ladies, Mrs. Vreeland's head sits independently on
top of a narrow neck and smiles at you. Everything about her
features is animated by amused interest: her nose as broad as an
Indian's, is boldly assertive; her eyes twinkly; her mouth emits the
most amazingly aggressive and masculine laugh, a red laugh that
is taken up by her cheeks, expertly rouged with an art that has
gone out of style and of which she is one of the remaining masters
(Beaton 1954: 312).

Vreeland's own journalistic talent lay in visualizing and styling photographic images. In 1960, while she was at *Harpers Bazaar* (prior to
her time at *Vogue* and the Met), Bettina Ballard, Vreeland's opposite
number at American *Vogue,* said of her:

> Working on a fashion photograph or a fashion show, Diana has
> never been content simply to present a costume; she must create
> the type of woman who might wear the costume, consider where
> she might wear it, possibly stop to ponder on the life story of the
> imaginary woman in the ready-made suit in front of her. Clothes
> are people to her, and her interest in them is deep and human
> (Ballard 1960: 293).

There is no surviving documentation to offer insight into Vreeland's
own perception of *Vogue*'s 1971 exhibition preview and photo shoot.
However, almost certainly she would have entirely approved. Vreeland
had known Berenson since childhood and had later nurtured her modeling career—much to the fury of Schiaparelli, who apparently wanted
her granddaughter to marry an aristocrat (Dwight 2002: 165–6). At
the Costume Institute, one of Vreeland's main objectives—often to the
chagrin of those she worked with—was to make historical dress appear
fashionable, beautiful, and "now" for the museum visitor (Dwight
2002: 209). In fact, Dwight quotes Vreeland as saying:

> "Who cares about Schiaparelli 1939 gloves with a 1974 black
> velvet Grès gown? The public isn't concerned about ponderous
> accuracy—they want spectacle, the illusive spirit" (Dwight 2002:
> 210).

Because Vreeland clearly adored Berenson, and in her capacity as a
curator would interpret dress, irrespective of period, in the fashion context of "now," *Vogue*'s approach was entirely in keeping with Vreeland's
own ethos. As described earlier, at the time it was also an accepted form
of museological interpretation. However, it was the only occasion upon
which *Vogue* created new and contemporary images of historical, worn
dress to review a fashion exhibition at the V&A.

How the V&A Exhibited Vreeland's Chanel Suit

When, in November 1970, Beaton outlined his ideas for the overall
"feel" of the show, he wrote: "I am so keen that when this display is
shown it will convey a feeling of elegance and romanticism that the
dresses pervaded in their own epochs."[11] The exhibition design, however, was entirely contemporary. At the suggestion of Ernestine Carter
from *The Sunday Times*, the V&A approached Michael Haynes, a
talented London display designer who had recently left Jaeger. A press
release promised that, with Haynes's involvement, the show would have
"all the originality and liveliness of the best shop windows in London."
In recent years the relationship between commerce and culture, retail
and the museum, have been critically examined (Silverman 1986;

Figure 3
Diana Vreeland's Chanel suit
displayed in the 1930s section
of the exhibition "Fashion: An
Anthology by Cecil Beaton,"
V&A, 1971. Private collection.

Belk 1995), but in 1971 this was an entirely modern and exciting approach for the display of fashionable dress within the context of the museum. *Vogue* advised its readers that the clothes "will be shown inside a big [Plexiglas] structure, grouped on revolving platforms with their contemporary props, the whole exhibition designed by Michael Haynes" (British *Vogue*, October 1971: 123).

The exhibition was divided into twelve sections which were identified by period, theme, or designer: Royalty; 1920s; 1930s; Schiaparelli and Surrealism in the 1930s; 1950s; Mainbocher; Dior; Givenchy;

Balenciaga; English Contemporary; Space Age; and Miscellaneous. Although Beaton was clearly fascinated by the women who had worn the clothes he collected (as were Vreeland and *Vogue*), the V&A's design-led emphasis prevailed within the exhibition. And, as with *Vogue*'s preview, the clothes were displayed on modern bodies—albeit in this case made of fiberglass—that bore no relationship to the owners' appearance. With the exception of items that had been worn by royalty, which were mounted on faceless, dressmaker-style mannequins, the exhibits were shown on a selection of contemporary shop window mannequins manufactured by Contour, Derek Ryman, Schlappi of Zurich, Barway Mannequins, and Adel Rootstein. Vreeland's pantsuit was displayed within the 1930s case, on a kneeling figure.

The Exhibition's Launch Party

In October 1971, soon after "Fashion: An Anthology by Cecil Beaton" had opened, Beaton updated Diana Vreeland on the exhibition (*Vogue* had not reported the opening) and the private view at which Patrick, Lord Lichfield had taken photographs. Vreeland knew Lichfield well; she had given him his photographic break when she invited him to work for American *Vogue*. "The exhibition is a huge and beautiful success," wrote Beaton. However, "Lichfield's photographs give no suggestion of the exhibits, except Queen Alexandra, but I suppose he went to photograph the people not the clothes" (Vickers 1993: 553). By the late 1980s, this focus upon the celebrity guests who attended the private-view parties of fashion exhibitions was a common occurrence, not only for *Vogue* which had always reported on arts social events, but also for the V&A itself.[12]

V&A Fashion Exhibitions and the Celebrity Image in *Vogue*

Since the 1890s, fashion designers have "placed" their product by lending or giving clothes to stylish celebrities to wear to high-profile public events (Latour 1958). In recent years, such events have increasingly included fashion exhibition openings at major international museums—now part of the annual social calendar.

As we have seen, in 1969 V&A Director John Pope-Hennessy advised against acquiring and displaying dress which had been worn by celebrities, fearing that the emphasis would shift from designed object to personality. While this did not occur within the Beaton exhibition itself, the object of Pope-Hennesy's advice, it was precisely the focus of the photographs taken by Patrick Lichfield at the private-view. By the late 1980s, with more fashion exhibitions scheduled into the V&A's

program, the private view parties were regularly featured on *Vogue*'s "People Page." Celebrity guests would often be clothed in dress related to the exhibition subject or fashion designer whose work was being profiled. Yet it was frequently the celebrities themselves, rather than specifically the fashions exhibited within the exhibition, who were the magazine's main topic.

In 2001, Chris Rojek's book *Celebrity* was published as part of Reaktion Books' "Foci" series, which addresses "the pressing problems, ideas and debates of the new millennium." Rojek's text discusses "attribution and distance rather than the innate qualities or characteristics of celebrity because I believe that mass-media representation is the key principle in the formation of celebrity culture. To us, celebrities often seem magical or superhuman. However, this is because their presence in the public eye is comprehensively staged" (Rojek 2001:13).

"Ferragamo: the Art of the Shoe 1927–1960" (1987–88)

In January 1988, *Vogue*'s "Eye on People" presented photographs of five famous guests who had attended the October opening of this exhibition, curated by Valerie Mendes (which went on to attract more than 125,000 visitors). As with most society reportage, *Vogue* readers were told that Mrs. Ferragamo wore a strapless taffeta dress designed by Lorcan Mullany, and that the Countess de Borchgrave was dressed in a full-length gown by Romeo Gigli. On this occasion, it was the fashion choices of famous women which were highlighted: their clothes, or the footwear they wore, were not linked to the exhibition.

"Fashion and Surrealism" (1988)

In September 1988, almost half of *Vogue*'s "People Page" was devoted to the famous guests who had attended the launch party of "Fashion and Surrealism," which was visiting from the Metropolitan Museum of Art and was coordinated by Valerie Mendes for the V&A, where it attracted over 120,000 visitors. The exhibition covered dress, fashion, and surrealism from the 1930s, and carried significant contemporary appeal because fashion designers were currently exploiting surreal devices and motifs in their seasonal collections. Once again, however, *Vogue*'s launch piece did not report on the exhibition subject, its design, or even the exhibits, as it had for the Beaton exhibition in 1971. Instead, it showed photographs of performance artist Leigh Bowery, bedecked in the dramatic crewel-and-sequin-embroidered costume he had created to wear on stage in Michael Clark's ballet, then showing at London's Sadler's Wells theater, fashion designer Georgina Godley wearing her "TV Dinner" dress, and milliner Kirsten Woodward wearing her own-design "Man's Torso" hat. Once again the self-presentation of famous guests and exhibitors, some of whom wore attire related to the exhibition theme, gave a vibrant contemporary element to the reportage, and brought a vital performative and celebrity dimension to the "People Page."

Figure 4
"Surreal Thing," *Vogue*'s
"People Page," British *Vogue*,
September 1988, p. 26.

"Versace at the V&A" (2003) and "Vivienne Westwood: 34 Years in Fashion" (2004)

The V&A's two most recent major fashion exhibitions, both curated by Claire Wilcox (appointed in 1999), were "Versace at the V&A" (visited by 165,000 people) and "Vivienne Westwood: 34 Years in Fashion" (170,000). These exhibitions obviously appealed to *Vogue*'s editorial panel, because the magazine published a six-page preview article profiling each designer, as well as photographing the famous guests who attended the private view of each exhibition.

Figure 5
"Viva Versace" in "People in Vogue," British *Vogue*, January 2003, p. 34. Nick Harvey/ British *Vogue*.

The Versace party was allocated a full page of "People in Vogue." Titled "Viva Versace," the text (bylined "O. F.") described:

> Celebrities galore, rhinestone-encrusted gowns, big jewellery— all the hallmarks of a Versace party were on full display for the private view of *Versace at the V&A* exhibition. Resplendent in one of her sexy signature dresses, Donatella Versace whipped up a paparazzi flashbulb frenzy when she toured the show with a power posse that included her daughter Allegra, Chelsea Clinton, Madonna and Lourdes (British *Vogue*, January 2003: 34).

Other photographed celebrity guests from the world of movies, theater, and fashion included Anna Friel, Patsy Kensit, Sophie Dahl, Joely Richardson, Lisa Butcher, Leah Wood, and Rachel Hunter. Although their clothes were not individually provenanced, the photographs indicated that they mostly bore the hallmarks of Versace design. In this instance, the *Vogue* reader could see almost the same clothes as those in the museum gallery, worn by celebrity guests.

"People in Vogue" coverage of the Westwood exhibition's launch party, similarly titled "Viva Vivienne," addressed an additional theme. As an *hommage* to the designer, and reflecting the prevailing fashion for "vintage" Westwood garments, many of the guests wore pieces from the designer's past collections. On this occasion, details of each outfit were carefully documented in the *Vogue* report. The earliest Westwood design photographed at the opening party dated from her Fall/Winter 1982 collection, and was worn to the party by Kate Moss. Denise Zamarioni wore items from Westwood's Spring/Summer 1997 collection, Erin O'Connor clothes from Fall/Winter 2002, and Sam Taylor-Wood from Fall/Winter 2003, while Westwood herself, Jerry Hall, and Leah Wood were all dressed from the designer's current collection. Writer Danielle Radojcin

suggested that, over and above the exhibition, "[p]erhaps the most fitting tribute, however, was the spectacular array of gowns worn by the crowd—the designs on display came from all periods of Westwood's long career. Proof, as if it were needed, of her enduring appeal" (British *Vogue*, June 2004: 49).

Unlike the clothes displayed on mannequins in the exhibition, which were assessed chronologically and in terms of their stylistic influences, these "vintage" Westwood fashions, worn to the launch party by top celebrities, lost the historical interpretation which draws visitors to see fashionable dress within the context of the museum. There they became mere "props" for the stars and the fashion press, bringing with them perhaps a vague sense of nostalgia.

In recent years, the V&A's approach to celebrity has come closer to that of *Vogue*. A special red carpet is rolled out across the pavement and up the steps to the museum entrance when celebrity guests attend, and they are photographed en route by the paparazzi. As a practice, it borrows much from Diana Vreeland's approach during her tenure at the Met.

"Streetstyle" 1994

In 1994 this author co-curated the "Streetstyle: From Sidewalk to Catwalk" exhibition, which displayed outfits worn by international members of subcultures (male, female, and revival styles) between 1954 and 1994, and revealed how these had stylistically inspired international catwalk fashions. *Vogue* published a fascinating article titled "From Street to Elite" which revealed, via photographs, this "bubble-

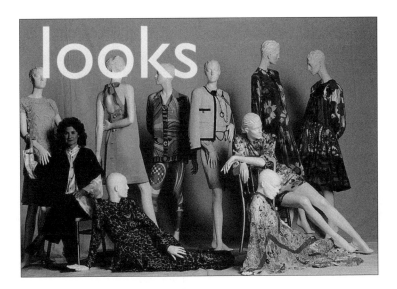

Figure 6
V&A donor Jill Ritblat, seated among mannequins dressed in garments she had worn since the 1960s. British *Vogue*, May 1997, p. 86. Snowdon/British *Vogue*.

up" process. A hypothetical garment formed the hook into the piece: "An item of clothing glimpsed in a film of the jerky rhythms of an underground music revolution can influence the way people dress more than the creative musings in a designer's head" (British *Vogue*, October 1994: 180). However, this extensively researched, diagrammatic and photographic article did not engage with the subcultural clothing that had been worn, nor did *Vogue* commission special photography. (The magazine did not report on the "Black Style" exhibition in 2004, curated by Carol Tulloch and Shaun Cole, which included many "worn" outfits, but did publicize the accompanying publication.)

"Peopled" Dress in Vogue: "One Woman's Wardrobe" (1998)
In 1997, arts patron Jill Ritblat donated the largest single gift of fashionable dress the V&A had ever received: it included almost everything she had worn in her adult life to date. A selection of these garments was exhibited in the V&A's Dress Gallery in 1998 as "One Woman's Wardrobe," curated by this author working closely with Mrs. Ritblat. Unlike the other exhibitions discussed, this was not a major show staged in the museum's exhibition galleries. None the less, this gift and the exhibition became the subject of a two-page preview in *Vogue* called "Out of the Closet," written by the magazine's fashion features writer, Lisa Armstrong (British *Vogue*, May 1997: 85–6).

With its primary emphasis upon aesthetics, the V&A has traditionally prioritized the creative process, working practice, and output of the designer, whereas this display prioritized the fashion client as consumer. As such, it provided an opportunity to explore the nuances of one woman's taste and sartorial requirements over thirty years, and to acknowledge the "real life" of clothes, once they have left the designer's studio or saleroom. The exhibition also considered the role of consumer as stylist, who juxtaposes clothes by various designers in her wardrobe and selects items from different seasons, to create a unique personal expression. This was a "real" process entirely ignored in Beaton's 1971 show, but always present in *Vogue*'s society coverage. Where it differed from *Vogue*'s standard coverage of the fashion choices of stylish women was that Armstrong also explored the clothes Mrs. Ritblat had worn over many years in the context of her biography and her motivation to preserve them.

Two color photographs illustrated *Vogue*'s article: a portrait by Henry Bourne of Ritblat dressed in an orange pleated ensemble by Issey Miyake, posing in front of an unattributed modern painting that highlighted her role as a collector of modern art. The other photograph, by Antony Armstrong-Jones (Lord Snowdon), pictured here, presents her seated wearing clothes designed by Shirin Guild, amid a group of nine mannequins dressed in clothing she had worn at various points in her life. These include her Christian Dior pink silk going-away ensemble from 1966; a Valentino dress worn at Royal Ascot, and the Chanel suit, customized with grosgrain ribbons, that she had worn for her wedding to John Ritblat. There were also fashions less explicitly associated with rites of passage and special occasions (which tend to dominate museum dress collections): printed silk jersey leggings and shirt by Pucci; a handpainted dress by Deborah & Clare; designs by Ossie Clark and Zandra Rhodes; and a leopard-print dress by Yves Saint Laurent. The problems we have discussed of displaying "real people's" clothes, not of the current season, on relatively tall, commercial display mannequins, their bodies and faces cast in contemporary ideals of beauty (in this case lent by Adel Rootstein) were overcome in this juxtaposition, because the *Vogue* reader actually saw the "real person" whose clothes were photographed, and later exhibited.

Lisa Armstrong's text explored the significance of Jill Ritblat's clothes as a collection which facilitated identification of her stylistic preferences, including her enduring love of cutting-edge tailoring and animal and floral patterned fabrics. Ritblat explained how she divided her wardrobe into two sections: "Husband Wardrobe" (formal and conventionally pretty—Chanel and Valentino), and "Wife Wardrobe" (for her own activities, "artsy" and cutting-edge—Comme des Garçons and Alexander McQueen). This gave the reader a fascinating insight into one woman's sartorial taste and specific consumption across the range of elite fashion in the late twentieth century. Armstrong's article also documented the donor's expenditure on fashionable dress in the context of her biography, identifying for example "the splurge she indulged in after her daughter was born." The article concluded by acknowledging the collector's justification for future acquisition: "She has masterminded a watertight excuse for buying as many clothes as she wishes. Her public will expect it" (British *Vogue*, May 1997: 86).

During the 1930s, the German-Jewish cultural critic Walter Benjamin noted that, while it might be socially desirable and academically more useful, the "meaning" of a collection was lost once it passed from its personal owner to a museum (Sherman 1994: 138). However, *Vogue*'s combination of Armstrong's insightful text and Snowdon's skilful image ensured that Jill Ritblat's collection of worn clothing retained its "meaning."

The "Versace at the V&A" (2003) and "Vivienne Westwood: 34 Years in Fashion" Exhibitions

The Versace and Westwood exhibitions, already referred to, were both previewed by *Vogue* in the form of six-page interview-style articles. These worked contextually to remind *Vogue* readers of the designers' fashion milestones and working practices, and additionally offered insights into their personalities and personal lives. Many of the photographs used had originally been published in *Vogue* and served to highlight the designers' historical and contemporary relationship with the magazine. However, for the main image of each piece, *Vogue* commissioned special photography.

The Versace preview, entitled "Master Class" and compiled by Charlotte Sanders, was introduced with a full-page photograph by cutting-edge fashion photographer Toby McFarlan Pond, who was also the photographer chosen by Jill Ritblat to photograph her clothes for the catalog that accompanied "One Woman's Wardrobe." For the Versace preview, McFarlan Pond photographed a full-length, pale blue Versace evening dress, adorned with two oversize pins. *Vogue*'s caption read: "Frock tactics: a frothy early-nineties ballgown displays both Versace's typical ebullience and his masterful technical skills in its drapes and folds" (British *Vogue*, October 2002: 361). Unlike a museum label, the caption does not give the provenance and precise date of the dress. What is known, however, is that the dress did not belong to the V&A, nor was it associated with the exhibition. McFarlan Pond's hauntingly beautiful photograph for *Vogue* includes a partial glimpse of the studio setting, in which the Versace dress is suspended by its shoulder straps on a sloping pole, defying gravity. Exquisitely styled (no individual stylist credit given), it emphasizes the contours of an absent feminine body: presented as "empty" dress, it is deliberately distinct from the fashion photography which dominates *Vogue*'s pages.

In 2004, to illustrate the interviews on Vivienne Westwood linked to the V&A exhibition and compiled by Sarah Harris, *Vogue* commissioned Mark Mattock to photograph a vinyl-trimmed black T-shirt, adorned with chicken bones chained together to read "Rock," bought in 1971 from Westwood's London shop "Let it Rock." (Again, no stylist is credited.) The garment is presented as hanging on a wooden coat hanger, held by a gloved hand implying the reverential hand of the

Figure 7
"God save the Queen," British *Vogue*, April 2004, p. 280. Mark Mattock/British *Vogue*.

museum curator. In 1971 this garment was worn as an act of subcultural rebellion; by 2004, it had become a rare and precious "object" which was to form part of the V&A's exhibition. *Vogue*'s photograph makes this transition explicit. The photographs used by *Vogue* for the Versace and Westwood previews render these garments as "other"—they are not presented as "vintage" fashion, nor are they modeled by a modern-day celebrity. Their status as "objects" is underlined.

Conclusion

Since 1971, British *Vogue* has reported on most of the major fashion exhibitions staged at the V&A.[13] In the late 1980s, the magazine's policy was to privilege the dress worn by celebrity guests attending the private-view parties over that shown within the gallery, while in recent years it has covered both. *Vogue* and the V&A still have very different remits but, as increases both in subscriptions[14] and the attendance figures for fashion exhibitions reveal, they share a growing audience for this subject.

For "Fashion: An Anthology by Cecil Beaton" *Vogue* photographed museum exhibits—historical, special-occasion clothes with biography—displayed on a living model whose personal appearance was, otherwise, entirely of 1971. By 2004, things had changed to the extent that a T-shirt, representing a fashion subculture and with no provenance subsequent to its point-of-sale, was styled and photographed as a revered "object." *Vogue* made it explicit that the garment was not offered as an item for consumption, or one to be imagined being worn; on the contrary, its editorial purpose was to raise questions. And, just as *Vogue*'s approach to historical fashionable dress echoes changes in fashion curation, so the V&A's attitude toward the famous men and women who wear fashionable dress has drawn closer to that of *Vogue*. This article has sought to highlight the implications of displaying, photographing, and interpreting fashionable dress that has been imprinted with wear, whether in the context of the decorative arts museum or on the glossy magazine pages of *Vogue*.

Acknowledgments

I am indebted to Avril Hart, Valerie Mendes, and Claire Wilcox for their insights and for answering my many queries about the exhibitions they have curated. For their support with related research, I would like to thank Helen Beeckmans, Andrew Bolton, Emily Owen, and Caroline Windsor. For valued advice on the themes of this manuscript I am most grateful to Professor Lou Taylor. For input on its style I acknowledge Martyn Oliver. At Vogue House, I would like to acknowledge the invaluable support of Janine Button, Harriet Wilson, and Nicky Budden. Finally, I would like to thank the London College of Fashion for my Senior Research Fellowship which has made this project possible.

Notes

1. Contemporary fashion was included in, but was not the focus of, "Britain Can Make It" (1946), and historical dress was the subject of "Six Wives of Henry VIII Costumes" (1970). Of the V&A's previous forty-two exhibitions, Cecil Beaton's anthology was the ninth most highly attended, and attracted higher audiences than subsequent exhibitions until "Faberge" in 1977 (V&A intranet).
2. V&A Registered Papers 70/375A.

3. Ibid.
4. Ibid.
5. Ibid.
6. Ibid.
7. An article titled "Debutantes in their Ball Backgrounds" (*Vogue* 1954: 54–7) is just one of many examples.
8. Interview with Avril Hart, May 29, 2005.
9. Ibid.
10. Avril Hart, unpublished lecture manuscript. This insightful lecture, planned as part of a study day to coincide with the National Portrait Gallery's Cecil Beaton exhibition in 2004, was reluctantly canceled by the Costume Society due to lack of subscription.
11. Beaton to Pope-Hennessy, November 11, 1970. V&A Registered Papers 70/375A.
12. In light of the success of the V&A's first major fashion exhibition, it is surprising that the museum did not generate another until 1987. In 1976 the museum hosted the Royal Scottish Museum's exhibition "Fashion 1900–1939" (*Vogue* included the show in its "Don't Miss…" listings of January 1976). In 1977 Valerie Mendes, the V&A's specialist textile curator, was asked to take responsibility for the Twentieth-Century Dress Collection, and held this position until 1990 when she was promoted to Chief Curator of the Textiles and Dress Collection. Mendes worked tirelessly to promote fashion at the V&A. Nonetheless, it was not until 1987 that the museum supported another internally generated major exhibition with fashion as its theme. "Ascher: Fabric, Art, Fashion" (1987) was curated by Mendes, and previewed in the May issue of *Vogue* (1987: 156).
13. *Vogue* did report on "The Cutting Edge: 50 Years of British Fashion" (a V&A exhibition which attracted over 230,000 visitors) in the form of short interviews with "fashionable faces" concerning traits within Britain's national fashion identity (British *Vogue*, March 1997: 85–6, compiled by Mark Holgate). As neither the article nor the exhibition explicitly engaged with worn clothes, this was not discussed in the main text.
14. *Vogue* does not have complete annual statistics until 1975. From January to December 1975, total sales of British *Vogue* were 230,227 (186,886 UK sales and 43,341 overseas). Sales from July 2004 to June (the most recent at time of writing) were 417,167 (UK sales 327,922 and overseas 89,245). Supplied by *Vogue*.

References

Ballard, Bettina. 1960. *In My Fashion*. London: Secker & Warburg.
Beaton, Cecil. 1954. *The Glass of Fashion*. Weidenfeld & Nicolson.

—— and Madeleine Ginsburg. 1971. *Fashion: An Anthology by Cecil Beaton.* London: Victoria & Albert Museum.

Belk, Russell. 1995. *Collecting in a Consumer Society.* London: Routledge.

Chase, Edna Woolman and Ilka, Chase. 1954. *Always in Vogue.* London: Gollancz.

Dwight, Eleanor. 2002. *Diana Vreeland.* New York: William Morrow.

Felshin, Nina. 1994. *Empty Dress: Clothing as Surrogate in Recent Art.* New York: Independent Curators Incorporated.

Jobling, Paul. 1999. *Fashion Spreads: Word and Image in Fashion Photography since 1980.* Oxford: Berg.

Kavanagh, Gaynor. 2000. *Dream Spaces: Memory and the Museum.* London: Leicester University Press.

Kopytoff, Igor. 1986. "The Biography of Things" in Arjun Appadurai (1986) *The Social Life of Things.* Cambridge: Cambridge University Press.

Kwint, Marius, Christopher Breward and Jeremy Aynsley. 1999. *Material Memories: Design and Evocation.* Oxford: Berg.

Latour, Anny. 1958. *Kings of Fashion.* London: Weidenfeld & Nicolson.

Martin, Richard and Harold Koda. 1993. *Diana Vreeland:Immoderate Style.* New York: Metropolitan Museum of Art.

Muir, Robin. 2004. *Norman Parkinson: Portraits in Fashion.* London: Trafalgar Square Publishing.

Ritblat, Jill. 1998. *One Woman's Wardrobe.* London: Jill Ritblat/Art Data.

Rojek, Chris. 2001. *Celebrity.* London: Reaktion Books.

Semin, Didier, Tamar Garb and Donald Kuspit. 1997. *Christian Boltanski.* London: Phaidon.

Silverman, Debora. 1986. *Selling Culture: Bloomingdale's, Diana Vreeland, and the New Aristocracy of Taste in Reagan's America.* New York: Pantheon.

Sherman, Daniel J. 1994. "Quatremère/Benjamin/Marx," in Daniel J. Sherman and

Irit Rogoff (eds) (1994) *Museum Culture: Histories, Discourses, Spectacles.* London: Routledge.

Taylor, Lou. 2002. *The Study of Dress History.* Manchester: Manchester University Press.

Vickers, Hugo. 1993. *Cecil Beaton.* London: Weidenfeld & Nicolson.

Vreeland, Diana. 1984. *DV.* London: Weidenfeld & Nicolson.

Wilcox, Claire and Valerie Mendes. 1991. *Modern Fashion in Detail.* London: Victoria and Albert Museum.

ROLAND BARTHES

The Language of Fashion

Fashion Theory, Volume 10, Issue 1/2, pp. 153–174
Reprints available directly from the Publishers.
Photocopying permitted by licence only.
© 2006 Berg.

"Over to You": Writing Readers in French *Vogue*

Agnès Rocamora

Dr. Agnès Rocamora is a Senior
Research Fellow and Lecturer
in Cultural Studies at the
London College of Fashion. She
has published articles on media
discourses on fashion and on
the work of Pierre Bourdieu.
Her current research interests
are in fashion journalism and
cultural mediation.
a.rocamora@fashion.arts.ac.uk

Introduction

Fashion companies and the fashion media, Wargnier observes, are
both addressed to "one and the same consumer-reader who 'consumes
fashion'" not only through the act of buying clothes in a shop but also
through that of reading magazines (2004: 15). However, little is known
not only about such processes of fashion-media consumption, but also
about the production by the media of fashion. Although there is, as
Hermes observes, a "small but steady stream of publications about
women's magazines" (1997: 10), comparatively little attention has been
paid to the subgenre of fashion magazines,[1] their production and recep-

tion, and the images and words that constitute them. This article is devoted to the latter: the words contained in fashion media's texts, here French *Vogue*. The words I am focusing on, though, are not those of the captions that accompany fashion images—what Barthes calls "written clothing" (1990)—nor are they the lengthier articles devoted to trends or designers. They are those published in the readers' letters page between March 1996 and December 2001, during which the section lasted.[2]

However, I do not see the readers I invoke throughout this article as readers "out there" and whose discourse would represent an actual readership. Rather, I see the section as offering insights into the way the reader's voice is melded into that of the magazine and appropriated by the French title to represent itself. As McKay observes, letters pages "are often good indicators of the tone of a magazine" (2000: 82). Situated at the beginning of *Vogue* before its three main sections—"Mode," "Beauté" and "Magazine"—the page offers an entry, both literally and metaphorically, to the magazine. Through the selecting, editing, or even, some would argue, manufacturing of readers' letters (see McLoughlin 2000: 56, but see also Davis 1994: 159–162, Morrish 1996: 135 on the editing of letters pages), a publication chooses to represent a certain voice of a certain reader—a preferred one—in a certain way, in the process also representing itself to its readership.[3] In the letters page, *Vogue* produces a "textualized" (Hartley 1996: 88) readership, that is, a readership given a reality on paper, in its constructed and mediated form in the text of the letters as published by *Vogue* and grafted into the chain of texts (Derrida 1997: 9) that make up the magazine. The letters, to borrow Bakhtin's terminology on the novel (1998: 262), are part of the "heterogenous stylistic unities" which "combine to form a structured" system and are "subordinated to the higher stylistic of the work as a whole," here *Vogue*. They reveal the magazine's voice—"the unified meaning of the whole," its "accent" (ibid.). Barthes' contention that "the text is a tissu of citations" (cited in Compagnon 1998: 53) is here particularly pertinent, for a letters page is nothing but an assemblage of citations. And if citations can be seen as helping those who appropriate them to put their point across by invoking another, the readers' words cited in a letters page can also be seen as allowing a monthly such as *Vogue* to better convey its own voice, that is, to better represent itself.

In this article then I use the letters page as a platform for reflecting on the way *Vogue* defines itself. I look at some of the different functions the section performs, commenting on both its organizational structure and the way the letters' values represent *Vogue* and its readership. In the first part I appropriate Habermas's notion of the public sphere to discuss the presence, in a consumer magazine such as *Vogue*, of a readers' page. In the second part, and drawing on the work of Bourdieu, I comment on the way the page participates in the production of the belief in fashion as a high art and the construction of *Vogue* as a magazine devoted to the field of high culture. Finally, in the last part, and further elaborating on the values and ideas that both inform and are conveyed in the letters, I discuss how *Vogue* can be defined, and defines itself, as French and more precisely Parisian.

Readers' Letters in the Consumer Press

In *The Structural Transformation of the Public Sphere*, Habermas (2003) discusses the appearance, in the eighteenth century, of what he terms "the public sphere." This bourgeois sphere encompasses a "public sphere in the world of letters"—"now more reasonably termed 'cultural'" Gripsrud argues (2000: 90)—and a "public sphere in the political realm" (Habermas 2003: 30). In both, "rational-critical debate" (108) is promoted; "the exchange of information and views on questions of common concern can take place so that public opinion can be formed" (Dahlgren 2002: 195). Although salons, coffee houses and periodicals were its key institutions, "the published word" became its "decisive mark" (Habermas 2003: 16), and "today, newspapers and magazines, radio and television" are its media (Habermas 2001: 102).

Within the press, the page allocated to readers' letters encapsulates perhaps more than any other sections the ideal[4] of the public sphere as a space where, as with the correspondence of which early journals were constituted (Habermas 2003: 20), the opinion of private people "who relate ... to each other in it as a public" (ibid. 28)—in *Vogue*'s letters page the readership invoked in the inclusive "us" of statements such as "Anything to do with high heels will always be well received by us, readers" (French *Vogue*, April 1998)—becomes public. It is a forum where critical discussions take place in the seemingly unmediated voice of the readers. That this voice is the product of an editorial selection, or even, some would argue of some publications, a fabrication, as mentioned in the introduction, is hidden from view, in favor of the ideal of the media as "a function of public opinion" (Habermas 2003: 2). Readers' pages play the role of a democratic platform, where, as *Vogue* tells its readers in the section's subheading: "La parole est à vous" (Over to you), an expression that conveys this democratic ideal, for *la parole* represents "the contradictory debate, discussion, argumentation" (Vernant, cited in Breton 2000: 35) central to democracy (Breton 2000: 33). This expression is also strongly evocative of another: *la prise de parole*—literally "the appropriation of speech," and which, as Certeau (1994) notes of the May 1968 *prise de parole*, can be seen as signaling a shift away from mere consumer to *homme*—this "human being" and "[reasoning] subject," of the public sphere (Habermas 2003: 29, 26). The distinction Certeau makes between consumer and critical human being also informs Habermas's account of the contemporary public sphere of the media. There, according to him, a shift in a direction opposite to that which Certeau identifies has taken place: the press is no longer "a mediator and intensifier of public discussion" but "the medium of a consumer culture" (Habermas 2001: 105).

This distinction between the world of critical debate—public opinion —and that of consumption has been problematized (see Gripsrud 2002; Dahlgren 2002: 196–197), but it nevertheless informs a distinction often made between magazines and dailies (see Neveu 2001: 29–33; Charon 1999: 80), and more specifically women's and fashion magazines as opposed to the broadsheets, where the former are attributed a low status, that of frivolous entertainment, as opposed to "serious" news, not least due to the low status, in the hierarchy of social positions, of the female realm they are associated with. This distinction is also expressed in the opposition between what is euphemistically known as "soft" news and "hard" news, which, as Hartley observes, structures much discourse on the media alongside oppositions such as substance vs. style, words vs. pictures, culture vs. consumerism, that is men's vs. women's issues (1996: 27).

A letters page allows consumer magazines, in line with the impera-tives of promotion of readers' participation and involvment central to successful magazine editorship (Morrish 1996: 46), to "create the relation to the reader by making her know and recognize the possibility of engaging in this relation" (Charon 1999: 80). But in such a page the shift Certeau identifies from consumer to human being is also promoted, which allows magazines to assert themselves as media devoted not simply to the pursuit of material goods and the realm of appearances, but as a platform for critical debate and public opinion; a public sphere for all to join, in line with the "theory of popular participation" which informed in late eighteenth-century Revolutionary Paris the development and practice of journalism (Hartley 1996: 86). A consumer magazine's low status recedes behind its acquired quality as a space devoted to the ideal of the press as site for the expression of "democratic energies" (77). Through a letters page, then, readers are constructed as active thinkers— a "critical public" (Habermas 2003: 26)—as implied in *Vogue*, which tells its readership: "Vos réactions nous intéressent" (Your reactions interest us), here also signaling dedication to the readers' opinions. Reaction is encouraged, which is also why *Vogue* does not content itself with publishing positive letters only. Not only does it show that, as with the women's magazine Winship discusses, *Vogue* "like any reputable retailer … also listens to its consumers' angry complaints as well as to their praise" (1987: 120), but it also shows that it is open to all debate, for any democratic space should be able to convey both praise and condemnation, including that aimed at the institution the letters are sent to.

Recurring objections concern the killing of animals for aesthetic appropriations, and the representation of women in fashion images. Thus one reader "note[s] that *Vogue*'s 'ideological discourse' is paved with contradictions" and, to "demonstrate the truth of my point," comments on fur and "emaciated young women" in the magazine (French *Vogue*, September 1997). However, such letters are often juxtaposed with letters whose content contradicts them, as in the March 1996 issue, for example, where a letter complaining that "Your magazine encourages wearing real fur" is immediately preceded by one in which the author laments the absence of fur in *Vogue*. "You should reflect the real woman," another reader observes (French *Vogue*, March 1997). "You and your colleagues from the women's press," yet another letter argues, "impose an image of women that is far from the reality" (French *Vogue*, August 2000); "Enough is enough, we are being treated like fools" writes another reader, complaining about *Vogue*'s endorsement of "ugly, unhealthy, anorexic women" as models (April 1998). Such criticisms are often addressed to fashion magazines, but the French *Vogue* exonerates itself from them through the regular publication of letters that celebrate its ability to foster dreams amongst its readers: "Carry on making us dream" reads a letter (French *Vogue*, February 1997). *Vogue* is a title "whose vocation is to make us dream" (March 2000). "To dream for us and to make us dream, that is your role" (French *Vogue*, February 2001), and in a rare response to a letter, *Vogue* writes that "the vocation of our magazine is to show dream clothes on sublime women" (March 1997). Accusations of a lack of realism in the pages of *Vogue* are disarmed, since *Vogue*'s aim, the magazine is saying here, is to sublimate reality and foster dreams. Present in *Vogue* to signify its openness to criticism and its status as an organ of public opinion, accusatory letters are nonetheless deflected. Their content is tempered by the positioning of the letters relative to each other and *Vogue*'s statement of intention, but also by the mass of non-condemnatory comments in which they are diluted.

The readership presented in *Vogue*'s letters page is an ideal audience of a "reader faithful to your magazine" (French *Vogue*, March 1996); an "unreserved supporter of your magazine" (February 1997); an "assiduous reader" (December 1998); and readers who "have been buying *Vogue* every month" (April 1999) "for about fifteen years" (February 1997) or even "for more than 30 years" (March 1996). In such statements, the strong link that unites *Vogue* to its readership is asserted. Continuity binds *Vogue* to its readers. Conveyed in the section both through expressions such as the ones above, but also through the reference made to past issues in both the letters and the images chosen to illustrate the section, continuity also binds together the different fragments of *Vogue* that are individual issues. The past of *Vogue* is always present, carried from one issue to the other through the readers' page, where it can be revisited, providing a smooth entry into a "new" *Vogue* which is never completely new but has an established presence in the field of fashion.

The faithful relation between *Vogue* and its readers is also conveyed through the expressions that signal in the letters an imaginary conversation between their author and the magazine. Statements such as "You're going to tell me" (French *Vogue*, 2001), "You'll say I'm quibbling" (May 1996), "You'll tell me it's a detail" (August 1996) transform the impersonal institution *Vogue* into an anthropomorphized "You" with whom readers establish a more intimate discussion. Intimacy, as Giddens notes, can be seen "as transactional negotiation of personal ties by equals," it "implies a wholesale democratizing of the interpersonal domain, in a manner fully compatible with democracy in the public sphere" (2002: 3). In the the public sphere of *Vogue*'s letters page, the relation between the title and its readers is constructed as democratized, allowing for an intimate relation between equals to take place.

In this section, I have looked at some of the functions a readers' page performs in a consumer magazine such as *Vogue*. I would now like to turn to a particular function as performed in *Vogue*, that which contributes to the belief in high fashion as a high art and, in the process, in the positioning of *Vogue* as a magazine devoted to high culture and the high art of fashion.

The Art of *Vogue*

A recurrent debate in discourses on fashion is concerned with the question "Is fashion art?," which according to some it is, whilst to others it isn't (see, for instance, Bok Kim 1998; Radford 1998). Fashion, as I have discussed elsewhere (Rocamora 2001; 2002), drawing on the work of Bourdieu, is not only the outcome of a process of material production whereby material things—clothes for instance—are produced, but also the product of a process of symbolic production whereby the "immaterial content" (Boselli 1998: 21) of fashion is created, and the "universe of belief" (Bourdieu 1993a: 12) attached to its products, agents, institutions, and rules is produced and reproduced, not least through the discourses of the varied players that constitute the field of fashion. One such belief is that according to which fashion is art. This belief, however, is not unchallenged, for, as Bourdieu has argued (see, for instance, 1993a), the legitimate values of a field are a permanent object of struggle between different agents and institutions, as the various attempts to offer a positive or negative answer to the above question illustrate. What is acknowledged as art is the outcome of a discursive construction informed by assumptions and values which are at stake in the field of culture. Moreover, Bourdieu (1993a; 1996) also shows, judgments on cultural objects are structured by the oppositions between, on the one hand form, mind, and disinterest—art for art's sake—and, on the other, content, the body, and interest—not least interest in commercial profit—where the former are valued over the latter. In discourses on cultural forms, legitimate "high" cultural products such as theater, opera or painting—the canonical arts—are traditionally attached to the first half of the binary pair, whereas "popular" cultural forms such as thrillers, pop music or soap operas are often linked to the latter halves and denied the status of art (on the divide between high culture/popular culture see also, for instance, Goodall 1995). As for fashion, as Bourdieu observes, it is a "minor art" and occupies "an inferior rank in the hierarchy of artistic legitimacy" (1975: 16, 17). In the field of journalism, this translates into the low status, as mentioned earlier, accorded to women's magazines and, within these, to fashion magazines—this "part of the mediasphere," as Hartley puts it, "where women readers tend to have the default-setting on literacy" (1996: 130).

French *Vogue*, however, is one of those institutions which contributes, not least through the readers' page, to the belief in fashion as a high art. In this page, in statements such as "Every month, I'm in a trance looking at the pants, the jackets, the skirts ... that, systematically, I want" (French *Vogue*, December 1996), "I even bought the silver Xuly Bët jacket" (September 1998), "I admit being very influenced by your magazine when I shop" (April 1997), fashion is acknowledged as an object of material consumption and *Vogue* as a consumer guide. However, letters carrying such statements are few compared to those on topics such as literature, opera, theater or the aesthetics of *Vogue* and its fashion images—the "aesthetic joy" (March 1996) it provides its reader. The letters page, echoing the editorial positioning of the title, most constantly represents *Vogue* as a magazine consecrated to—at the same time as it consecrates—the high art of fashion and high culture more generally.

The positioning, in *Vogue*, of fashion as a major art alongside architecture, painting, and other "serious" and "noble" topics such as science and philosophy, materializes itself in the pages of the magazine, where fashion images and fashion writing are juxtaposed with many articles dealing with high culture. The section "On en parle," for instance —a round-up of recent cultural events including fashion—is largely devoted to the field of art, as in the February 1999 issue, for example, which includes news on a theater play by Christa Wolf, the sculptures of Philippe Berry, and choreography to the music of Ligeti and Hurel. In *Vogue*, the realms of fashion and high culture are brought together, intertwined in the structure of the magazine to become one and the same: the high art of fashion. In *Vogue*, as the Editor notes, "Art feeds fashion" (French *Vogue*, 2000).

This melding of realms into one another is reproduced in the readers' page. There, letters on fashion are regularly juxtaposed with letters on exhibitions, ballet, and other topics of high culture, allowing *Vogue* to signify its status as a "serious" magazine not simply devoted to the frivolous topic of fashion: "I particularly love your articles on the art market" one reader writes, "it's the first section I read each time" (French *Vogue*, June 1999). "I love seeing the original art works," writes another, "often selected by art lovers (one can feel it), which you choose to illustrate the horoscopes" (French *Vogue*, October 1996), whilst the author of another letter writes to express how pleased she was to see that "my favorite magazine" wrote an article on theater director Luc Bondy (October 1996), and yet another praises an article on Alexander Liberman, who "was a sort of aesthete that no longer exists: spiritual inheritor of a bygone Europe, intuitive artist … a refined and deliberately elitist intellectual" (April 2000). The seriousness of *Vogue* is further asserted in letters that draw attention to *Vogue*'s interest in other "noble" subjects such as science, as in one letter where the author notes "I'm very happy to see that you also look into serious and delicate topics" such as genetics (September 1999).

Recurrent analogies with art, in letters on fashion, also contribute to legitimate *Vogue* and its fashion as serious and noble. A past issue, for example, was "a lovely lesson on history, art and elegance" (French *Vogue*, March 1996). One reader enthuses, in a stylistic crescendo whereby the status of fashion is raised to that of art: "It's more than fashion, your story 'State of Grace,' it's cinema, it's painting, it's art" (French *Vogue*, April 1996). Some fashion images "were like a profound breath, a long moment of poetry and grace" (French *Vogue*, September 2001). A fashion spread "is dazzlingly beautiful, of a perfect aestheticism. It is pure force, elegance, poetry, charm … an ecstatic pleasure for the eyes" (French *Vogue*, December 1998). The analogy which some readers make between fashion and the field of art—through the metaphor of poetry for example—also often informs *Vogue*'s fashion discourse in the other sections. The headline of an article on designer duo An and Filip, for instance, invokes their "true and poetic universe" (French *Vogue*, February 1999). A fashion story entitled "Performance" is "a good pretext for stage direction, a fashion orchestrated like a creation of the German choreographer Pina Bausch" (French *Vogue*, February 2000). Georges Lamblin "creates jewelry like others compose, paint, or write" (French *Vogue*, March 2000). Weaver Luc Drouez is a "young virtuoso" whose creations are "symphonies of fabrics" (French *Vogue*, April 1997), while a fashion spread entitled "In the Eye of the Poets" (Figure 1), invokes Cocteau, Buñuel, Man Ray, and Dali (May 1998). Poetry, ballet, classical music, and painting are mentioned, inscribing fashion in the field of high culture. Although some concessions are made to popular culture, in cinema and music reviews for example, in the French magazine, fashion is made understandable through high art references. As in the French field of high fashion Bourdieu discusses, throughout *Vogue*—and this includes the readers' page—"the references to noble and legitimate arts, painting, sculpture, and literature" made in the representations of fashion provide it "with most of its ennobling metaphors," while at the same time being "so many *hommages* that the 'minor art' gives to the major arts" (1975: 16). Such references, like the juxtaposition of fashion features with articles on high culture,

Figure 1
"Dans l'oeil des poètes." Photo courtesy of French *Vogue*.

"bring the work into an interminable circuit of inter-legitimation" (Bourdieu 1996: 53). They "lend dignity" to the object of discourse (ibid.), fashion, but also to *Vogue*, a dignity also conveyed through the melding in the readers' page of the field of fashion with that of high culture. As one reader puts it, *Vogue* is "serious, competent" (French *Vogue*, November 1996), another arguing that the quality of *Vogue*'s fashion images in a past issue prove that "fashion is a worthy object of reflection" (September 1996).

Further dignity is lent to *Vogue* through the reference the letters page makes to its male readership, that is to the high sociocultural space of masculinity. The readers' page is "le courrier des lecteurs," the morpheme "eur" indicating, in French, masculine presence. This presence allows *Vogue* to further establish itself as a magazine not simply devoted to fashion and the female readership usually associated with this field, but as a magazine whose interest in high culture can legitimately claim—as it is legitimated by—a male readership. Thus most issues include at least one letter attributed to a man.

Moreover, in the letters page the readers' high "cultural capital" (Bourdieu 1996) is regularly displayed, which further reinscribes *Vogue* and its fashion in the field of high culture. The letters show readers endowed with a high capital of fashion knowledge as in this letter, for example, where photographer Herb Ritts is praised for having "shown discernment with the talent he is known for" (French *Vogue*, February 2000) or the letter on shoes where the author argues that *Vogue* neglects the creations of "Vivienne Westwood, Mugler, Véronique Leroy, Cyd Jouny, etc." (May 1997). But they also show a readership endowed with a high capital of high culture. In the readers' page as in the bourgeois public sphere Habermas discusses, one can read "the critical reflections of a public competent to form its own judgments" (2003: 90). Thus, for instance, a reader who praises the "diversity" and "erudition" of the philosophy section invokes Plato in an argument about the philosophy of naturism (French *Vogue*, January 1999). *Vogue*'s article "Buy Me a Painting," a reader notes, commenting on, among others, Tzara, Dada, and Titian, "has inspired me with some reflections I would like to share with you" (French Vogue, February 1998). In his letter on ballet another reader quotes Kandinsky: "The human soul must be made to vibrate and be refined" (French *Vogue*, March 1998), while another engages with the work of Irigaray to discuss an article on the gender of philosophy (June 1998). *Vogue* is legitimized as a magazine addressed not simply to the fashion *connoisseur*, but to the connoisseur *tout court*, whose "critical discussion" is "sparked by the products of culture" (Habermas 2003: 29) reported in *Vogue*. As one reader puts it, "I'm not one of those women (I'm not criticizing) who wear what you show ... but I value 'seeing,' 'knowing,' 'judging'" (French *Vogue*, August 1996). In the letters page, readers, who have mastered, like the bourgeois avant-garde Habermas discusses, "the art of critical-rational public debate" learned in the "elegant world" (29)—the high cultural space attached to the readers' high social position[5]—but also the elegant world of *Vogue*—become cultural commentators like *Vogue*'s journalists. The distinction of writer/reader is bypassed. As *Vogue* tells the readers in the first letters page: "Our readers write too. For the first time we are publishing them" (French *Vogue*, March 1996). The distance between the text—*Vogue*—and its audience is bridged through the enlightened discussion—"art criticism as conversation" (Habermas 2003: 40)—that takes place between the two.

If, in the letters page, readers are represented as enlightened and critical, *Vogue* is celebrated as the ultimate "magazine of reference for the world of fashion and culture" (French *Vogue*, February 2001) as one reader puts it. Thus, "Thanks to you, I've discovered a fabulous author I didn't know" (French *Vogue*, May 1999); "You have fulfilled your role: allowing one to see, to feel, and to learn" (April 2000); "On top of being beautiful, your magazine has a pedagogic value" (October 2000). *Vogue* is acknowledged that lead which defines fashionable subjects, but the magazine is also legitimized as a title whose "authority and prestige" (French *Vogue*, May 1999) one can rely on in one's quest for a higher cultural capital. It is "a first-class magazine" (French *Vogue*, October 1996), "an absolute reference" (April 2001).

In the readers' page, then, *Vogue* displays readers endowed with the high cultural capital that allows them to critically engage with the field of high culture, to whose products the magazine devotes many pages. They are also readers whose high economic capital allows them to acquire the luxury goods produced by the designers featured in *Vogue*. The correspondence between the high points of, respectively, the field of fashion, the field of culture, and that of social class is established and, in the process, *Vogue*'s high position in these fields asserted, in line with the magazine's "ethics" of "luxury" (*Vogue* media kit). French *Vogue* is, as some letters put it, "pointu" (see, for instance, March 2000, April 2001, September 2001), the word *pointu* meaning "sharp, highly specialized," but also "à la pointe," literally "at the peak" or "in the vanguard." *Vogue* evidences the consumption pattern of social elites. Their "tastes of luxury" lead them to consume goods that have a homologous position in their respective fields (Bourdieu 1996), here the luxury goods of high fashion and "that other category of luxury goods, the goods of legitimate culture such as music, poetry, philosophy, and so on" (Bourdieu 1995: 132). All these goods endow their beholders with "the symbolic signs of 'class'" and distinction (Bourdieu 1975: 29).

Although *Vogue* has become an international brand whose key concepts of fashion and luxury have crossed national borders, these concepts, like those of other international media brands (Charon 1999: 6; Jost 2004: 35), are also adapted to the sociocultural context of the different countries where it is published. The cultural values conveyed in *Vogue* cannot be seen outside of the values that inform French culture and society, as I now discuss.

Paris, France

Amongst the values at play in French culture is that according to which one's high capital of high culture—"the supreme fetish" (Bourdieu 1996: 250)—is a sign of distinction and class, as Bourdieu argues in *Distinction*, where he also underlines the "particularity of the French tradition" (1996: xi, but see also Chartier 2000). In France, high culture is a highly valued source of prestige and "symbolic capital" (Bourdieu 1996: 282). Thus, in response to a letter drawing attention to a mistake which, its author suggests, *Vogue* made in an article about a sixteenth-century tapisserie on "Lot and his daughters," *Vogue* replies that they "trembled at the assaults on" their cultural knowledge (French *Vogue*, April 1997). The magazine then goes on to demonstrate the validity of its point, hence reestablishing its authority and status in the field of culture as an erudite magazine.

That in France high culture occupies a dominant position in the hierarchy of cultural values is reflected in the meaning of the word "culture" itself. For the English "culture" cannot simply be translated into the French "*culture*," the latter being often conflated with the more restricted "high culture." Thus Gauthier distinguishes two definitions of the concept "culture". One is inspired by Anglo-Saxon anthropology which:

> includes all that which participates in an ensemble of repre-
> sentations, images, symbols, myths, rules of social organization,

Figure 2
"Paris, France." Photo courtesy
of French *Vogue*.

practices of everyday life interiorized by the members of a same
group. Another definition—which is actually a French particularity—sees culture as the set of products of the mind [*esprit*].
Thus the Ministry of Culture … reunites more or less the same
activities which in the Fourth Republic used to belong to the
department of Art and Literature. Add cinema (but not TV, an
interesting prejudice), and a few scientific activities, and we get
an idea of what Edgar Morin used to call pleasantly "cultivated
culture," that is the dominant representation of culture: what one
needs to master to be cultivated (Gauthier 1997: 114).

I later come back to the word "*esprit*." Its many meanings—"the mind"
but also "wit," "intelligence," "the spirit"—cannot be captured in only

one equivalent English term. The reader should keep in mind that, in French, all these connotations are present in the meaning of the word. The valuing in France of spiritual development and the activities of *l'esprit* is also epitomized in the compulsory learning of philosophy in French colleges, in preparation for the examination of philosophy at the Baccalaureate.

Thus, according to French author Jean-Louis Harouel, "True culture is of course culture in its noble and classical sense," it "carries the idea of the formation and the edification of the mind [*esprit*] ... the health of its soul. This is the humanist conception of culture" (1998: 21) whereby, in France, "the products of the human spirit [*esprit*]" (Fumaroli 1991: 33) are attributed a superior value. It is this culture as high culture or "culture cultivée" (Morin 1982: 20) which in France has established itself as the dominant model. The French sociologist Yonnet even talks about "the French ideology of Great Culture" which has "extended and crystalized itself over a wide range of the population to the point where it has reached an almost total domination of its field" (1985: 195, 197, but see also Rigby 1991: 4). It has been conveyed by a wide range of institutions ranging from education to the government (197) and, one could add, magazines such as French *Vogue*.

In *Vogue*'s letters page too "the edification of the mind" which informs "the French ideology of Great Culture" is celebrated. One reader, for example, notes that it is "marvelous that you [*Vogue*] have decided to also be the messengers from the outposts of the mind [*esprit*] (French *Vogue*, March 1999). Another writes that "Rare are the magazines you leave feeling satiated, at last uplifted" (French *Vogue*, February 1999). The magazine is "*pointu* and enlightened" (French *Vogue*, April 2001), it knows how to "render intelligence fashionable" (March 1999). Even models, in *Vogue*, "look more acute than is usual today" (French *Vogue*, June 1996). A take on bourgeois fashion is "full of intelligence [*esprit*]" (French *Vogue*, June 2001), and a parallel is made between *Vogue* and the French highbrow newspaper *Le Monde*, both "great minds [*esprit*]" (May 1998). *Vogue* regularly invokes, in other sections, this valued *esprit*. The designer Dominique Sirop, for instance, is said to "create like he lives: with spirit [*esprit*]" (French *Vogue*, June 1997); Eric Bergère is the "spiritual inheritor" of Saint-Laurent, "his personal dramaturgy has no less nobility" (November 1999). A fashion spread reads "It is with a touch of wit [*esprit*] and lots of humor that we take on the winter's graphic prints ... we prefer the cultural alibi: Vasarely paintings, the Pucci years, 60s kinetic experimentions ... a studied and sophisticated chic for urban and cultivated women" (French *Vogue*, August 2000). The material dimension of fashion is transcended. Fashion is raised to the valued spiritual world of the artists celebrated in *Vogue*, whose readers hail its intelligence (see also, for instance, French *Vogue* March 2000, September 2000, September 2001, December 2001), further legitimizing the French magazine as a "serious" magazine.

However, in the French cultural hierarchy of high culture, one cultural form stands out from the others for the high status it is attributed: literature, also standing out "against literary culture elsewhere" (Parkhurst Clark 1991: 9). In France, mastery of the written word is a key component of one's cultural capital, the source of a high symbolic capital (27). For a monthly such as *Vogue* to gain a high status, that is, to position itself in the field of high culture, it is central to be perceived as well-written. Thus, as the magazine makes clear in a profile on its contributors (in December, 1999), Michel Braudeau, *Vogue*'s book critic, is the "*éminence grise* on books at *Vogue*," a "man of letters and culture" who "has published no less than eleven novels, was awarded the Médicis Prize and has also dipped into the arcana of psychiatry for erudite translations." A recent *Vogue* media kit also highlighted the presence, in the magazine, of "major signatures," and "reputed writers."

The letters page conveys to the readership this high value attributed to literary culture. One letter states, for example, "What a pleasure to see that fashion does not rhyme with the frivolous and superficial only ... most fashion magazines neglect their texts," but "you take care of the written words" and "seek out true writers." The reader then exhorts *Vogue* to "continue to offer us quality texts" (French *Vogue*, March 1996). "What a pleasure for your readers," another writes, "to have access within the same 'bible' to both sumptuous images and soaring texts" (French *Vogue*, December 1998). One reader read an article in the science page—a "poetic" page—"like one reads a short story" (French *Vogue*, September 2000), while another, commenting on the work of *Vogue*'s book critic, writes about her pleasure in coming across "someone so sensitive, so well acquainted with literature ... Such respect for authors and such an elegant approach in a fashion magazine deserves to be hailed" (June 1999). "Thanks to the orchestrated magic of the correspondences between texts, subjects, and images," a past issue "attains to the work of art for its coherence and the sensation of generosity that emanates from its pages" (French *Vogue*, March 1999). In *Vogue*, and contrary to the shift which some argue is taking place in the press away from the written word toward the image as "main conveyor of sense" (Yats 2003: 71), the readers' page suggests that attention to the written text is paramount. As one reader puts it, "I have always loved Vogue's style of talking about art, an elegant, light style, so near the fashion we like" (French *Vogue*, September 2001). Elegance in written style is as valued as elegance in sartorial style. "The moral authority of literature" (Parkhurst Clark 1991: 35) is respected, *Vogue* presented as a fit inheritor and defender of "literary France" (ibid.).

In the French magazine, as in the eighteenth-century salons of the literary public sphere—the salons were those "of the fashionable ladies" (Habermas 2003: 3)—the world of fashion and that of intellectuals are connected. It is the elite world of "those who possess Culture ... '*les cultivés,*' '*les intellectuels,*' '*les esthètes*'" (Rigby 1991:7), and who make up "the fashionable social and cultural world of Paris" [*le tout Paris de la culture*] (ibid.). The letters section is the fashionable salon where intellectuals meet in the elegant world of *Vogue*'s pages, a Parisian world, as I next discuss.

Vogue Paris

Frenchness is a recurrent theme in French *Vogue*, or *Vogue* Paris, whether it is in the special issues, articles and spreads devoted to French fashion and culture (see, for instance, French *Vogue* September 1996, April 1997, May 1998, p. 93) or in the letters page, where, for example, a reader notes: "I really like your article on *Vogue* women, all those creatures we dream we look like and who perfectly epitomize chic *à la française*" (March 1996), or where the model Laeticia Casta's ability to "represent contemporary French fashion" is praised, the magazine calling her, in response to this statement, "a real French beauty" (October 1997). She is, the author of another letter notes, "a sort of synthesis of beauty 'à la française': elegance, sensuality, spirit [*esprit*]" (French *Vogue*, 1996). However, the Frenchness invoked in *Vogue* is one often circumscribed to a specific version of it—the Parisian. As Lucien Vogel, founder of Condé Nast France in 1921, said: "*Vogue* must be a real Parisian magazine. But Parisian, Parisian … a magazine that couldn't be made either in Rome, nor in London, nor in New York (cited in *Vogue*'s media kit).

Yats notes that the title of a magazine is its "first exponent" and "initiator of meaning," it is "the announcement of a content, and the utterance of that which contains" (2003: 68). "Monemes like 'Elle,' 'Femme,' ou 'Donna,'" he adds, announce "a preoccupation within a wide or narrow editorial approach: the feminine condition. A 'Vogue' has no precise contractual obligation, it can be adapted to various concepts: fashion, glamour, celebrities" (ibid.). For Bonnet and Richoux-Bérard it is "a name that has become timeless," evocative of "prestige, glamour, ideas of luxury and refinement" (1994: 11). This title might well be "timeless" as Bonnet and Richoux-Bérard argue, but it is not, and contrary to Hartley's contention that the French *Vogue* provides "postnational identifications to readerships whose allegiances are no longer defined by their territoriality" (1996: 130), unbound to territoriality. In French *Vogue*, allegiance to French and more specifically Parisian territory is regularly expressed, not least in the title itself. French *Vogue* is the only one of the fifteen editions where the name of the capital constitutes part of the title, with the word "Paris" inscribed in the "o" of *Vogue* (Figure 3). If *Vogue* means fashion, it also means Paris fashion, the fusion between the three being neatly encapsulated in the title: *Vogue* is fashion is Paris.

Figure 3
"*Vogue* Paris. Mode et Art."
Photo courtesy of French
Vogue.

Paris has for long been seen and constructed as the center of high fashion (see, for instance, Kawamura 2004; Steele 1998), an idea captured and reproduced in the title of fashion magazines: *Modes et Manières du Jour à Paris*, in the late eighteenth early nineteenth centuries, *Parisiennes* under Napoléon III, or *Les Elégances Parisiennes* at the beginning of the twentieth century, are some examples (see Monfort 2004: 19–22 for an overview of some of France's fashion titles). In France, Paris is the high point of fashion and culture more generally, in a model inherited from the centralism of court society where Parisian culture became elevated as the only culture, all culture, the French Court instilling "an invincible prejudice against provincial mud" (Parkhurst Clark 1991: 30, see also Bourdieu 1996: xi; Chartier 2000; Steele 1998). As Lemert notes in reference to the common French expression *le tout Paris*, literally "all of Paris" but an expression which refers to Paris's cultural fashionable elite), "in France, *tout Paris* is *tout*" (1981: 5). The cultural capital which, Hartley argues, the French have capitalized "in style" through *Vogue*'s "global sales" (1996: 130) is a Parisian cultural capital.

The homology which exists between the position of high fashion and that of high culture in their respective fields also links these two positions to that of Paris in the French geographical space: in France Paris is to *la province* what high fashion is to fashion and high culture to culture; it is in a dominant position. It is also the space where high fashion, high culture, and the high social classes meet, as *Vogue* regularly shows in the section "L'oeil de *Vogue*," where le tout Paris—"les tout-parisiens" as the magazine puts it in this section (French *Vogue*, February 2000)—is regularly featured. Sociocultural spaces, as Bourdieu notes, materialize into geographical spaces, an idea epitomized in the parallels made between the binary pairs Paris/*province*; chic/not chic; culture/lack of culture (1993b: 160–162): In France *la capitale* is "the place of capital … where the positive poles of all fields … are concentrated: thus it can only be conceived adequately in relation to the provinces (and the 'provincial'), which is nothing but the privation (strictly relative) of *la capitale* and capital' (162) as well as that of style, what reader Flora D. Tarquin of Paris calls "provincial naffness [*ringardise*]" (French *Vogue*, October 2001), and which, implicitly, contrasts with what another calls "Parisian elegance" (August 1998). As Ferguson also observes, *Harpers and Queen* and *Vogue* itself are "consciously *classy* titles which segregate their elite followers from the common cultists" (1983: 188), the latter being epitomized, in France, with the *provinciaux*.

A letter published in the September 2000 issue illustrates the privation of fashion and cultural capital Bourdieu talks about. The author notes "I live in the provinces … At the beginning of each month, seeing your magazine at my newsagent is a real pleasure. I need to catch up with all the new fashion of course, but also new beauty, culture, cinema" (French *Vogue*, September 2000). To catch up with *Vogue* is to catch up with Paris and its culture. As another reader, from Mandelieu, puts it, "I miss Paris a bit, and your magazine brings me 'the breath of life,' all the novelty I miss" (French *Vogue*, December 1999); Paris, through *Vogue*, brings life—fashionable and intellectual—to provincial existence.

Thus many articles are devoted to the actuality of culture and fashion as taking place in the French capital, le "Paris Parisien" as *Vogue* puts it on the cover of the November 1996 issue. The section "On y va" (The places we go/Let's go), for instance, about new places, is almost exclusively devoted to Parisian places, and in a short but significant article on the opening of a Mary Quant boutique in Paris, a journalist writes: "We'll be able to grab, here, in Paris her Eye Opener" (French *Vogue*, May 1997). In *Vogue* "here" means Paris. The many referents to which "here" could possibly be attached are excluded, the signifier "here" anchored to the particular Parisian territory. In *Vogue* there is only one here: Paris. *Vogue*, then, is first and foremost "a real Parisian magazine" as the magazine puts it in its media kit. Its Parisianism is also emphasized in the letters page through the specification of the reader's geographical origins, Paris being the most represented city (thirty-six percent of all letters). *Vogue* is not so much addressed to *la française* as it is to *la parisienne*,[6] the mythical figure of French literature and of course fashion (see, for instance, Steele 1998). As Carine Roitfeld, *Vogue*'s Editor, told the press in a statement that draws attention to the discursive construction of *la parisienne*, the imagined reality produced by institutions such as the fashion media, "We're speaking to *la parisienne* as we imagine her .... A sparkling woman with personality, who follows fashion, easily goes to New York or Berlin. Through our choices, we create a world for people to want to belong to" (cited in Baudriller 2002: 44). Similarly, *Vogue*'s former editor, Joan Juliet Buck, wrote in an editorial: "This season ... will be chic. But a sublimated and never immediate chic. A symbol of that elegance captured through the prism of idealization: la parisienne, or at least a certain version of la parisienne" (French *Vogue*, February 2000).

Conclusion

Hartley notes that "what makes the reputation of journalistic institutions such as *The Times* is clearly a combination of its meanings (what it says) with its readership (who reads it), but in the end it's the readership, both real and imagined, that matters most" (1996: 13), not least because, one could add, in a section such as the letters page, it too contributes to the production and reproduction of a title's editorial positioning and definition of itself. In *Vogue* this page also participates, like many other pages, in the production of the belief of fashion as high culture.

Elsewhere I have shown how, in its writing on high-fashion shows, another key French institution, *Le Monde*, also contributes to this belief, in contrast with *The Guardian*'s positioning of high fashion in the field of popular culture (Rocamora 2001). *Vogue*, like the French daily, participates, in the readers' page as elsewhere, in the construction of French fashion as what McRobbie argues is "an elite thing" defined by the "elitism of the fine art world" (1998: 8, 36). *Vogue* and *Le Monde* occupy a homologous position in their respective fields of fashion journalism and dailies—both are established institutions addressed to an elite readership and with a reputation of authority in their field—and this homology translates into a homology of fashion discourses. These are only two among the many institutions that form, in France, the chain of production of the symbolic value of fashion. Other discursive sites could be studied to best capture the values that structure the French field of fashion, the way they are produced and reproduced, but also questioned, in the struggles for the definition of the field.

Fashion discourses in different cultures collude to create different versions of fashion, and more work needs to be conducted on such discourses for a better understanding of the different national fashion cultures that now make up the global field of fashion. This might entail comparative analysis, the like of which I conducted on *Le Monde* and *The Guardian*. Fashion magazines do not just belong to purely internal signifying systems. They are caught in a network of transnational relationships where the meanings they invest in fashion arise from a system of national differences. These meanings are themselves part of "the international struggle for the domination in cultural matters," a struggle that "finds its roots in the struggles within each national camp, in struggles where the dominant national definition and foreign definition are themselves involved" (Bourdieu 1999: 227). With its fifteen editions worldwide, *Vogue* is a particularly rich site for such a comparative analysis and, as I have attempted to show in this article by way of a discussion of the functions performed by the readers' page in French *Vogue*, the interrogation of the way a country's fashion culture feeds into and is informed by its cultural norms and values.

Notes

1. For the distinction between women's and fashion magazines see Jost (2004: 36), Charon (1999: 59).
2. The issues I analyzed cover the same period. The arguments put forward in this artcle on the construction of fashion as high culture still seem relevant to *Vogue* since the section ended. Although it looks like more references are made to the field of popular culture (albeit perhaps an elite popular culture), references to high culture still abound in *Vogue*'s discourse, and as Tamsin Blanchard recently put it in the *Observer Magazine*, "American *Vogue* is where you will read the stories, see the celebrities and get the scoops. French *Vogue* is where you might get a bit of highbrow intellectual stimulation alongside your Dior and Saint-Laurent' (August 15, 2004).
3. Mallarmé's *La Dernière Mode* offers a clear illustration of this blurring of the distinction between readers' and editorial voices. Although the magazine was "a real journal, with real subscribers," it was also primarily a one-man production, Mallarmé himself filling it with articles he penned using various pseudonyms (Furbank and Cain 2004: 5). This is why, in the correspondence section, it is nearly impossible, as Furbank and Cain observe, "to distinguish fact from fantasy" (5). The letters, they note, "frequently came, *or purported to come*, from countesses, duchesses and the titles generally; and it was a tacit assumption throughout the magazine that readers were mainly interested in, if they did not actually move in, 'high-life'" (5, my emphasis).

4. Some authors have drawn attention to the idea of the public sphere as an ideal as opposed to an actual empirical reality (see Dahlgren 2002; Gripsrud 2002: 231).
5. *Vogue* is "a magazine in strong affinity with the very high income target, company directors and living in the Paris area" (*Vogue*'s 2004 media kit, but see also *Vogue* AEPM 1999, 2000, 2001 studies of readers' profiles as well as, for instance, Ipsos 1999 and 2001 studies of *Vogue*'s readership profile).
6. Forty-three percent of *Vogue*'s readers live in the Paris area (*Vogue*'s media kit).

References

Bakhtin, M. M. 1998. *The Dialogic Imagination*. Austin: University of Texas Press.

Barthes, R. 1990. *The Fashion System*. Berkeley: University of California Press.

Baudriller, M. 2002. "La Tentation du Luxe," in *Stratégies*, 1235, May 3, pp. 43–44.

Bok Kim, S. 1998. "Is Fashion Art?," in *Fashion Theory* 2(1): 51–72.

Bonnet, F. and Richoux-Bérard (eds). 1994. "Avant-Propos," in *Glossy: Mode et Papier Glacé*. Marseilles: Images en Manoeuvres Editions.

Bourdieu, P. with Y. Delsaut. 1975. "Le Couturier et sa Griffe. Contribution à une Théorie de la Magie," *Actes de la Recherche en Sciences Sociales*, 1: 7–36.

Bourdieu, P. 1993a. *The Field of Cultural Production*. Cambridge: Polity Press.

—— 1993b. *La Misère du Monde*. Paris: Editions du Seuil.

—— 1995. *Sociology in Questions*. London: Sage.

—— 1996. *Distinction*. London: Routledge.

—— 1999. "The Social Conditions of the International Circulation of Ideas," in Shusterman, R. (ed.), *Bourdieu: A Critical Reader*. Oxford: Blackwell.

Boselli, M. 1998. "Pitti Immagine's Role in the Creation of a Culture for the Textile and Clothing Industry," in G. Malossi (ed.), *The Style Engine*. New York: Monacelli Press.

Breton, P. 2000. *La Parole Manipulée*. Paris: La Découverte.

Certeau de, M. 1994. *La Prise de Parole*. Paris: Seuil.

Charon, J-M. 1999. *La Presse Magazine*. Paris: La Découverte.

Chartier, R. 2000. "Trajectoires et Tensions Culturelles de l'Ancien Régime," in A. Burguière and J. Revel (eds), *Histoire de la France*. Paris: Editions du Seuil.

Compagnon, A. 1998. *Le Démon de la Théorie*. Paris: Seuil.

Dahlgren, P. 2002. "The Public Sphere as Historical Narrative," in D. McQuail (ed), *McQuail's Reader in Mass Communication*. London: Sage.

Davis, A. 1994. *Magazine Journalism Today*. Oxford: Focal Press.

Derrida, J. 1997. *Limited Inc*. Evanston: Northwestern University Press.

Ferguson, M. 1983. *Forever Feminine*. London: Heinemann.

Fumaroli, M. 1991. *L'Etat Culturel: Essai sur une Religion Moderne*. Paris: Fallois.

Furbank, P. N. and A. M. Cain. 2004. "*La Dernière Mode*, and its Prehistory," in *Mallarmé on Fashion*. Oxford: Berg.

Gauthier, G. 1997. "Culture et Citoyenneté," in D. Lecourt et al. (eds). *Aux Sources de la Culture Française*. Paris: La Découverte.

Giddens, A. 2002. *The Transformation of Intimacy*. Cambridge: Polity.

Goodall, P. 1995. *High Culture, Popular Culture*. St Leonards: Allen & Unwin.

Gripsrud, J. 2000. "The Aesthetics and Politics of Melodrama," in P. Dahlgren and C. Sparks (eds), *Journalism and Popular Culture*. London: Sage.

Gripsrud, J. 2002. *Understanding Media Culture*. London: Arnold.

Habermas, J. 2003. *The Structural Transformation of the Public Sphere*. Cambridge: Polity.

Habermas, J. 2001. "The Public Sphere: An Encyclopedia Article," in M. N. Durham and D. Kellner (eds), *Media and Cultural Studies*. Oxford: Blackwell.

Harouel, J. L. 1998. *Culture et Contre-Cultures*. Paris: Quadrige.

Hartley, J. 1996. *Popular Reality*. London: Arnold.

Hermes, J. 1997. *Reading Women's Magazines*. Cambridge: Polity.

Jost, H. 2004. "Economie de la Presse de Mode," in S. Richoux-Bérard F. and Bonnet (eds), *Glossy: Mode et Papier Glacé*. Marseilles: Images en Manoeuvres Editions.

Kawamura, Y. 2004. *The Japanese Revolution in Paris Fashion*. Oxford: Berg.

Lemert, C. C. 1981. *French Sociology*. New York: Columbia University Press.

McKay, J. 2000. *The Magazines Handbook*. London: Routledge.

McLoughlin, L. 2000. *The Language of Magazines*. London: Routledge.

McRobbie, A. 1998. *British Fashion Design*. London: Routledge.

Monfort, P. 2004. "Image de Mode," in S. Richoux-Bérard and F. Bonnet (eds), *Glossy: Mode et Papier Glacé*. Marseilles: Images en Manoeuvres Editions.

Morin, E. 1982. *L'Esprit du Temps 1. Névrose*. Paris: Grasset.

Morrish, J. 1996. *Magazine Editing*. London: Routledge.

Neveu, E. 2001. *Sociologie du Journalisme*. Paris: La Découverte.

Parkhust Clark, P. 1991. *Literary France*. Berkeley: University of California Press.

Radford, R. 1998. "Dangerous Liaisons: Art, Fashion and Individualism," *Fashion Theory*, 2(2): 151–164.

Rocamora, A. 2001. "High Fashion and Pop Fashion: The Symbolic Production of Fashion in *Le Monde* and *The Guardian*," in *Fashion Theory*, 5(2): 123–142.

—— 2002. "Le Monde's *Discours de Mode*: Creating the *Créateurs*," in *French Cultural Studies*, Vol 13(1): 83–98.

Rigby, B. 1991. *Popular Culture in Modern France*. London: Routledge.

Steele, V. 1998. *Paris Fashion*. Oxford: Berg.

Thompson, J. B. 1993. "The Theory of the Public Sphere," in *Theory, Culture and Society*, Vol. 10: 173–189.

Wargnier, S. 2004. "Eloge de l'Intermédiaire," in S. Richoux-Bérard and F. Bonnet (eds), *Glossy: Mode et Papier Glacé*. Marseilles: Images en Manoeuvres Editions.

Winship, J. 1987. *Inside Women's Magazines*. London: Pandora.

Yats. 2003. "Magazines Féminins: Le Sens et L'Espace," in *Etapes Graphiques*, March 1: 63–72.

Yonnet, P. 1985. *Jeux, Modes et Masses: 1945–1985*. Paris: Gallimard.

Other documents consulted

Vogue's media kit (2004).

"Vogue Audiences Etudes sur la Presse Magazine" (AEPM), 1999, 2000, 2001 (documents provided by French *Vogue*).

"Profil du Lectorat de Vogue," Ipsos Hauts Revenus, 1999, 2001 studies (documents provided by French *Vogue*).

Fashion Theory, Volume 10, Issue 1/2, pp. 175–204
Reprints available directly from the Publishers.
Photocopying permitted by licence only.
© 2006 Berg.

In Russia, At Last and Forever: The First Seven Years of Russian *Vogue*

Djurdja Bartlett

Djurdja Bartlett completed
her PhD research on Fashion,
the Spectre That Haunted
Socialism at the London College
of Fashion, and is currently
preparing it for publication.
djurdjabartlett@blueyonder.co.uk

The first issue of Russian *Vogue* was published in September 1998. It featured Kate Moss and Amber Valetta with a single blurb on the cover that read: "In Russia, at last." Announcing the arrival of the legendary fashion magazine, the streets of Moscow were plastered with posters carrying the same message. A party hosting the most important and glamorous international fashion players and the domestic elite was planned for the launch, which was preceded by carefully planned preparations. But all did not go as planned. A major financial crisis broke out on September 2, shaking the Russian economy.[1] The lavish party that was supposed to have taken place at "Number One, Red Square" was canceled. *Vogue* found itself in alien territory. Normally, its various national editions are smoothly-run operations, supported by a complex network of relationships between international and domestic advertisers and skilled editorial teams. In contrast, Russian *Vogue* experienced the uncertainties of extreme modernity, a phase that Russia entered with the fall of socialism.[2] Paradoxically, Marx's prophetic prognosis "that everything that was solid melts into air," which supposedly announced the imminent fall of capitalism, was realized in the early 1990s in Russia when sweeping changes dissolved the petrified socialist system.

Western fashion, which had colonized Soviet women's subconscious for decades, had finally arrived. "The empire of seduction" in its role of a "euphoric gravedigger for the great ideologies,"[3] appeared in its glitziest version, represented by the leading fashion houses and prestigious fashion magazines.[4] *Vogue*, the highest representative of the empire of seduction, could not simply be a fashion magazine in a country in which fashionable woman had officially been forced into the position of a permanent Other for decades. But could *Vogue* fulfill its ambition to bring fashion to Russia? Two obstacles stood in its way: the economically and socially unstable circumstances, and the lack of any sophisticated traditions for the dresses presented in *Vogue* to draw on. According to *Vogue*'s Director of International Editions, Anna Harvey, when *Vogue* began its operation in Russia, there were no collaborators with the necessary knowledge and skills. She herself acted as the Editorial Director in the first couple of years, in order to establish *Vogue*'s profile in Russia at the standards expected by the magazine's international status.[5] The arrival of *Vogue* announced a change in the politics of style, imagery, gender representations, and consumption practices. However, the Russian version of *Vogue* was itself influenced by the former socialist cultural patterns. In the next four sections, I analyze these four topics to reveal a series of negotiations between the well-established international *Vogue* brand and post-socialist Russian society, which eventually shaped it into a Russian product.

The Politics of Style

By the time *Vogue* arrived in Russia the ideological barriers to fashion had disappeared, but most women still did not have access to fashionable dress for economic reasons. With the economic collapse in the fall of 1998, the budding middle classes lost a large part of the material possessions that symbolized their middle-class status and enabled them to negotiate new consumption practices. The very rich, the other usual segment of *Vogue*'s readership, had a negative image in Russia, as many of them had accumulated their wealth in various murky businesses, yet they were the only customers of the luxurious brands that the magazine promoted. However, *Vogue* could not have relied solely on the small new class of the very rich, which would have alienated it from other potential readers and would also have tarnished its reputation. The intelligentsia, which had tried to preserve its relations with the West throughout socialist times, tended to dismiss *Vogue* as just another glossy magazine.[6] Historically wary of conspicuous consumption and any display of material wealth even before the arrival of socialism, the intelligentsia had hoped that some higher intellectual values would eventually come from the West when the doors finally opened. The early relationship between *Vogue* and its new territory therefore started under huge pressure. Editorially, the magazine tried to manage the dialectics between the elements of partnership, colonization, and liberation. Stories about well-known actors and classical ballerinas, as well as features on the giants of Russian literature such as Ivan Turgenev and Anna Akhmatova, showed that *Vogue* did not want to be known just for excessive luxury. The inclusion of the prominent writer Tatyana Tolstaya, with her literary reminiscences on the socialist times, not only referred to the recent past, but also supported the appearance of seriousness that *Vogue* craved.[7]

While a fragile balance between topics on the previous times and the new reality could be established in some fields, socialist dress codes and beautifying practices were not useful for *Vogue*. For more than seven decades, Russia had been obliged to follow a slow master narrative. All change had been controlled by the powerful bureaucracy, which ruled through a rigid, hierarchically structured and over-centralized system.[8] Fashion could not develop under circumstances in which all change was viewed with suspicion. The system prevented fashion trends from emerging because of its impenetrable organization, which consisted of numerous boards and committees within the field of fashion design and production. Neglecting seventy years of socialism—a period during which the phenomenon of Western fashion was officially opposed— Russian *Vogue* was involved, from its first issue, in a complex process of negotiating western meanings and practices in relation to post-socialist dress and beautifying rituals. Guy Debord had recognized as early as 1970 that: "The society which carries the spectacle does not dominate the underdeveloped regions only by its economic hegemony. It dominates them as the society of the spectacle" (Debord 1995: thesis 57). In its first issue, *Vogue* published "*Vogue*'s Photo Album: 106 Years of Fashion" and a feature on the history of the magazine, ironically announced as "A Short Course in the History of *Vogue*."[9] While the Russians had in the past been used to "short course" directives coming from their Party leaders, *Vogue*'s "short course" brought an entirely different ideology and aesthetics. The iconic Western fashion images displayed the work of the most famous photographers, while the equally iconic models and actresses fulfilled the long-standing craving for fashion and beauty.[10] In order to conquer its new territory, *Vogue* had to emphasize the import- ance of its own history, and fashion's history in general. Those frozen moments of perfection nevertheless confirmed, by their incredible diversity, fashion's total dependence on change. In contrast, the socialist relationship with fashion was rooted in an ontological anxiety about the fluidity of time and depended on its attempts to control and tame change.

Images from *Vogue*'s archive presented the sort of dress and woman-hood that Russians had not been able to enjoy and share under socialism.[11] But those pictures neglected not only the preexisting imagery, but also negated all everyday practices through which Russian women had negotiated fashion during the socialist times. While dreaming of Western fashion, they had developed a series of tactics in their everyday lives, from having a seamstress to sewing their own dresses; to using the services of the state-owned fashion studios, and establishing connections in clothes shops in order to beat the crowds when desirable goods eventually appeared. But *Vogue*'s readers did not need that type of knowledge, as the twenty-five-page fashion story "Moscow Holidays" published in the first issue of Russian *Vogue* demonstrated.[12] In the story, shot in Moscow by Mario Testino, Kate Moss and Amber Valetta showed the latest fashion trends from the leading Western fashion houses, with familiar Moscow scenery and social situations in the background. Kate Moss attended a typical Russian wedding ceremony, while Amber Valetta was pictured among young cadets. Other fashion images included Moscow streets, a visit to the theater, the Ostankino palace in the suburbs of Moscow, and the woods surrounding it. The familiarity could not conceal the message that money and sophistication were necessary prerequisites in Moscow as well as in Paris and New York. The latest trends simultaneously recognized the crucial role of change and made it clear that large sums of money were needed to keep up with it. Neither an experienced seamstress nor simple DIY techniques could compete with such perfection. The most expensive and smartest Western fashion had not come to Moscow for a holiday, but had come to stay.

Through the distorted process of economic transition in Russia, a small minority had amassed enormous wealth. They were to become the magazine's readers, and Russian *Vogue* recognized its educational role toward this new elite right from the start. *Vogue*'s Editor, Aliona Doletskaya, personally penned a column called "Protocol" in the first couple of issues, advising her readers on the importance of the right fashion accessories for specific social functions, the meaning of "RSVP," the style of e-mail messages, and the proper use of mobile phone. The short course in sophistication was meant for everybody, but would eventually be practiced only by those who could afford the dresses and accessories that *Vogue* promoted, as if they had to deserve them in some higher way than by just paying for them. Traditionally, culture had been a channel for social promotion in the officially classless Soviet society, and knowledge of literature, art, or science would secure a higher economic and social status for its otherwise obedient pos-

Figure 1
"In Russia, at Last," Cover of
the first issue of Russian *Vogue*,
photographer Mario Testino,
Moscow, September 1998.

sessors. But *Vogue* presupposed a new type of knowledge, and in its educational drive aimed to connect the new economic capital with a new symbolic capital. Significantly, *Vogue*'s new symbolic capital was informed neither by domestic high culture nor by domestic popular culture. Although in an ideal *Vogue*-world it would also embrace a conventional knowledge of literary classics, the new symbolic capital was not defined by it. While it was related to frivolities such as proper appearance and etiquette, the new symbolic capital was nevertheless too sophisticated and complex a set of rules to bear any resemblance to the expressions of popular culture. The real and symbolic scarcities, shortages and absences, which had characterized the previous system, had left a void, which *Vogue* urgently had to fill by introducing the most refined Western styles of dress and makeup. The magazine's credentials, as well as the credentials of its glossy advertisers, depended on how fast the new rich Russians could be taught the subtleties, half shades, and fine distinctions of *Vogue*'s style. It was a difficult task in a country that had officially disparaged differences in looks for decades. Hiding behind democratic ideals of equality, socialism had only produced uniformity. In the West, where real democratization in fashion had taken place with a greater diversification and better quality of mass production, the truly fashionable and truly rich had long since learned to differ from the mass in tiny details, which just happened to be very expensive. Historically, *Vogue*'s most critical purpose has been the preservation of nuances. In Russia, *Vogue* had first to introduce a set of nuances, especially because there was a threat of a new type of uniformity.

Vogue wanted to get rid of the prevailing image of the overly madeup New Russian, clad from head to toe in Versace, without alienating its readership. The magazine had to introduce its own concept of luxury. The expressions of the most extravagant opulence had had a long history in Russia, starting from the tsarist times, and surviving all the way through socialism. Magazines presenting elitist clothes had existed throughout the socialist period, regardless of the official ideology, which advocated modesty and restraint. Historically, the luxury of the 1920s NEP period had been highly visible but was ideologically condemned.[13] Later, the socialist elites enjoyed their luxury in secrecy. Luxury, which magazines such as *Fashions of the Seasons* had promoted from the late 1930s to the end of socialism, mirrored the totalitarian aspirations of the Soviet regimes and the unquestionable power of their elites. Practiced by the privileged few in the context of timelessness and secrecy, Soviet luxury was elitist, but also traditional, conventional, and old-fashioned. *Vogue*'s sophisticated and fashion-conscious aesthetics corresponded neither to the totalitarian glamour of the socialist elitist magazines nor to the very public excesses of the New Russians. Luxury and the inclination toward bold decoration had to be recoded to suit the post-socialist times as *Vogue* and its advertisers perceived them.

Vogue's luxury is subject to change and evolves with the spirit of the times and with new proposals from the market-conscious luxury brands. Ideally, *Vogue*'s luxury is also democratic and accessible. It is supposed to be readily available at a local shop and embodied in a designer's dress or the latest-style handbag, with money being the only discriminatory factor in obtaining a desirable item. In contrast, needs and wants had been complicated by a differentiated access to goods during socialism, and income counted less than access in promoting social distinctions. In a situation in which not all social groups could procure what they needed or wanted with equal facility, "the distinction between wants and needs constituted the discourse of power" (Bauman 1991: 113). The fact that New Russians could easily acquire any sartorial item they wished demonstrated the new rules on the politics of style. *Vogue* carefully orchestrated the New Russians' emblematic travel from the practices of haphazard conspicuous consumption toward the acquisition of the symbolically more complex expressions of luxury. *Vogue*'s Editor, Aliona Doletskaya, emphasized that her biggest challenge was the education of the reader, who would eventually develop into a "*Vogue* person."[14]

The New Imagery

In its attempt to educate its public in all the refineries of luxury, *Vogue* dedicated many pages to the presentation of luxurious clothes and accessories. The informative picture stories on the most prominent representatives of opulence, such as John Galliano, Karl Lagerfeld, Valentino, and Julien MacDonald, appeared from the first issue. The regular column, "Retail Therapy" presented only the most expensive shoes, jewelry, handbags, furs, and clothes, while the haute couture collections were continually presented from the very beginning. Knowing the material wealth of its readership and its aesthetic preferences, *Vogue* indulged in opulence, limiting itself only to its most precious expressions. In the 2004 issue dedicated to power, *Vogue*'s leading fashion story, "Power to Luxury" presented haute couture dresses by John Galliano for Dior, Chanel, Lacroix, Givenchy, Gaultier, and Valentino. The story was opened by Dior's long blue silk dress, embellished with silver lace and a rich fur strip running along its hems.[15] A story on the "Magical Power of Precious Stones," which presented the latest pieces of jewelry by Cartier, Van Cleef and Arpels, Boucheron, and Tiffany, was published in the same issue. These features provided guidance for *Vogue*'s rich readers on the better things of life by showing the most refined examples. They also allowed for a new social context for luxury. Whereas previously luxury was secretive and hidden behind closed doors, it now became transparent and on open display, and was available for all at a price.

But *Vogue*'s educational role went beyond presentations of the latest haute couture extravagances and the most expensive diamonds. Once the phenomenon of fashion had been established through its most recognized and most acceptable representatives, *Vogue* dared to offer different and more radical fashions to its fast-learning readership. In June 2001, *Vogue* advised precise dress codes for a series of newly opened smart cafés and restaurants. While Chanel, Hermes, Valentino, and Louis Vuitton featured prominently, some restaurants were best served by clothes from Roberto Cavalli, Etro, Kenzo, and even by the Belgian avant-garde designer Ann Demeulemeester and the minimalist Calvin Klein.[16] A fashion story promoting minimalist style had already appeared in the first issue, and features replete with photographs of designers who challenged fashion conventions, such as Helmut Lang,

Nicholas Ghesquière and Yohji Yamamoto, were published alongside stories on the representatives of opulence.

But the crucial change in *Vogue*'s imagery happened in April 1999, when the most notable Soviet celebrity Alla Pugacheva appeared in *Vogue* dressed in Yohji Yamamoto.[17] Pugacheva had just celebrated her fiftieth birthday, after spending twenty-five years as the most important performer of the specific socialist phenomenon called "estrada."[18] Yeltsin had just pinned the highest state order on the lapel of this singer who had made Russia cry with her heartbreaking ballads, joking that he was happy to live in Pugacheva's times.[19] The celebrated diva had accumulated enormous wealth, traveled in a white, chauffeur-driven stretch limo and was enjoying her fourth marriage, to a colleague, singer Philip Kirkorov, eighteen years her junior. In 1999, the mass public still adored her and identified with her continual efforts to slim down, her love life, her Soviet looks, her big body wrapped in shapeless vaguely ethnic tunics, her strong makeup and her untidy, badly dyed hair. The encounter between *Vogue* and Pugacheva was bound to be challenging, but *Vogue*'s gamble paid off. Pugacheva's own style was so deeply rooted in Soviet times that she had completely missed the phenomenon of Western fashion. *Vogue* generally did not address that generation of women, but their post-socialist daughters. The mothers' generation suffered a double exclusion, the first related to age discrimination and the other one being ideological. The mothers' everyday lives, from their appearance to their practices of consumption, were impregnated with Soviet aesthetics to such a degree that they totally clashed with *Vogue*'s imagery and its set of values.

As Russia's only authentic superstar belonged to that generation, dressing her up in a conventionally smart and luxurious Paris haute couture dress would be wrong. Pugacheva needed clothes that would transcend Western fashion's rules on beauty and femininity. Yamamoto was the right choice, as he seriously challenged all concepts of Western fashion, from cuts and shapes to concepts of femininity and luxury. Pugacheva's transformation into an avant-garde fashion icon announced the final victory of *Vogue*'s imagery, and confirmed that there was no relevant Soviet or immediate post-Soviet sartorial reference that would suit the rarefied world of *Vogue*'s fashion pages. By dressing Pugacheva in Yamamoto's clothes, this editorial demonstrated how fast symbolic progress has been in Russia, at least in *Vogue*'s world. While the West agonized about the dangers of Japanese avant-garde fashion at least for a decade during the 1980s, finding its restrained aesthetics shocking as well as a serious threat to the Western canon of beauty and femininity, it took Russian *Vogue* less than a year to make the leap not only from the concept of Soviet uniformity to the highly sophisticated expressions of the latest Western fashion, but also to embrace the intellectual austerity of avant-garde fashion. In his conversation with Wim Wenders in the film *On Cities and Clothes*, Yohji Yamamoto declared an old photograph of a poor Russian woman in a thick winter coat as his inspiration. The beauty of that coat was, for Yamamoto, in its necessity. [20] The circle was closed with Alla Pugacheva dressed in a plain black Yamamoto dress, an embodiment of the Russian woman with her round Slavic face and body. Due to *Vogue*, the return to severity and restraint was not informed by any political directive, as in the past, but was mediated through the spectacle of consumption.

The expressions of extreme luxury continued to be a permanent aesthetic statement in *Vogue*, but luxury was increasingly accompanied by cutting-edge novelty. Such fashion stories demonstrated that *Vogue* was gaining in self-confidence and that its educational efforts were successful.[21] On the conceptual level, they showed that *Vogue*'s readers, who had been deprived of both luxury and novelty for decades, were slowly starting to switch their favors from a space-bound category of luxury toward a time-bound category of novelty. In the immediate post-socialist Russia, luxury was understood in terms of plenty. While luxury was perceived as a physical category, which was simply supposed to feed the urgent need for huge quantities of long-craved goods, a change in the concept of time, on the other hand, presupposed a serious social and political change. Socialism had been served by a culturally slow flow of time. It tended to abolish novelty or, at least, strictly control it. Aesthetic categories, such as beautiful, pretty, balanced, classical, and measured, which had defined Soviet dress in the domestic media, demonstrated the immutability of official dress codes. But Western fashion had already left the binary opposition between beautiful and ugly in the middle of the nineteenth century,[22] in favor of other, more exciting binary oppositions, like interesting and dull, or new and old.

A new post-socialist, fast and fragmented concept of time needed to be ingrained into consciousness and everyday life practices before novelty in dress could be appreciated more, or at least equally, as luxury. The fashion story "Double Agent" presented an anxious model against the background of a dark and empty Moscow underground. Her uneasiness was palpable while she quickly paced by the miles of long marble walls and journeyed deep down as the only passenger on otherwise vacant escalators. As the story developed, becoming increasingly threatening page after page, the model, dressed in Hussein Chalayan, Viktor and Rolf, and Martin Margiela, appeared more and more convincing as a fashion agent bringing cutting-edge looks and fashion to Russia. [23] Metaphorically, the fashion story "Double Agent" proposed a new concept of time for post-socialist Moscow. It could have been a metaphor for *Vogue*, which had already been involved in changing the perception of time for five years when that story was published.

Almost all of *Vogue*'s visual references in the various fashion stories and features about fur, smart sports, films, cinema stars, and beauty icons belonged to Western iconography. Due to its backward past, Russia had yet to develop its own fashion industry and to establish its own creative contribution to the cosmopolitan world of international fashion, which was still dominated by the big players in Paris, Milan, and New York. *Vogue* had little choice but to present Western dresses that met its standards of quality and style, and which also sold in Moscow's new designer shops, thus meeting the approval of its advertisers.[24] The new Russian fashion designers, on the other hand, were still struggling with the production side of their budding businesses. The country did not have the decades needed to establish a flexible and highly skilled manufacturing base and to nurture the talent and creativity required to turn the city into a fashion capital. Moscow lacked these prerequisites, and being short of time was unable to follow that route. However, it took the city just a few years to become a recognized capital of consumption on the global fashion map.

Vogue promoted the transformation of Moscow from a retail back-water into an extraordinarily exciting space of consumption. Its success depended on that change, and its growing confidence was confirmed with the self-assured blurb "In Russia, forever" on the cover of its fifth anniversary issue. However, *Vogue*'s awareness that it did not pro-vide homegrown Russian fashion was apparent in this issue. Aliona Doletskaya had announced in her editorial letter that the readers would experience a wholly Russian issue, claiming that the fashion stories were either shot in Russia, motivated by Russian topics, or inspired by the Russian woman.[25] Yet the important summary article "Glory to Russia" republished several fashion pictures from previous issues, which demonstrated that Russia only served as a picturesque backdrop for shots of the latest Western fashions.[26] In fact, the anniversary issue did not feature any fashion stories presenting Russian designers.[27]

The first fashion story that featured clothes by Russian fashion designers, "The Russian Century," appeared in February 2005.[28] *Vogue* chose designers and fashion houses which had already become household names through their catwalk shows at the Russian Fashion Week and other media events: Julia Nikolaeva, A&V, Tatiana Parfenova, Julia Dalakyan, Chistova and Endourova, Igor Chapurin, and Nina Donis. This fashion story offered models of imaginative national identity, which not only preceded Soviet times but were also positioned in some cherished premodern past. Thick braids, which framed the models' fresh young faces, represented the eternal beauty of a Russian woman. Yet, the models wore decadent dresses in opulent settings filled with antiques. The highly sexualized and visible Agent Provocateur access-ories, from corsets to suspenders, spoilt the old-fashioned romance. The kinky sashes, on which expensive pieces of jewelry were pinned in place of medals, also disturbed the idyllic atmosphere. This post-totalitarian pastiche of different styles and periods resembled the totalitarian aesthetics of the 1930s, when Stalinism had filled a barren present with a visually rich and picturesque, albeit invented, tradition. The photo-grapher, Egor Zaika, cleverly played with the aesthetics of that period

Figure 2
"Russian Century,"
photographer Egor Zaika,
Vogue, Moscow, February
2005.

and with its mythical nature. The grand 1930s narrative offered him an alluring and picturesque atmosphere for a century of Russian fashion that had never happened. But in sharp contrast to Stalinism, *Vogue* did not try to pretend that its story was the final and only truth. It was invented in all its playfulness.

New Technologies of Gender

One of the most challenging issues for *Vogue*, on its arrival in Russia, was its relationship to a heritage of complex gender issues, which stemmed from the early Bolshevik abolition of sexual difference between genders by political decree. Fashionable dress and makeup had been identified as serious threats to the social body throughout the socialist times during which a puritanical concept that advocated modesty and unadorned simplicity had prevailed.[29] The recognition of the fashionable woman and of femininity became an irresolvable problem for socialism after Khrushchev promoted an official reconceptualization of gender during the Cold War, in an effort to catch up with Western everyday cultures and lifestyles. This new concept connected the old puritanical ideas on modesty and simplicity with new categories such as prettiness and elegance, in order to offer a concept of womanhood closer to the real desires of Soviet women. The regime's failure to generate a new socialist everyday culture, as well as the repression of the market and its competitive and changing ways in offering desirable images of femininity, contributed toward the official reintroduction of gender difference in its most traditional and fixed form from the 1960s on. A woman could be pretty but not sexy. She could be beautiful but not fatal. She could be adorned but not in excess. An inner beauty was more appreciated than its exterior version.[30]

Soviet women, however, did not appreciate the way in which the state controlled and suppressed their longings for seriously fashionable clothes and luxurious grooming.[31] The conventional concept of femininity was never questioned or challenged by women in Soviet Russia, as they were too busy struggling with the regime to let themselves indulge in the rites of traditional womanhood. Soviet women had been genuinely unaware of the bourgeois commercialization of beauty and fashion, and they craved the artificiality of Western femininity and dress in place of the ideologically imposed naturalness.

From being a suppressed phenomenon under socialism, femininity in post-socialist times went in a completely opposite direction. Just a year before *Vogue* arrived, *The New York Times* reported on an "extravagant form of femininity" in Russia:

> Women have mostly ignored the kind of understatement and comfort now fashionable in the West. J. Crew is not a popular look in Moscow; the ideal is Nolan Miller, who designed the femme fatale clothes worn by Joan Collins in "Dynasty." They eschew the natural-looking blond highlights for vivid henna and improbable gold tresses. Lipstick is red, foundation is thick, eyeliner is black and luxuriant. Even in the parliament, where the dull grey business of the government goes on, female employees can be seen wearing spangly cocktail dresses. Pants are unthinkable" (Stanley 1997: 3).

These highly visible expressions of femininity demonstrated the extent to which the boundaries between the private and the public had shifted. The new overexposed rituals of femininity and sexuality could be interpreted as a liberating and healthy reaction to the previously imposed deritualization of sexual behavior. The Russian feminist, Larissa

Lissyutkina, argued that "Sexist stereotypes in the West are accepted by Russian woman as a return to individuality and to the forcibly wrested feminine 'I'" (Lissyutkina 1993: 277).[32]

Western-style beauty contests were introduced in 1988, during Perestroika, organized by official institutional networks, such as the branches of the Communist Youth organization and the first Soviet entrepreneurs. The contests were approved because of the interest in developing business connections with the West. The media emphasized that beauty contests generally were profit-making events. The winners were presented as excellent pupils, well-read girls and loving daughters. This perception changed with the first All-Union contest for the first Miss Russia in 1989, at a time when pornography had begun to appear openly in the Russian media.[33] After the earlier enthusiasm about the perfect pairing of beauty and business, the image of the beauty queen quickly began to lose its allure. Following decades of the public invasion of the private sphere in the socialist times, the private now entered the public arena in even more transgressive ways than in beauty contests. High-class prostitutes became highly visible and embodied Western-style fashion and beautifying rituals in their most sexualized versions.

Officially, prostitution had not existed in Soviet Russia, but the liberalization processes during Perestroika opened up a space for the phenomena of prostitution and pornography in the domestic media in the late 1980s. A series of voyeuristically flavored reports appeared about the high life and the stylish and groomed looks of high-class prostitutes. They revealed the fascinating milieu of the *Intourist* hotels, in which high-class prostitutes mingled with Westerners, dressed in sexy miniskirts and high heels, with their youthful beauty enhanced by expensive perfumes and skillfully applied makeup.[34] Their appearance emphasized an image of a woman who dared to be sexually provocative in public. The high-class prostitute was perceived not only as a feminine and sexy woman, but also as an independent businesswoman, a pioneer of the market economy (Lissyutkina 1992). In 1988, *Intergirl: A Hard Currency Prostitute*, by Vladimir Kunin, became a literary bestseller, and a very successful film. Its heroine Tanya, the Russian version of *Pretty Woman*, knowledgeably dropped the names of the brands Chanel, Max Factor, Christian Dior, Nina Ricci, and Cardin into her conversations. She and her colleagues seemed to announce a new sort of Russian woman: they swam in the morning, played tennis, lunched with business partners, and learned English, Italian, French, and Finnish. They also managed to earn one hundred dollars with each client, a huge sum in Russia (Kunin 1991: 8–9). Tanya's adventurous leap into the new world nevertheless meant that she experienced the dangers, alienation, and coldness of the foreign culture firsthand. She married her rich Swedish client, only to be killed in a car accident soon afterward.

This post-Soviet relationship between a high-class prostitute and fashionable dress can be compared to the introduction of bourgeois fashion

Figure 3
"Beauty Queens," photographer
Steve Hiett, *Vogue*, Moscow,
June 2004.

in the nineteenth century in Western Europe. A few authors dealing
with that fashion period—from Philippe Perrot (1994) to Georg Simmel
(1997) [35] and Werner Sombart—recognized the *demimondaine* as a
brave promoter of fashion. Claiming that luxury production and luxury
consumption gave birth to capitalism, Sombart argued that the courtesan
was a catalyst of that development, as she promoted "all the follies of
fashion, luxury, splendor and extravagance" (Sombart 1967: 57). When
Vogue had to deal with the relationship between the concept of highly
sexualized femininity and the world of commodities in the specific
context of Russian capitalism, the magazine's aesthetic approach was in
fact meant to protect the image of its advertisers and to accommodate
their presence on the domestic market. Regardless of their social provenance, the courtesans that Perrot and Sombart observed operated in a
highly sophisticated world with long traditions in the production and
consumption of luxury goods. In Russia, which lacked such traditions
during seventy years of socialism, high-class prostitutes flounced around
in expensive Western clothes and cosmetics before *Vogue*'s arrival. How
did such a loud visibility affect the brands themselves? The provincial
Soviet Perestroika papers praised the sophistication of the high-class
prostitutes and the most coveted Western cosmetic brands entered the
vocabulary of post-Soviet literature, but *Vogue* had to affirm a concept
of sexualized femininity following its own aesthetics. In fact, *Vogue* had
to reclaim that sort of femininity back from the *demimonde* world, and
grant it respectability and credibility.

One fashion story, "Beauty Queens," played with an event well known to the domestic public: a beauty contest.[36] The story presented a group of beauty queens engaged in different activities during the contest. While posing for a photo shoot, lounging by the swimming pool, preparing for the catwalk and chatting, they were dressed in evening gowns, sexy swimwear, and flowery, feminine dresses. The luxuriant scenery of a Miami hotel helped to immediately transfer the story far away from the amateurish and doubtful context of the earlier Russian beauty contests. Yet, it referred to them by the numbered disk that all the models wore on their wrists like a sort of bracelet. That little detail was an ironic reminder of the rather patchy reputation that beauty contests had acquired in post-Soviet Russia. Nevertheless, the polished, debutante looks of the young girls in expensive clothes demonstrated how successfully *Vogue* had managed to introduce new signifying practices, and organize its representational strategies around smart and expensive commodities that the magazine promoted.

Many fashion stories showed that *Vogue*'s most significant task was to recode and reclaim the highly sexualized female image, because it effectively united the female body as a site of pleasure and a site of consumption. Aliona Doletskaya strongly denied that the sexualized female image was the most important for *Vogue*.[37] The sexually charged images nevertheless dominated the magazine. Yet, any hints of sexuality as a natural force were tamed through a process of naturalization into femininity practiced in a series of highly codified grooming rituals. While opposing the past, the new sexualized femininity was nevertheless in the service of the most developed capitalist market strategies. The socialist regime attempted to impose modesty and to control desires from afar, and so its bureaucratic gaze only surveilled fully clothed bodies. However, the new iconography, informed by the processes of commoditization, allowed for the fetishistic gaze over a body's exposed parts. While under socialism the commodity had been a fetish, the body became a fetish once the commodity lost its mysterious, opaque nature. The division of the body into fetish-like partial objects, and the enlargement and isolation of particular bodily parts in beauty pages— breasts, waist, feet, nails, lips, eyes, hair—showed that the market economy had finally arrived. The image that symbolically embodied the unity of the fetishized aesthetics and the free market presented a carefully pedicured foot with each nail painted in a different shade of nail varnish. The foot was held by an equally preciously manicured and nail-varnished hand, with each finger sporting a huge diamond ring. This was *Vogue*'s unique touch on an otherwise conventional beauty page, which was, apart from a foot and a hand, crammed with bottles of nail varnish of different brands.[38]

Although the sexualized images corresponded to the current trends, they were still haunted by the earlier memories of suppressed sensuality and suppressed sexuality. The fifth anniversary issue presented what it

Figure 4
"Trapped by Temptation,"
photographer Oliviero Toscani,
Vogue, Moscow, September
2003.

supposed to be three types of Russian womanhood: a strong woman in
Helmut Newton's images, a weepy Slavic girl in Henrik Halvarsson's
fashion story, and Oliviero Toscani's interpretation of a tomboy.[39] In
these stories the previous Russian meanings of strength, emotion, and
the tomboy were, however, overpowered by new images that either
subverted or negotiated conventional values. In Helmut Newton's story,[40]
the aggressive, sexualized strength of his signature woman dressed in
black leather differed radically from the Russian socialist concept of a
strong woman, whose strength was informed by a puritanical morality.
Halvarsson's story ("What If This Is Love?"),[41] set in Saint Petersburg,

portrayed a young, emotional, and highly-strung girl who resembled the Soviet film heroines from the 1960s, and shared their vulnerability, tenderness, and youthfulness. The story recaptured a rare moment of socialist fashionability. The invasion of Western youth culture and music was unstoppable, and so Soviet looks, now embellished by miniskirts and slender bodies, correspond to the Western cultural model.

In contrast, in his fashion story "Trapped by Temptation,"[42] photographer Oliviero Toscani presented a uniquely Russian version of the tomboy. Neglecting the Soviet period, this story attempted to establish a narrative continuity with pre-Revolutionary times. A delicate and graceful girl, dressed in feminine clothes and accompanied by a squadron of sailors, could only be perceived as a tomboy through its cultural reference to Natasha Rostova, the aristocratic heroine of Tolstoy's novel *War and Peace*. She was as cheerful and flirty as the young Natasha, and was dressed in similarly feminine lace and long silk dresses. This image demonstrated the specifically Russian construction of gender difference, which had far less to do with appearance than with character and social context. An independent-minded and intelligent girl could make friends with boys and have some innocent fun with them, but her femininity and delicacy, represented by romantic dress, could not be sacrificed.

In pre-Revolutionary Russia, the tomboy did not wear pants. Almost one hundred years later, that phenomenon was reflected in post-socialist *Vogue,* where pants could hardly ever be found on women's bodies. In the collective Russian memory, trousers remained a metaphor for the forced Soviet masculinization of women. Under early Bolshevism, both the New Man and the New Woman had been modeled on the Nietzschean *Übermensch*. The early Bolshevik concept of masculinized womanhood had not only violated the notions of traditional femininity, but had also blocked the arrival of the dynamic exchange between female and male wardrobes that had taken place in the West. There, in contrast to the socialist masculinization of the social body, an opposite process of feminization of the social body had occurred, and women's borrowing from men's closets eventually changed the dress codes of both.[43] However, the Soviet concept of femininity, reintroduced in the late 1950s, remained caught in traditional practices. In the Khrushchev period, women were encouraged to become ladylike once again, and were strongly discouraged from wearing pants. Books on beauty, taste, and culture of dress that started to appear in that period stressed that pants not only jeopardized a woman's femininity but also her modesty. Pants were supposed to be worn only for sports, physical work, and travel, and even then only by young girls.[44] Pants were eventually accepted as a practical option for women in the Perestroika period. By avoiding having women in pants on its fashion pages, *Vogue* ensured that its readers were not bothered with the functionality of their clothes. However the magazine simultaneously obeyed the earlier socialist cravings for the most traditional expressions of Western femininity.[45]

Figure 5
"A Brief Encounter,"
photographer Pablo Alfaro,
Vogue, Moscow, October,
2002.

The story "A Brief Encounter" was a rare example that offered a fashionable choice between a skirt and pants.[46] Women in fedoras and pantsuits competed with others dressed in fur coats, transparent black dresses, and high heels. The subheading of the story read: "Woman or man? Does it still mean anything?"[47] It obviously still did since *Vogue* had had to borrow its tomboy from pre-Revolutionary times. Thus, *Vogue* had a further task to accomplish: to convince its readers that women can also be graceful and feminine in pants. In Western fashion, the boyish look had increasingly developed into a distinctive genre of female dress from the 1930s. Women had learned to play with the sexual ambivalence of androgyny, but it was an androgyny that evolved to emphasize an idealized youth rather than any expression of masculinity.[48]

Vogue and the Arrival of Sophisticated Market Capitalism in Russia

In an interview that announced the arrival of *Vogue* in Russia, the chairman of Condé Nast, Jonathan Newhouse, stated: "In Russia today nearly every important designer and beauty house has opened and is selling. Advertisers with whom we have had a long relationship need us to open their markets. They asked us to come into Russia" (Binyon 1998: 41). The Western media had already relentlessly reported on the excessive shopping habits of the newly rich Russians, and the new lavishly decorated shops stocked with luxury goods that served them. A typical customer from that social group, Galina Grishena, as reported in American *Vogue* in 1995, would spend from $10,000 up to $50,000 a month on luxurious Western-branded clothes, jewelry, and accessories in such shops. Cartier and Versace were her favourites. Grishena justified her choices, stating: "Versace is bright and attention-getting, and I don't want to be lost in the crowd ... I know it's not practical to go to our country house in high heels, but I do it because it's beautiful. Our rich women now do not want to be modest" (Singer 1995: 352).[49] Global luxury brands had found their ideal customers, fabulously rich and hungry for fashion. But there were some problems to be resolved.

It was not surprising that the newly rich could not control their desires. Two types of modernity, Western and socialist, provided different histories of modern desire. In socialism, state power confronted modernity by simultaneously forcing desire into a collective project, and postponing it as an individual drive. The complex relationship between state power, free-floating human desires and unobtainable Western objects resulted in a specific form of socialist commodity fetishism. The social life of many fashion items had been transformed through the black market, and the smuggling and hunting for them in the understocked shops, but the relationship with the commodity became more conventional in post-socialist Russia. Commodities lost their preciousness, their previous thrilling social life. The task of Alla Verber, the Fashion Director of the newly refurbished luxury department store TsUM in the center of Moscow, was to fill its huge space of 377,000 square feet with the most exquisite and expensive Western fashion goods.[50] However, she still remembered the deprivation under socialism: "Before, when you came to TsUM you would buy what you could get. If they had red shoes, you got red shoes. Now to come to one place and have such massive choice is exciting ... Minimalism doesn't work for us. When people come into a boutique and see no product, they get suspicious. They think things are being hidden from them"(Goldstein Crowe 2005).

While the rich Russians' gathering of huge quantities of luxury goods was the result of an earlier material deprivation,[51] their indiscriminate shopping patterns were driven by an enforced symbolic deprivation, due to decades of isolation from the West. Luxury goods companies faced the problem of positioning their brands in Russia, as their new customers lacked the necessary selective and sophisticated knowledge about the products they were buying so ardently. Uprooted, by their new wealth, from the modest Bulgarian and Polish clothes that they had praised in the recent socialist past,[52] the newly rich attempted to justify their Western luxury shopping extravaganzas by comparison with the excessive spending of the pre-Revolutionary elites, or simply by evoking the alleged Russian national disposition for overindulgence and over-decoration. These strategies clearly attempted to reestablish a discontinued narrative with pre-socialism and its penchant for the conspicuous display of wealth.

But global luxury had evolved into novel modes of understatement and discretion. *Vogue*'s task was to educate the newly rich about the new and sophisticated ways of spending money, by carefully nurturing their enthusiasm for the best and the most expensive goods. The magazine's columns dedicated to shopping—"Shopping Therapy," "Wanted," "Spy," "Choice," "Purchases," and "Gold Reserve"—served as a catalyst in an alchemical process of turning new money into old as fast as possible. While some similar columns also exist in other national editions of *Vogue*, the Russian edition included more of them, and presented only the most exclusive fashion goods available in Moscow's most luxurious shops.[53] By targeting only the richest among its readership, the column "Gold Reserve," dedicated to the most precious pieces of jewelry, demonstrated what sort of wealth some of *Vogue*'s readers possessed, and were prepared to spend.

Vogue enabled its rich readers to learn and to acquire a totally new symbolic capital in a short space of time. Western and domestic media mocked their lack of style and sophistication in the late 1990s. The disturbing Dostoyevskian background of crime, squadrons of bodyguards, armored cars, and armed guards at the entrances of luxury shopping temples, made their excessive shopping sprees only more entertaining for Western magazines. But the Russian super-rich eventually gained new respect. Stories in the Western media continued to emphasize the fabulous sums that the wealthy Russians spent, but also praised their newly acquired style. They began to be perceived as saviors of the luxury market, and their outrageous shopping sprees became an anchor for the ailing global luxury brands, which had to survive a recent downturn in the Middle and Far East. Once they had learned about limited editions and customized pieces, the incredibly wealthy Russians started to buy the most special goods. *Vogue* played a significant role in the development of this style, which eventually succeeded in combining money with up-to-date knowledge about the latest trends. The journey that took the newly rich Russians from a merely expensive object to a rare and expensive object was already named "oligarch chic" (Croft 2004:18).

The super-rich Russians became globally recognized as one of the most influential consumer groups in the world. In 2004, Giorgio Armani

Figure 6
"In Russia Forever," the Fifth Anniversary Cover, *Vogue*, Moscow, September 2003.

claimed that the Russian customer was becoming increasingly sophisticated and stated that his fashion house "sold more beaded evening gowns in Moscow than in many other principal cities in the world." The Moscow headquarters of the most prestigious luxury companies could hardly praise them enough. "If it comes in suede or lizard, they'll take the lizard," observed the Hermes representative, while his Yves Saint-Laurent counterpart said: "They want the most special pieces, the stand-out items" (Croft 2004: 18). Jean-Paul Gaultier convincingly expressed his feeling of gratitude toward his new Russian customers. After visiting Ukraine and Russia for the opening of his shop in Moscow, his 2005/06 haute couture collection was heavily inspired by Russian and Ukrainian folk heritage.[54]

For *Vogue*, its mission was accomplished. By educating the wealthy Russian customers in the finer things of life, the magazine saved the most precious asset of the luxury brands: their aura. Moreover, the world of exquisite luxury was transferred to virgin territory to start a new life. It was fortunate timing for the luxury industry, as the West had grown tired of luxury brands and the type of luxury they represented.

Conclusion

Vogue arrived in Russia in 1998 under conditions of economic collapse and many commentators doubted its chances of surviving in such an environment. *Vogue* proved them wrong. The economic and social circumstances in Russia seemed light years away from the magazine's sophistication, apparently based on delicate lace and precious embroidery, but *Vogue* is a tough and resilient product that embodies the society of the spectacle in all its moneyed power. Assisted by the most important advertisers, *Vogue* entered its new territory with great determination.

It initiated its readers in the latest styles of dress and looks by introducing a completely new imagery. In this article I have analyzed the highly symbolic content of that rapid process, through which *Vogue*, in less than a year, made the leap not only from the concept of Soviet uniformity to the highly sophisticated expressions of the latest Western fashion, but also embraced the intellectual austerity of avant-garde fashion.

The introduction of a type of femininity that would suit the most refined requirements of *Vogue*'s advertisers was a more complex task. *Vogue*'s concept of femininity, as I have shown, was established by partially recognizing the influence of the previous cultural patterns on post-socialist practices (by avoiding pants in a woman's wardrobe), but also by negating the old socialist models of modesty (by overemphasizing sexuality). Yet, *Vogue* affirmed a concept of sexualized femininity following its own aesthetics, reclaiming that sort of femininity from the *demimonde* world, and granting it respectability and credibility.

Vogue arrived in Russia as a representative of the most advanced market capitalism and its advertising and retail strategies. Its politics of style were intended not only to promote its advertisers, but also to protect the allure of their image in socially unfavorable surroundings. *Vogue*'s educational efforts toward its wealthy but unsophisticated readership were also informed by that task. In order to fulfill it, *Vogue* connected the new economic capital possessed by the Russian super-rich with a new symbolic capital. It consisted of a type of knowledge that *Vogue*'s readers had not been acquainted with, due to the previous material and symbolic shortages. *Vogue*'s presentation of luxurious dresses and accessories also allowed for a new social context for luxury. Whereas previously, luxury was secretive and hidden behind closed doors, it now became transparent and on open display, and was available for all at a price.

Acknowledgments

I would like to thank Amy de la Haye for her invitation and encouragement during the writing of this article. I am grateful to Anna Harvey, *Vogue's* Director of International Editions, for briefing me about the start-up of Russian *Vogue*; to Aliona Doletskaya for a most helpful interview; to the Picture Editor of Russian *Vogue*, Natalia Chernova, and to assistant picture editor Maria Sorokina; and for Russian *Vogue's* permission to publish four images that accompany this article. I am indebted to photographers Oliviero Toscani and Steve Hiett (and his agent Kenny Burns from D + V Management), who gave permission for the use of their images in this article. I was privileged to use *Vogue's* London library during my research, and I would like to thank Janine Button for her assistance there.

Notes

1. There have been many reports related to the launch of Russian *Vogue* under the circumstances of economic collapse. See for example: Crawshaw, S. "Retail Therapy in Novosibirsk," *The Independent*, September 24, 1998. Isabella Blow offered her personal account in "Tsars in Her Eyes: Isabella Blow Goes Mad in Moscow," *Style*, *The Sunday Times*, February 7, 1999.
2. Talking about the post-socialist experiences, Daniel Miller observed: "... the bewildering experience of that extreme modernity that arises when the criteria for value are cut from beneath one" (Miller 1995: 7).
3. See Lipovetsky 1994: 210.
4. *Vogue's* publisher, Condé Nast, was very cautious and only introduced the magazine to Russia after other Western fashion magazines had already established themselves there: *Cosmopolitan* (1994), *Elle* (1996), and *Harper's Bazaar* (1996), *L'Officiel* (1988).
5. Interview with Anna Harvey (London, March 24, 2005). In her advisory function, Anna Harvey used to spend one week each month in Moscow.
6. This was also emphasized in my interview with *Vogue's* editor Aliona Doletskaya (March 24, 2005, by telephone).
7. In my interview with her, Anna Harvey acknowledged that the Russian edition of *Vogue* contained more features on high culture than other editions. That followed the advice of the Moscow editor Aliona Doletskaya, who considered that such topics were important

in order to establish the status of *Vogue* on the Russian market (Interview, March 24, 2005).

8. Khrushchev's and Gorbachev's reforms did not succeed, because the changes they planned did not suit the ruling bureaucracy. For an overview of the role of bureaucracy in the Soviet Union, see Lewin 1995.

9. "*Vogue*'s Photo Album: 106 years of Fashion," pp. 29–32; Buck, J. J. (text) and Muir, R. (picture editor), "The Short Course of *Vogue*'s History," *Vogue*, September 1998, N 1.

10. The photographers included in "A Short Course in the History of *Vogue*" were: Horst, Irving Penn, Richard Avedon, Norman Parkinson, Lord Snowdon, Arthur Elgort, Patrick Demarchelier, Peter Lindbergh, David Bailey, Helmut Newton, and Steven Meisel, while the models and actresses included Lisa Fonssagrives, Audrey Hepburn, Marlene Dietrich, Sophia Loren, Twiggy, Jerry Hall, Linda Evangelista, Naomi Campbell, and Helena Christensen.

11. There was not a single visual reference to Soviet times, while, for example, Cecil Beaton photographed the most prominent Soviet ballerina, Maya Plisetskaya, for *Vogue* in 1964.

12. "Moscow Holidays," photographer Mario Testino, Russian *Vogue*, September 1998, N 1, pp. 174–199.

13. The New Economic Policy (the NEP), established with the approval of Lenin in 1921, and abolished in 1929, recognized private ownership and entrepreneurship and signaled the return of capitalistic practices and a bourgeois way of life.

14. Interview March 24, 2005.

15. "Power to Luxury," Russian *Vogue*, September 2004, N 9, pp. 352–365.

16. Russian *Vogue*, June 2001, pp. 92–95. "Dress Code" was published on page 95.

17. "The Queen Mother," Russian *Vogue*, April, 1999, N 4.

18. Estrada was a form of Soviet romantic pop music delivered by a singer accompanied by a large orchestra. Alla Pugacheva was the most important exponent of estrada during the 1970s and 1980s.

19. Yeltsin referred to an earlier popular joke, which asked how Brezhnev would be remembered in twenty years. The answer was: as a political figure that lived in Pugacheva's times.

20. Yohji Yamamoto's statement in Wim Wender's film *On Cities and Clothes*. For an overview about the relationship between the traditional haute couture and the phenomenon of post-fashions, see: Vinken 2005.

21. In an interview with *The Times* fashion editor Lisa Armstrong in 2001, *Vogue*'s Editor Aliona Doletskaya stated that the Russians did not dress in Versace and Moschino from head to toe any more, and that they grew more sophisticated and wore Martin Margiela's and Yohji Yamamoto's clothes (*The Times*, London, May 28, 2001).

22. In the mid-nineteenth century, Charles Baudelaire was the first to recognize that novelty is the most important ingredient in fashion, and that beauty is not only a transitory but also a fleeting phenomenon. The later authors, such as Georg Simmel at the beginning of the twentieth century, and Gilles Lipovetsky toward its end, also stressed novelty as the key element of fashion.

23. Fashion Story "Double Agent," photographer Alex Cailey, Russian *Vogue*, September 2003, pp. 346–361. The story also presented clothes by Gucci, Alberta Ferretti, and Givenchy.

24. Only a handful of the defunct socialist textile giants had been successfully restructured after their change of ownership, but they were restricted to the production of mass-market clothes. A few new domestic fashion entrepreneurs also directed their efforts toward the same mass consumer market. These new local businessmen understood the Russian mass market well, as they mainly started their careers already under socialism, when their entrepreneurial attempts could get them into jail, being qualified as black market activities. One of them was Anatoli Kilmin, the owner of the clothing company Tom Klaim, who successfully sold showy, inexpensive clothes to middle-income young working women.

25. Doletskaya, A. Editorial: "For the last five years we've wanted to do an issue on Russia, a one hundred percent Russian issue. And it's taken us and the country five years to see that dream become a reality" (Russian *Vogue*, September 2003, p. 32).

26. "Glory to Russia," Russian *Vogue*, September 2003.

27. In *Vogue*'s first five years, domestic fashion designers had regularly appeared in news stories, presented mainly as personalities. *Vogue* also covered the budding activities of Russian seasonal fashion shows, establishing a certain hierarchy of values within the slowly emerging domestic fashion scene. See *Vogue*'s articles: "The Cast," photographer Helena Christensen, October 1998, N 2, pp. 164–171; "USSR All-Stars," September 2003, pp. 140–146; "The Designers," September 2003, pp. 300–301; "Made in Russia: Russians Arrived," September 2004, pp. 106–110. Most of articles on Russian fashion designers were written by Olga Mikhailovskaya, who started with *Vogue* and eventually developed into an appreciated critic of the domestic fashion scene.

28. "Russian Century," photographer Egor Zaika, Russian *Vogue*, February 2005, pp. 257–267. The significant investment in the production of that fashion story demonstrated *Vogue*'s dedication to the cause of the budding Russian fashion industry. The designers covered in the story (except for Igor Chapurin) still struggled to maintain their production even on a small scale and were not regular *Vogue* advertisers.

29. Different notions of womanhood also appeared. The dramatic difference between the concepts of the austere and unadorned

Bolshevik woman and the over-decorated NEP woman demonstrated the huge schism within the Soviet social body throughout the 1920s. Within the Stalinist petit-bourgeoisification of society during the mid-1930s, the New Woman was transformed into a Superwoman, with femininity and other attributes of traditional womanhood added to the list of her duties.

30. Advice in the Soviet women's magazine *Working Woman* would usually underplay individuality, femininity, and sex appeal.

31. For an overview, see: Azhgikhina, N. & Goscilo, H. 1996: 94–121.

32. Lissyutkina argued that even men's small courtesies toward women, such as holding a door for her, helping her from a car or kissing her hand, were not perceived as retrograde and hypocritical by Russian women, but considered instead to be the precious recognition of a gender difference that had be denied to them for too long.

33. In 1989 the All-Union contest for the first Miss Russia was planned, without any irony, for the highly symbolic date of March 8, on which International Women Workers' Day and Mother's Day were both celebrated, demonstrating the high esteem in which beauty contests were held during Perestroika. The contest was finally delayed to May 1989, because of many organizational problems. For an overview of beauty contests during Perestroika, see Waters 1993.

34. Inhotel is the shortened version of the name for the hotel that exclusively hosted foreigners. See the media reports on prostitution in Waters 1989: 7–8. While accusing prostitution of alienation and labeling it as a serious social problem, these reports in the Perestroika newspapers nevertheless presented it as glamorous and exciting.

35. "In the matter of dress, the demimondaine's social and material existence required her to risk ridicule, to flaunt excess and to dare to impose the latest extravagance, in short, to introduce fashion … Their function was to exalt the prestige of their lovers by displaying spectacular finery, the emblems of their own success and the wages received for their keep," emphasized Philippe Perrot (1994: 168). Georg Simmel arrived at a similar conclusion: "The fact that the *demi-monde* is so frequently the pioneer of new fashion is due to its distinctively uprooted form of life" (Simmel 1997: 198).

36. "Beauty Queens," photographer Steve Hiett, Russian *Vogue*, June 2004, pp. 146–157.

37. Doletskaya stated that the concept of womanhood changed with the latest fashion trends, moving from the sexualized toward the romantic. She insisted that the role of *Vogue* was to open Russia to the beauty of life, by imprinting beauty on the souls and minds of its readers (Interview, March 24, 2005). Her attempt to connect the socialist concept of a beautiful soul with the reality of post-socialist poverty might be a strategic statement. In domestic interviews, Doletskaya is ritually asked about the context of *Vogue*'s luxury

within post-socialist poverty. Belonging to a genre of fashion magazines, *Vogue* can neither influence nor address these issues.

38. "Feet and Hands" (Beauty column), Russian *Vogue*, June 2004, p. 112.

39. Doletskaya defined the young, romantically dressed girl from Toscani's story as a metaphor for the Russian tomboy (Interview, March 24, 2005).

40. "The Power of Woman," photographer Helmut Newton, Russian *Vogue*, September 2003, pp. 330–339.

41. "What If This Is Love?" photographer Henrik Halvarsson, Russian *Vogue*, September 2003, pp. 372–385. This fashion story borrowed its plot and name from the 1961 Soviet film with the same title and scenario, which featured an unhappy love story between the young couple.

42. "Trapped by Temptation," photographer Oliviero Toscani, Russian *Vogue*, September 2003, pp. 316–329.

43. For an overview, see Hollander (1994).

44. In the late 1950s and early 1960s, when the back-to-femininity-campaign was at its fiercest stage, women could even be fined for wearing pants. Khrushchev's mouthpiece on women's issues, the weekly *Little Flame (Ogonek)*, also advocated that only slender, tall, and young women should wear pants, preferably at home (see especially *Ogonek*, March 4, 1962, N 10, p. 31). In his 1962 travel book *House Without a Roof: Russia After 43 Years of Revolution*, Marcel Hindus also reported that women struggled to wear pants and shorts but were prevented from doing so, except at home (London: Victor Gollancz, pp. 377–378). I am grateful to Olga Vainshtein for discussing with me everyday practices concerning the wearing of pants during socialism.

45. Maintaining the earlier concept of practicality, post-Soviet popular Russian magazines, such as *Lisa* and *Burda*, regularly published fashion images with women wearing pants (the paper patterns were attached in *Burda*). *Vogue* eventually approved pantsuits for businesswomen in a supplement dedicated to them ("Business," Russian *Vogue*, N 10, October 2001, pp. 176–186).

46. "A Brief Encounter," photography Pablo Alfaro, Russian *Vogue*, October, 2002, pp. 246–259. The model in story "Double Agent," which was dedicated to the avant-garde fashions, was also dressed in pants (Russian *Vogue*, September 2003, pp. 346–361).

47. "A Brief Encounter," Russian *Vogue*, N 10, October 2002, p. 246.

48. Roland Barthes observed: "When noted, the *boyish look* itself has more a temporal than a sexual value. It is the complementary sign of an ideal age, which assumes increasing importance in fashion literature … it tends toward androgyny; but what is more remarkable in this new term is that it effaces sex to the advantage of age (Barthes 1983: 257–258).

49. Grishena explained to the reporter that she never mixed the brands between themselves, always opting just for one at a time.
50. TsUM (The Central State Department Store) started as a Scottish-owned department store in the late 1800s under the name Muir and Merrilies. During socialism it was Moscow's second-largest department store, after the nearby GUM. TsUM's exciting post-socialist period started in 2002 after it was bought by the domestic luxury group Mercury. GUM was already owned by the other main Russian luxury retailer Bosco di Ciliegi, and so Mercury hired the ex-Selfridges maverick Vittorio Radice to turn TsUM into the most exciting shop in Moscow.
51. See also: Oushakine, S. (2000).
52. Dresses from the Eastern Bloc countries, such as Poland and Bulgaria and, especially, Yugoslavia and Czechoslovakia, were considered fashionable in comparison to Soviet clothes.
53. Compare with American and British editions of *Vogue*, which, in contrast, publish regular features on cheap chic, or even separate supplements dedicated to affordable clothes and accessories.
54. The Western and Russian media covered Gaultier's haute couture fashion show with great interest, especially because the Ukrainian first lady Kateryina Yushchenko was seated in the front row (see: Alexander, H. (2005) "Inspired Gaultier Creates a Fairytale from the Steppes," *The Daily Telegraph*, July 9, p. 15; Willard A. (2005) "Fashion Guru Inspired by Russia," *The Moscow Times*, July 15, p. 7. After Gaultier's haute couture presentation, the Paris, New York, and Milan 2005/06 ready-to-wear collections also chose Russian folk motifs as one of their key inspirations.

References

Azhgikhina, N. and H. Goscilo. 1996. "Getting Under Their Skin: The Beauty Salon in Russian Women's Lives", in H. Goscilo and B. Holmgren (eds), *Russia, Women Culture*, pp. 94–121. Bloomington: Indiana University Press.

Barthes, R. 1983. *The Fashion System*. Berkeley: University of California Press.

Bauman, Z. 1991. "Ideology and the Weltanschauung of the Intellectuals," in A. Kroker and M. Kroker (eds), *Ideology and Power in the Age of Lenin in Ruins*, pp. 107–120. New York: St. Martin's Press.

Binyon, M. 1998. "Fashion Victims," *The Times Magazine*, September 12, pp. 40–43.

Croft, C. 2004. "From Russia with Cash," *Style, The Sunday Times*, April 18, pp. 18–19.

Debord, G. 1995. *Society of the Spectacle*. New York: Zone Books.

Goldstein Crowe, L. 2005. "Moscow: Not Red and Not Square," *The Times*, June 23, 2005.

Einhorn, B. 1993. *Cinderella Goes to the Market: Citizenship, Gender and Women's Movements in East Central Europe*. London: Verso.

Hobsbawm, E. 1983. "Introduction: Inventing Traditions," in E. Hobsbawm and T. Ranger, *The Invention of Tradition*, pp. 1–14. London and Cambridge: Cambridge University Press.

Hollander, A. 1994. *Sex and Suits*. New York: Alfred A. Knopf.

Kunin, V. 1991. *Intergirl: A Hard Currency Prostitute*. New York: Bergh Publishing.

Lewin. M. 1995. *Russia/USSR/Russia: The Drive and Drift of a Superstate*. New York: New York Press.

Lipovetsky, G. 1994. *The Empire of Fashion*. Princeton: Princeton University Press.

Lissyutkina, L. 1993. "Soviet Women at the Crossroads of Perestroika," in N. Funk and M. Mueller (eds), *Gender Politics and Post-Communism: Reflections from Eastern Europe and the Former Soviet Union*, pp. 274–286. New York and London: Routledge.

Lissyutkina, L. 1992. "Lieber Hure als Feministin" (Rather a Prostitute Than a Feminist) in: *Deutsches Allgemeines Sonntagsblatt*, May 8.

Miller D. 1995. "Introduction: Anthropology, Modernity and Consumption," in *Worlds Apart*, pp. 1–22. London and New York: Routledge.

Oushakine, S. A. 2000. "The Quantity of Style: Imaginary Consumption in the New Russia," in *Theory, Culture & Society*, Vol. 17, N 5, pp. 97–120.

Perrot, P. [1984] 1994. *Fashioning the Bourgeoisie: A History of Clothing in the Nineteenth Century*. Princeton: Princeton University Press.

Singer, N. 1995. "The New Russian Dressing," American *Vogue*, October, pp. 348–355.

Simmel, G. 1997. "Fashion, Adornment and Style," in D. Frisby and M. Featherstone (eds). *Simmel on Culture*, pp. 187–217. London: Sage Publications.

Slobin, G. 1997. "Ona: The New Elle-Literacy and the Post-Soviet Woman," in G. Brinker-Gabler and S. Smith (eds), *Writing New Identities: Gender, Nation, and Immigration in Contemporary Europe*," pp. 337–357. Minneapolis: University of Minnesota Press

Sombart, W. 1967. *Luxury and Capitalism*. Ann Arbor: University of Michigan Press.

Stanley, A. 1997. "Democracy in Russia: Women's Lib is Just Cosmetic," *The New York Times*, May 11, 1997, p. 3.

Vinken, B. 2005. *Fashion Zeitgeist*. Oxford and New York: Berg.

Waters, E. 1993. "Soviet Beauty Contests," in I. Kon and J. Riordan (eds), *Sex and Russian Society*, pp. 116–134. London: Pluto Press.

Waters, E. 1989. "Restructuring the "Woman Question: Perestroika and Prostitution," *Feminist Review*, No. 33: 3–19.

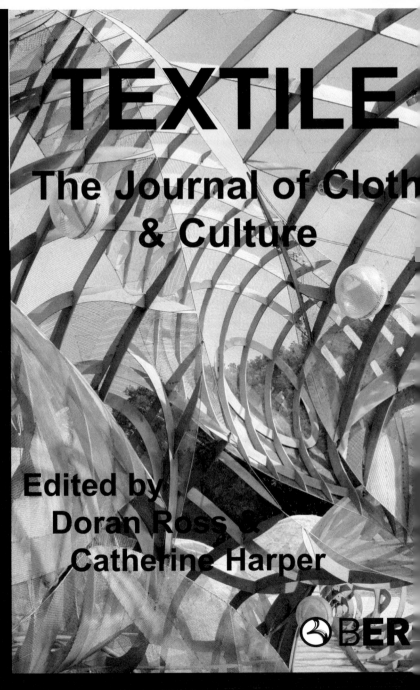

2005
ALPSP/ Charlesworth
AWARDS

ALPSP
WINNER

Winner of the 2005 ALPSP/ Charlesworth Award for Best New Journal

'Accessible, with diverse contribu- tions in a readable format ... Textile shows that wider cultural interest in 'the crafts' comes when we dare to move beyond the narrow concerns of tradition and technique.' **Crafts**

TEXTILE

The Journal of Cloth & Culture

Edited by
Doran Ross &
Catherine Harper

BER

Fashion Theory, Volume 10, Issue 1/2, pp. 205–224
Reprints available directly from the Publishers.
Photocopying permitted by licence only.

Glossy Words: An Analysis of Fashion Writing in British *Vogue*

Anna König

Anna König is a lecturer in cultural studies at the London College of Fashion. She writes for *The Times* and contributed to the anthology *Reading Sex and the City* (I. B. Tauris, 2004). Research interests include representations of fashion through text and patterns of consumption—including ethical consumption—within the fashion industry.
a.konig@fashion.arts.ac.uk

Introduction

Within international fashion publishing, no title resonates with authority and history the way that *Vogue* does. Although *Vogue* can now, quite rightly, be considered a global fashion phenomenon, the focus here is on British *Vogue*, a magazine launched in the fall of 1916 (Harvey 1991: 17) that firmly belongs to a tradition which links fashion with status, class, and wealth. Given the magazine's long and illustrious history, it is astonishing that the lexical peculiarities of "Voguespeak" (Steele 1997: 245) have attracted little more than fleeting glances from interested parties within academe (Borelli 1997).

To analyze and comment on the text of *Vogue* throughout its entire existence would be an extensive project well beyond the scope of a single research paper. The aim here, therefore, is to identify the most distinctive or enduring elements of fashion text appearing in *Vogue* for a specific period of time, namely, 1980–2001. Such a selective focus makes close analysis of content, tone, lexicon, and cultural references possible, leading to the identification of patterns of continuity and change in the text for the time period sampled. Having established the parameters of this lexical territory, it becomes possible to contextualize findings within a framework of existing work in this area, and to discuss broader cultural issues pertaining to the language of fashion and textual constructions of the fashion world.[1]

Fashion Writing: Uncharted Territory

The establishment of cultural studies as an area of legitimate academic investigation had a huge impact on the study of women's popular culture.[2] For the first time, women's magazines became the focus of critical examination, prompting evaluations and interpretations, not merely of their manifest content, but of their mediating roles in the cultural lives of women. While fashion is only one of many topics covered by women's magazines, the literature on this subject provides some clues as to how fashion writing came to be so undervalued, in both consumer and academic circles.

Historically, women's magazines and the subjects therein belong to a private realm of femininity, a world that is full of opinion and views, yet a world that only ever talks to itself. For some feminists, the very notion of a publication aimed specifically at women is problematic because "The medium is still a message in itself and that message continues to be that women are uniquely different, they require separate treatment and instruction in ways that men do not" (Ferguson 1983: 190). Paradoxically, this stance reduces women's magazines to a lowly status by failing to recognize the role of readers as participants in the whole process: they become little more than subscribers to the "cult of femininity" (Ferguson 1983: 184). If some feminists have found this kind of writing to be without value, it is hardly surprising that within a broader cultural context this kind of writing has been given little recognition, for "Aesthetic products have traditionally been … diminished in value if their audience or consumers were thought to be women" (Wilson 1992: 5).

However, other academics have been more sympathetic to women's magazines as a genre, acknowledging that the readership plays an active role in the consumption of this cultural product. In her exploration of women's magazines, Janice Winship hypothesizes, "How much more lonely and difficult life would be for many women without the support of magazines" (Winship 1987: 80). More recently, Joke Hermes has reflected on the role of the academic in assigning or denying cultural validation to particular forms of media, indicating that: "It needs to be accepted that readers of all kinds (including we critics) enjoy texts in some contexts that we are critical of in other contexts" (Hermes 1995: 2). Fashion writing is a perfect example of such a text, tied to the "trivial" world of womanly things, yet still consumed on a daily basis, sometimes guiltily, by millions of readers, male and female. It is possible that the feelings of ambivalence generated by these "guilty" texts have contributed to the lowly status of fashion journalism, in the eyes of readers and academics alike, for it is far easier to dismiss ambivalence than to explore its complexities.

Magazine Text

Appearance and image are the driving forces within the fashion system, so one might be forgiven for believing that fashion is nothing more than a visual phenomenon. Yet while visuals, primarily in the form of photographs, dominate the presentation and representation of fashion in magazines and newspapers, text has a critical mediating role to play. Of the many consumer magazines currently on offer in the UK, very few present fashion without using text to accompany images.[3] The ongoing use of fashion writing, despite huge technological advances in photographic reproduction and print techniques, suggests that fashion text is more than "just filler."[4] Text contributes to an understanding of fashion by assigning descriptive or interpretive meanings to the objects and images presented on fashion pages, thereby mediating a cultural understanding of the phenomenon. Given that text has such a pivotal interpretive role within the fashion system, it is curious that to a large extent it has been ignored, even by fashion academics.

Instead, there has been a focus on the "language of clothing," that is, the semiotic interpretation of actual items of clothing, an approach found in the work of Dick Hebdige (1987) and Alison Lurie (1981). Even when academic texts such as Paul Jobling's (1999) *Fashion Spreads* look at print representations of fashion, the focus is on images. The implication is that there is nothing of interest to be said about written fashion, particularly within the "throwaway" print media of magazines and newspapers

The most notable text that does address the linguistic peculiarities and conventions of fashion writing is the work of Roland Barthes. First published in 1967, *The Fashion System* deconstructs what he calls the "written garment" (by which he means the text that appears alongside fashion images in French magazines such as *Elle* and *Le Jardin des Modes*), formulating a system to explain the linguistic conventions that appear to govern such writing.

According to Barthes, the language of written fashion is inextricably bound to the feminine world. His study suggests that fashion writing is different from other forms of journalistic or creative writing, that it performs specific functions and that it obeys its own linguistic rules and conventions. No one before or since has examined the writing of fashion magazines in such close detail.

More recently, Angela McRobbie (1998) has evaluated fashion writing in the context of a much wider economic system, one that sustains the production and consumption of fashion through the fashion media. She argues that the economic systems regulating the production and consumption of fashion prevent fashion writing from being little more than effusive babble, and concludes that:

> Fashion writing is informative or celebratory, it is never critical, only mildly ironical … The editors and journalists rarely break ranks and produce more engaged and challenging writing on this subject (McRobbie 1998: 173).

Her assessment is a harsh indictment of the fashion industry in general and fashion journalism in particular.

Agnès Rocamora's (2001) study of fashion writing in *Le Monde* and *The Guardian* finds that: "In both newspapers a field of fashion is constructed that is articulated around different beliefs: the belief in fashion as popular culture in *The Guardian* and the belief in fashion as high culture in *Le Monde* (Rocamora, 2001: 124). Meanwhile, Laird Borelli's (1997) study of the writing in American *Vogue* between 1968 and 1993 attributes the style and tone of fashion text to the different personalities of consecutive *Vogue* editors and Leslie Rabine (1994) focuses on how changing attitudes to the readership are reflected, and finds that magazines from the latter part of the sample "invite the reader to be more self-reflexive about her relation to fashion' (Rabine 1994: 59).

Although most of the relevant literature focuses on women's magazines, in recent years this body of work has been supplemented and greatly enhanced by a number of texts that address men's magazines. Foundations laid by Frank Mort (1996) and Sean Nixon (1996) in their discussion of masculinities and consumption have enabled Ben Crewe (2003) to make a detailed analysis of the men's magazine market. Yet even here the focus is on the politics of publishing and editors' personalities, rather than the contents of magazines.

This study challenges some of the assertions of Barthes, McRobbie, and Rocamora by questioning the notion of fashion writing as a fixed form of textual representation. More importantly, it sets out to explore the forces and processes that shape the conventions of fashion writing, if indeed such conventions exist.

Unpicking Vogue

Constructing a Methodology

The lack of research into fashion writing means that methodology is not straightforward, but it is possible to draw on the most successful elements of previous work. Close attention to authentic text, combined with an attempt to place it within a broader cultural context, necessitates looking beyond fashion-specific work to the subject of mass, communication research.

Content analysis is the approach that has dominated research into mass media. Traditionally, when used by Berelson, "one of the fathers of content analysis" (Smith et al. 1975: 14) or, more recently, by members of the Glasgow Media Group,[5] it is a strictly quantitative method involving the counting of column inches devoted to specific subjects or the recording of the frequency of key words. While this approach aims to be methodologically rigorous and objective, it can be problematic, not least because "it produces results whose relation to the actual media experience of producers and audiences is unclear" (van Zoonen 1994: 73).

For a study such as this, the value of counting column inches or the frequency of certain words is debatable: one is left with arbitrary numbers. Furthermore, fashion reportage is a very specific form of journalism and has more in common with feature writing than news journalism. The expansive, often literary style of feature writing suggests it would be more productive to look toward literary criticism for a methodology. Yet an approach designed for critiquing a lengthy novel is unlikely to be entirely successful when applied to a two-hundred-word magazine article.

In light of these issues, a methodological compromise has been reached, and the approach taken here is akin to that advocated by Virginia Berridge in her work on nineteenth-century journals and readership attitudes reflected therein (1986). With specific reference to newspapers, she argues that:

> The paper ... presents a particular form of reality to its readership, albeit they make sense of it, or "decode" it, in different ways. The "world view" of readers is both reflected and reinforced by newspaper content (Berridge 1986: 207).

In recognizing the importance of the relationship between publication and readership perceptions, her view is similar to that of Rocamora (2001) in her work, discussed earlier, and to that of Smith et al. (1975) in their comparative analysis of two popular newspapers over a period of thirty years. The benefits of utilizing a more literary approach as opposed to conventional content analysis are thus outlined:

> Literary-critical, linguistic and stylistic methods of analysis are ... more useful in penetrating the latent meanings of a text, and they preserve something of the complexity of language and connotation which has to be sacrificed in content analysis in order to achieve high validation (Smith et al. 1975: 15).

They argue that although reoccurrences of words or phrases are not necessarily quantified, "The analyst learns to 'hear' the same underlying appeals, the same 'notes,'" being sounded again and again in different passages and contexts (Smith et al. 1975: 15).

Yet some form of categorization was necessary in order to deal with the sheer volume of text being analyzed, and so four categories were used to create a framework for the process of analysis: content, tone, lexicon, and cultural references. "Content" is self-explanatory, but it is probably worth saying more about the other three terms. I have borrowed Smith et al.'s explanation of "tone": "A rich and complex mode of linguistic registration. It indicates to the reader an evaluative 'set,' or stance, towards a certain topic" (Smith et al. 1975: 23). The category "lexicon," meanwhile, encompasses not only specific uses of vocabulary and terminology, but also phraseology. This means that there is some overlap between "tone" and "lexicon," but the categories are intended as guiding parameters rather than strict definitional terms. The final grouping, that of "cultural references," aims to capture aspects of the text outside the central subject matter of the article. This has been included in order to highlight the assumptions made by the publication about the wider cultural knowledge of the readership.

The time period chosen—twenty-one years, divided into three-year intervals[6]—was felt to be sufficiently long to tease out the idiosyncrasies and subtle nuances of the publication without making the study unwieldy.

Content

This sample indicates an increase in the volume of fashion text in *Vogue* since 1980. In the early 1980s, fashion text predominantly took the form of verbose captions that accompanied multi-page photo shoots. An average of four fashion-shoot stories per edition was accompanied by the occasional longer article, product profile, or designer interview ("Gloria Vanderbilt," British *Vogue*, June 1980: 126). By comparison, later editions contain more text relating to the catwalk origins of specific high street trends, reflecting a desire to explain rather than present fashion (Holgate, British *Vogue*, March 1998: 229, 223; MacLeod, British *Vogue*, March 1998: 231; Picardie British *Vogue*, March 2001: 127–130).

International show reports, including the Paris and Milan couture shows ("Paris Pleasures," British Vogue, March 1986: 255; Mower, British *Vogue*, April 1989: 33; Quick, British *Vogue*, October 2001: 249), are a perennial inclusion, and given the magazine's elitist history, it is hardly surprising that the exclusive fashions of the couture shows are given prominence. Long lead times in the production of a monthly magazines mean that *Vogue* is unable to produce reports with a sense of immediacy in the way that a daily, or even a weekly, publication can, so instead it gives a digested interpretation of shows, such as fashion shoots based upon a particular collection ("Paris Pleasures," British *Vogue*, March 1986: 255). Another strategy is to generate a sense of the catwalk atmosphere by featuring a behind-the-scenes photo shoot from the previous season's collections, thus keeping readers attuned to the rhythms of the fashion year (Bartley, British *Vogue*, March 2001: 141–144).

Interviews with designers are a recurrent feature and they follow a format: a description of training and work history followed by a look at recent work. As interviewees aim for maximum impact, the language becomes elevated, illustrated by the following excerpt from an interview with Isaac Mizrahi: "'It's such a modern, like, archery look ... oooh, I'm going outta my mind! How about you?'" (Mower, British *Vogue*, September 1989: 316). Similarly, Alberta Ferretti exclaims that "Night is the only time a woman can be a woman" (Mower, British *Vogue*, June 1992: 86). Reported speech adds a sense of immediacy, but this often impacts on the tone and lexicon.

Articles on fashion history and related exhibitions were found across the sample, but have changed qualitatively from lengthy, scholarly explorations of subjects such as costume conservation ("Costume Conservation," British *Vogue*, April 1983: 130–133), to brief paragraphs commenting on how it is fashionable to visit fashion exhibitions ("Sole Searching," British *Vogue*, March 1998: 49). This is an interesting example of a shift in the magazine's focus from actual fashion garments to less tangible notions of the perception of fashionability.

"Men in *Vogue*" makes an appearance in two of the earliest issues included in the sample (Crome, 06/80, p.165-194; British *Vogue*, June 1980: 165–194; Gimlette, British *Vogue*, March 1986: 365–403). Yet there is no evidence of a similar section in later issues, a finding that can be attributed to the growth of men's style magazines throughout the 1980s (Jobling 1999: 49; Crewe: 2003), which removed the imperative to append men's fashion to that of women's in order to obtain editorial exposure.

"Insider" aspects of the fashion industry are a distinctive development in the content of *Vogue*. Articles or whole sections focus specifically on subjects such as backstage activities prior to catwalk shows ("Backstage Countdown," British *Vogue*, March 2001: 199–200), the phenomenon of Trunk shows (Armstrong, British *Vogue*, August 1995: 116–119), and fashion adages entitled "Overheard in the Changing Room" (British *Vogue*, March 1998: 210). Items like these are significant in terms of shaping readers' perceptions of the fashion world, a subject discussed in more detail later in this article.

Tone

Vogue frequently strikes the tone of the informed voice of authority imparting wisdom. Examples include: "Lessons for fashionable beginners in how to be a sophisticated *ingénue*" ("More Dash Than Cash," British *Vogue*, March 1986: 192) and "The message from the collections is clear: fussy is out, simple is in" ("The New Chic," British *Vogue*, August 1995: 78). The implication is that fashion may be difficult for readers to comprehend, but that *Vogue* can be trusted to help them master the "rules": "Easy steps to a complete outfit" ("Great Good Buys," British *Vogue*, August 1995: 138); "The key to wearing this look is to keep it streamlined" (Holgate, British *Vogue*, March 1998: 233); "The New Rules of Short" (British *Vogue*, October 2001: 330). The use of the imperative also gives weight to this authoritative voice, as well as creating a sense of urgency: "Grab a fur" (Reinhardt, British *Vogue*, October 1983: 274); "Snap these up now" ("Snip: Economy Class," British *Vogue*, October 2001: 269). In recent years, the expression "Forget X and think Y" has become a frequently occurring imperative, exemplified by "Forget grunge and think precious pieces" ("Earth Girls," British *Vogue*, December 1998: 192).

From the late 1980s to the mid-1990s, there is a noticeable tendency for *Vogue* to reflect the disparity between the high fashion of the catwalk and the everyday wardrobe of its readers: "The true test of fashion is in the wearing—how will it suit the living woman?" ("*Vogue*'s-Eye View," British *Vogue*, April 1989: 163); "But for normal women operating without the help of dressers" (Spencer, British *Vogue*, January 1995); "The Nineties passion for simplification means women want more mileage from their clothes" (Armstrong, British *Vogue*, August 1995: 118). This relatively sombre tone reflects, perhaps, some of the economic concerns facing the British population at this time.[7]

The notion of fashion as a source of pleasure for women emerges in the text right across the sample: "A woman can revel in revealing lissom limbs without compromising herself or her position" (Mower, British *Vogue*, September 1989: 271); "I discovered that wearing leather and a short hemline can be a complete power trip" (Cosgrave, British *Vogue*, March 2001: 162). One photo shoot is accompanied by the caption: "Her man's fled. She faces dinner alone. But what the hell—with silk and cashmere to hand, life's not all bad." ("Single White Female," British *Vogue*, January 1995: 68), reflecting an alternative view of relationships to that which is usually expressed in women's magazines.[8]

The growing tendency for writers to make slightly mocking, ironic comments about the "fashion world" and its inhabitants is an interesting development: "The New York fashion set, martyrs to overexcitement" (Mower, British *Vogue*, September 1989: 316); "Fashion editors are a reckless breed when it comes to practicalities" (Armstrong, British *Vogue*, January 1995: 121). In recent years, irony has been used so liberally that it can recognized as a significant indicator of shifting attitudes toward fashion.

Lexicon

One linguistic style that disappeared from *Vogue* between 1980 and 2001 is what I describe as the "word salad."[9] Used in captions, this style of writing is typified by an unconventional use of syntax: "White cotton bloomers that blossom vastly from waist to knee, Saint-Laurent's these" ("*Vogue*'s-Eye View of Golden Opportunities," British *Vogue*, May 1980: 103); "Current pleasures too: the irresistible wit of reinvention" ("Paris Pleasures," British *Vogue*, March 1986: 255); "Extreme shape, pert hat, a bow and a breast of precious medals" ("Evenings – What More Can One Add?" British *Vogue*, October 1983: 236). Definite and indefinite articles are omitted, and at other times sentences have no verbs, factors which combine to generate the sense of a mythic rather than a real garment. The words become hypersensual representations of the garments they describe: "Cream of cotton knit" ("*Vogue*'s-Eye View of Golden Opportunities," British *Vogue*, May 1980: 103); "Crepuscular fox muffs" ("Evenings – What More Can One Add?" British *Vogue*, October 1983: 238); "Crumpled butterfly wings of twisted sleeve" ("Shapeliners Nouveau," British *Vogue*, March 1986: 286). It is intriguing that this use of syntax vanished completely by the late 1980s; as the content of *Vogue* started to focus on "real women," so the language became more straightforward.

Assuming that the *raison d'être* of fashion magazines is to showcase new styles, it comes as no surprise that words relating to newness are a perpetual feature of the *Vogue* lexicon: "fresh," "modern" and "contemporary" are used to emphasize the novelty and therefore the desirability of styles. However, notions of the "new" are often tempered with the word "classic," a lexical device which simultaneously encourages and reassures the reader: "New Generation Classics" (British *Vogue*, March 1986: 400); "A contemporary spin on ... historical allusions" (Armstrong, British *Vogue*, September 1992: 188); "Now that classics are back in fashion" (Sykes, British *Vogue*, August 1995: 16). In this way, the cycles of fashion are alluded to without the writer explicitly stating that the design idea is an old one. Similarly, expressions such as "prettiness meets city tough" ("More Dash Than Cash," British *Vogue*, June 1992: 94) or "a judicious mix of the sophisticated and the laid-back" ("Take It Away," British *Vogue*, August 1995: 108) meld together two familiar ideas to create the impression of something entirely new.

Fashion-specific and textile terminology decreases markedly across the sample. In the 1980s, the construction of garments was highlighted: "The gentle curve of a lightly frilled rever" ("Summer Life Silles," British *Vogue*, May 1980: 118), a "black spencer"[10] ("Black and White Newsnight," British *Vogue*, April 1983: 139) and "sharpened peplums" ("Paris Pleasures," British *Vogue*, March 1986: 255). Similarly, fabrics and even the finishes on them were specified: "navy wool barathea" [a fine woollen cloth] ("Modern Britain: Active Style," British *Vogue*, August 1986: 178); "slubbed silk, nubbly linen" (Mower, British *Vogue*, April 1989: 33); "flowered silk cloque" ("On the Scent of Summer

Nights," British *Vogue*, June 1980: 96). But by the 1990s, this lexical set had disappeared, reflecting a shift in emphasis from what garments are composed of to how they look.

A distinctive feature of the *Vogue* lexicon in recent years has been the hyphenated adjective. Whereas writing in the earlier half of the sample often had a smooth, dreamlike quality, in later years the prose takes on a decidedly choppy, syncopated rhythm, attributable, at least in part, to the increasing use of adjectival hyphenation. In the late 1980s, there was occasional use of phrases such as "high-performance womanhood" (*"Vogue*'s-Eye View," British *Vogue*, September 1989: 281), but this reaches a peak in 2001, with references to "roll-in-a-bag, temperature-sensitive wardrobes" (Muir, British *Vogue*, October 2001: 60) and "hot-pants-and-boob-tube stage outfits" (Quick, British *Vogue*, March 2001: 76). The reader is left mentally gasping for breath, dizzy with the excitement of all the *stuff* that is being described, although one is often left unsure of what the garment might look like. This lexical trend engenders a sense of fun, pleasure, and spontaneity, qualities that editors possibly see as central to current readership perceptions of fashion.

The changing usage of non-English vocabulary is also noteworthy. Whereas earlier editions use French words to indicate fabric types such as "crêpe de Chine" ("Black and White Newsnight," British *Vogue*, April 1983: 137) or specific garments like "maillot" (*"Vogue*'s-Eye View," British *Vogue*, August 1986), later editions use French words for ironic effect rather than meaning. Thus there are instances of *"mère"* and *"moue"* being used arbitrarily (Mower, British *Vogue*, September 1989: 316) and *"Il faut souffrir pour etre belle"* (Spencer, British *Vogue*, January 1995: 55) being inserted into the text in a somewhat gratuitous manner. Used in this way, the words subtly remind readers of fashion's Parisian roots while mocking that same tradition. This use of language might also be seen as a deliberate educational assertion on the part of the writer, an active response to the "brainlessness" so often attributed to fashion.

Cultural references

Vogue draws on figures from literary and artistic circles, indicating an expectation that the readership has a knowledge of, and interest in, such subjects. This manifests itself in various ways, with articles about surrealist influences on fashion ("Dressing for Dinner," British *Vogue*, September 1989: 276) and the impact of Russian constructivism and literature on design ("Tsars in their Eyes," British *Vogue*, October 2001: 33). Thus, *Vogue* can be seen to aspire to "high culture" rather than "popular culture," which, according to Rocamora (2001), follows the French as opposed to the English model of fashion journalism.

Similarly, *Vogue* expects its readers to have a comprehensive knowledge of contemporary and historical figures within the fashion world. Models are often referred to on a first name basis, as if there could only possibly be one "Gisele" or "Erin" ("Backstage Countdown," British *Vogue*, March 2001: 200). More traditional fashion figures are also mentioned, with references to "the Daisy Fellowes maxim" ("Gloria Vanderbilt," British *Vogue*, June 1980: 127), Veruschka ("Circus," British *Vogue*, September 1989: 282) and Loulou de la Falaise (Sykes, British *Vogue*, August 1995: 19). By referring to individuals such as these, *Vogue* reasserts its image as a traditional and well-established magazine whose primary focus has always been fashion.

In recent years, however, there has been a decline in fashion-specific references, with writers focusing instead on celebrities. Thus actors such as Julia Roberts (Sykes, British *Vogue*, January 1995: 53), Patsy Kensit (MacLeod, British *Vogue*, December 1998: 161) and Sarah Jessica Parker (O'Donnell, British *Vogue*, March 2001: 182) are all given a namecheck, often in conjunction with specific designer labels (O'Donnell, British *Vogue*, March 2001: 179). This trend not only underlines a shift from "high culture" to "popular culture" as the frame of reference, but also hints at the nature of the relationship between the content of editorial copy and issues around advertising revenue.

The Changing Language of Fashion

The writing in *Vogue* changed dramatically over the time period examined, and the May 1980 edition reads very differently from the October 2001 issue. As indicated, this is reflected in the decreasing use of rarefied or technical language, the marked increase in celebrity referencing and irony, and the overall increase in volume of fashion text, with a discernible shift toward a larger number of shorter articles. This suggests that the fashion writing in *Vogue* is not as fixed a form of expression as has been argued by Barthes (1990) and McRobbie (1998). While certain elements, such as the use of imperative language and hyperbole have continued, the frames of reference and vocabulary used to express this have undergone numerous changes, as outlined in the previous section.

The urgent, emphatic, and overblown language that Barthes (1990) and McRobbie (1998) describe is still a dominant force in the fashion text of *Vogue*, but vocabulary and references have changed radically, even since the early 1980s. The rarefied, lyrical unreality of the "word salad" has been replaced by a much brisker style of writing, but the imperatives linger on. Barthes regarded the use of emphatic language as an acknowledgment of "the arbitrariness of its decisions," the textual equivalent, perhaps, of overstating one's case (Barthes 1990: 270). Yet while expressing a theoretical explanation for the phenomenon, he fails to address the reasons why individual writers should persistently be compelled to express fashion in such a uniform manner, an issue that requires some consideration.

The catwalk show has made a substantial contribution to the distinct-ive features of fashion language. Typically, journalists see each outfit for a matter of seconds, yet their remit is to "capture" the essence of the garment and translate it into copy that will engage the reader. Newspaper journalists are expected to file reports within hours, and though writers for monthly and weekly publications have more time to hone their text, there is still a pressure to present it as "news." This leads to a style of writing that is more akin to linguistic note-taking than conventional prose: rich in hyperbole, but lacking detail as the emphasis is on impact, rather than transferral of information. Catwalk shows only account for a small proportion of fashion features, but they are given a privileged status and are, therefore, the most influential articles in any fashion publication.

Quoted speech has also had an impact on the prose of fashion features, particularly with regard to setting tone and lexicon. Stock phrases such as: "Think: X" or "It's X meets Y" appear frequently, expressing visual ideas in a very condensed linguistic form, yet they dominate the text. As Braham notes in his discussion of the fashion system: "In all this the opinions of the designers themselves are made to occupy a pivotal posi-tion: their pronouncements ... are often greeted with the sort of respect usually accorded to international statesmen" (Braham 1997: 132). The pressured and frenetic nature of the fashion industry means that designers, buyers, and retailers do not have the time, nor the skills, to contemplate linguistic subtleties. Their primary concern is to attract the attention of readers (and potential customers), and this manifests itself in excited exclamations and florid declarations. Given the increased volume of fashion text in recent years, the cumulative effect is that the same lexical set appears repeatedly, exacerbating fashion writing's reputation for cliché and hyperbole. Of course, such criticisms could similarly be made of the myopic and often self-important language of other creative discourses, such as art or architecture, so perhaps this is yet another manifestation of a general societal belief that fashion is not a legitimate form of cultural expression.

The use of irony may be indicative of an uneasy relationship between fashion writers and their subject. On the one hand there is a realization that a particular look or trend is not actually "important" in any real sense and that fashion is widely regarded as trivial, even in comparison to other cultural entities such as popular music. Yet on the other hand, fashion writers have a role within the industry and that is to produce copy that is appropriate to the readership demands of the publication they work for. By incorporating ironic statements about fashion into their text, writers avoid the pitfalls of looking sycophantic whilst neatly sidestepping the job-threatening issue of being openly critical of the fashion system. The growing dependence on irony may also be a reflection of writers' awareness that they are presenting a simulacrum of the fashion world: they don't believe in it, so why should the readers?

Similarly, the attribution of qualities such as "wit" or "intelligence" to clothing may also be due to writers' discomfort with the seemingly frivolous nature of fashion. An item labeled "witty," has more cultural substance than a mere garment and the implication is that these qualities will be transferred to the wearer. Thus, the skirt and its wearer fleetingly become "witty," in a postmodern transference of essentiality (Wilson 1992: 6). Perhaps, by association, the writer may also hope to gain such attributes in the eyes of the readership, thus liberating them from the yoke of fashion's longstanding reputation for narcissistic vacuity.

The decreasing use of technical fashion and textile terminology is indicative of a number of changes occurring elsewhere in the fashion system. Whereas in the past many readers would have had a working knowledge of the language of garment construction—most likely based on personal experience of home sewing—it is meaningless to the average reader of today. This reflects a decline in the skills associated with the production of clothing, whether in a domestic or a commercial setting.

To some it might seem risible to consider the notion of "dumbing down" in relation to fashion, for it is not a subject that has ever garnered much respect among the general population. Yet this analysis indicates that from the mid-1980s to the early 1990s, publications like *Vogue* did publish more scholarly or "high cultural" pieces, often commissioning non-staff writers with specialist fashion knowledge (Rocamora 2001). However in recent years, when socio-historical factors are mentioned, this is done in a simplistic, perfunctory manner, with a tendency toward populist ideas rather than scholarly ones.

Whereas even twenty years ago there was a degree of variation in the content, language, and tone of *Vogue*, it has become today remarkably homogenous. This can in part be attributed to operational factors within publishing houses: it is expensive and time-consuming to commission freelance contributors when in-house ones are already being paid. More importantly, fashion editors are unlikely to risk alienating advertisers by printing features that are even slightly critical of any aspect of the fashion industry, as this could jeopardize precious advertising revenue.

In recent years, many of the traditional feature-based women's magazines have been losing readers to newer publications whose focus is celebrity gossip. This suggests that readers, and subsequently editors, are turning away from in-depth fashion writing, preferring instead the "snippet" style of journalism that now dominates. A Mintel report dating from October 2000 found "a small but significant decline for all women's magazines, except celebrity weeklies, since 1998" (Mintel Executive Summary, October 2000). Magazine editors, including Alexandra Shulman at *Vogue,* would have been aware of reports such as these and are likely to have altered the content and tone of the publication in order to capitalize on readership preferences and therefore stabilize magazine sales. Thus the increasing use of short, image-driven pieces is unsurprising, as articles of this nature form the core content of the celebrity magazines that have captured such a large share of the women's magazine market.

Cultural Constructions of "The Fashion World"

It has been argued that the notion of a single cultural entity entitled the "fashion world" is erroneous, rather there are a number of very different worlds, each one of which has a very different role within the fashion industry (Braham 1997). Through the close analysis of text in this study, it has been possible to identify some of these disparate elements. Moreover, this process has demonstrated how language can be used to maintain, obfuscate or indeed fabricate these worlds.

The most easily recognizable of these is "the world of high fashion inhabited by designers and store buyers alike" (Braham 1997: 126). This is the one that is referred to frequently on the pages of *Vogue*. Although often referred to in a slightly ironic tone, this "place" (for its actual location is unclear) is presented as the natural home of fashion, even though it is exclusive and difficult to gain access to. The inhabitants of this world speak rapidly and emphatically, using the exaggerated language highlighted earlier in this paper. The fashion writer, meanwhile, is granted limited access and provides readers with insights, his (or, more usually, her) authority enhanced by sheer proximity to this fashionable never-never land. The presentation of "insider" items on fashion pages perpetuates the idea that it is a desirable, though inaccessible realm, marshaled, no doubt by the fictitious "fashion police." The boundaries of this consociation are defined by slippery notions of fashionability, rather than actual clothing, making membership all the more elusive.

But how real is this world? Although it may be true that senior writers and editors are participants in the glamorous fashion world portrayed on the pages of their publications, junior staff and freelance fashion writers often lead a very different existence. The hierarchy that exists within fashion journalism is something that, as is the case with many other professions, is opaque to all but those directly involved. While the identities of a few high-profile fashion editors may be known to publications' readerships, there is a surprising degree of anonymity in fashion journalism. This may be due to a perceived need to prioritize publication identity and consistency of product over individual voice. Alternatively, it may reflect the rate of staff turnover at fashion publications, or the widespread use of freelance contributors and interns.

A separate, but more practical fashion world is constructed around, and for the benefit of, the readership. This is where the ideas of "real women" are presented and where their diverse body shapes and varying economic circumstances are most likely to be acknowledged. Whereas

Rabine optimistically found a "new self-reflexivity" (Rabine 1994: 61) in her study of fashion magazines, there was little evidence of an equivalent development in the fashion text examined in this study. There may have been a phase during the late 1980s and early 1990s, the time period covered by Rabine's work, when more critical, reflective views of fashion were expressed in British publications. But in recent years, in *Vogue* at least, reflexivity has been replaced by irony and postfeminist rhetoric.

The fashion world least well represented in *Vogue* is the one concerned with production, a significant omission given that "as well as being a matter of creation, consumption and identity, [fashion] is also a matter of production, distribution and retailing" (Braham 1997: 121). This disinclination to deal with the production process leads to an impression that garments simply appear from nowhere, ready to be consumed. *Vogue* relies heavily on the goodwill, and more importantly, the hard cash, of advertisers who are unlikely to be delighted at seeing their products alongside articles on sweatshops or issues around free trade.

Of course, the same can be said of any consumer commodity, so why should fashion be expected to demonstrate a transparency that no other industry shows? One might argue that this is yet another demonstration of the ongoing tendency for fashion to be criticized for its triviality and preoccupation with the self. But this is a hollow defence. In recent years there has been a growing consumer interest in issues around the production of sportswear (Klein 2000: 365), so who is to say that other sectors of the fashion industry will remain immune from such scrutiny? In November 2002, for example, *The Evening Standard* ran a report on "sweatshops" in London that supply the successful high street chain Topshop, although it did not appear on the fashion pages (Fletcher, 19/11/02, www.thisislondon.co.uk).

Conclusions

Within the last twenty years a multitude of styles, lexicons, and cultural references have been utilized in *Vogue* to explain, promote, and at times, criticize the entity which we call fashion. So written fashion has shown itself to be less rigid and predictable than has previously been suggested by scholars of the subject, such as Barthes. The language of fashion journalism—exemplified by *Vogue*—might best be regarded as multidimensional, with a range of different qualities and conventions utilized at different times and in different contexts.

Yet over the past twenty years there has been a definite shift toward less critical and more homogenous fashion writing, confirming McRobbie's bleak outlook that we should not expect too much of fashion journalism. In many respects, this change mirrors changes in the fashion system itself. Postmodernity may appear to offer multiplicity, yet often it delivers little more than multihued variations on a theme and the high street ends up being full of stores offering very similar wares.

As the Mintel report cited earlier suggests: "Magazines must not only continually rejuvenate and refresh their content and style to maintain readership, but also address these issues in order to move forward" (Mintel Executive Summary; ibid.). The findings of this study suggest that over the years, *Vogue* has tried to move on from its traditional and somewhat elitist roots and yet one cannot help wondering if this has, at times, been at the expense of an assured and recognizable identity.

As the respective fates of publishers and retailers become increasingly intertwined due to commercial pressures, perhaps it is inevitable that variations in content, tone, lexicon, and cultural references will be gently erased, leaving a product with copy as flawless as a cover girl's skin. Fashion magazines such as *Vogue* may not be world-changing documents, but they do have a role in everyday cultural life. Given that words mediate our understanding of fashion, the subject's scope could well be impoverished by a lack of linguistic variety. If fashion is truly a vehicle for fantasy, pleasure, and self-expression, should that not be reflected in the language used to discuss it? With the "crumpled butterfly wings of twisted sleeve" ("Shapeliness Nouveau," British *Vogue*, March 1986: 286) comes the possibility of flight.

Notes

1. This study has been adapted from research carried out for my Master's degree in which the fashion writing in three publications was analyzed: *Vogue*, *The Guardian*, and *Draper's Record*.
2. Established in 1964, The Centre for Contemporary Cultural Studies at Birmingham University has been a particularly influential institution (Turner 1996).
3. One exception is the magazine *Rank*, which even lists credits in a separate insert, thus maintaining "pure" images, uncluttered by text of any kind.
4. According to Laura Craik, Fashion Editor at London's *Evening Standard*, "We know that fashion isn't real news, unless a company buys one of its rivals. Every newsdesk knows that it isn't news, it's just a nice picture. The words are just filler" (Porter, 17/09/01, www.guardian.co.uk).
5. The Glasgow Media Group researches the content of broadcast and print journalism, focusing primarily upon "hard" news issues such as racism and biases in reports on industrial action (Eldridge 1995).
6. Two months were selected at random for each of the years sampled in order to counter the effects of the fashion calendar.

7. Following the boom years of the 1980s, Britain was immersed in a recession during the early 1990s.
8. In their comprehensive study of women's magazines, Ballaster et al. (1991) found the maintenance of a heterosexual relationship to be a powerful and recurring theme.
9. Originating in psychiatric terminology, "word salad" refers to a jumble of seemingly random words or phrases.
10. A short, close-fitting jacket worn by women at the start of the nineteenth century.

References

Ballaster, R. et al. 1991 *Women's Worlds: Ideology, Femininity and the Woman's Magazine*. London: Macmillan.

Barthes, R. 1990. *The Fashion System*, trans. M. Ward and R. Howard. London: University of California Press.

Berridge, V. 1986. "Content Analysis and Historical Research on Newspapers," in M. Harris and A. Lee, *The Press in English Society from the Seventeenth to Nineteenth Centuries*. Rutherford NJ: Associated University Presses.

Borelli, L. 1997. "Dressing Up and Talking about It: Fashion Writing in *Vogue* from 1968 to 1993," *Fashion Theory*, Vol. 1 (3): 247–260. Oxford: Berg.

Braham, P. 1997. "Fashion: Unpacking a Cultural Production," in P. du Gay (ed.) *Production of Culture: Cultures of Production* London: Sage in association with the Open University.

Crewe, B. 2003. *Representing Men*. Oxford: Berg.

Eldridge, J. (ed.). 1995. *Glasgow Media Group Reader, Volume 1: News Content. Language and Visuals*, London: Routledge.

Ferguson, M. 1983. *Forever Feminine: Women's Magazines and the Cult of Femininity*. London: Heineman.

Harvey, A. (ed.). 1991. *Vogue: 75 Years*. London: Condé Nast.

Hebdige, D. 1987. *Subculture: The Meaning of Style*. London: Routledge.

Hermes, J. 1995. *Reading Women's Magazines*. Cambridge: Polity.

Jobling, P. 1999. *Fashion Spreads: Word and Image in Fashion Photography Since 1980*. Oxford: Berg.

Klein, N. 2000. *No Logo*. London: Flamingo.

Lurie, A. 1981. *The Language of Clothes*. New York: Owl Books.

McRobbie, A. 1998. *British Fashion Design: Rag Trade or Image Industry*. London: Routledge.

Mort, F. 1996. *Cultures of Consumption*. London: Routledge.

Nixon, S. 1996. *Hard Looks*, London: Routledge.

Rabine, L. W. 1994. "A Woman's Two Bodies: Fashion Magazines, Consumerism, and Feminism," in S. Benstock and S. Ferriss (eds.), *On Fashion*. New Jersey: Rutgers University Press.

Rank. London: Dazed Group.

Rocamora, A. 2001. "High Fashion and Pop Fashion: The Symbolic Production of Fashion in *Le Monde* and *The Guardian*," *Fashion Theory*, Vol. 5 (2): 123–142. Oxford: Berg.

Smith, A. C. H., E. Immirzi and T. Blackwell. 1975. *Paper Voices: The Popular Press and Social Change 1935–1965*. London: Chatto & Windus.

Steele, V. 1997. "Letter from the Editor" *Fashion Theory*, Vol. 1 (3): 245–246. Oxford: Berg.

Turner, G. 1996. *British Cultural Studies* (second edition). London: Routledge.

van Zoonen, L. 1994. *Feminist Media Studies*. London: Sage.

Wilson, E. 1992. "Fashion and the Postmodern Body" in J. Ash and E. Wilson (eds). *Chic Thrills: A Fashion Reader*. London: Pandora.

Winship, J. 1987. *Inside Women's Magazines*. London: Pandora Press.

Vogue

"The American Fashion Buyer," British *Vogue*, March 1998: 215.

Armstrong, L. 1992. *Vogue*'s-Eye View," Vogue September 187–189.

—— 1995. "Great Good Buys," British *Vogue*, January: 120–121.

—— 1995. "On the Road," British *Vogue*, August: 116–119.

—— 1995. "Great Good Buys," British *Vogue*, August: 134–138.

"Backstage Countdown," British *Vogue*, March 2001: 199–200.

Bartley, L. 2001. "Show Business," British *Vogue*, March 141–144.

"Black and White Newsnight," British *Vogue*, April 1983: 136–146.

"Circus," British *Vogue*, September 1989: 282–295.

Cosgrave, B. 2001. "A Fetish for Fashion," British *Vogue*, March: 159–162.

"Costume Conservation: A New Initiative," British *Vogue*, April 1983: 130–133.

Crome, E. 1980. "Men in *Vogue*," British *Vogue*, June. 165–194.

"Double Exposure," British *Vogue*, March 1998: 49.

"Dressing for Dinner," British *Vogue*, September 1989: 276.

Dyson, J. 1998. "Soft touch," British *Vogue*, December: 157

"Earth Girls," British *Vogue*, December 1998: 192–197.

"Evenings – What More Can One Add?" British *Vogue*, October 1983: 234–243.

"Fashion Cue," British *Vogue*, May 1980: 95.

Gimlette, P. 1986. "Men in British *Vogue, Vogue*, March: 365–403.

"Gloria Vanderbilt: In Her Own Fashion," British *Vogue*, June 1980: 126–127.

"Great Good Buys," British *Vogue*, August 1995: 134–138.

Holgate, M. 1998. "Field Work," British *Vogue*, March: 229.

—— 1998. "Trackstars," British *Vogue*, March: 233.

MacLeod, K.S. 1998. "Grey Daze," British *Vogue*. March: 231.

—— 1998. "The House That Ben Built," British *Vogue*, December: 161.

"Modern Britain: Active Style, City Suits," British *Vogue*, August 1986: 176–180.

"More Dash Than Cash. The Suitable Seven," British *Vogue*, March 1986: 192.

"More Dash Than Cash," British *Vogue*, June 1992: 88–94.

Mower, S. 1989. "Light as a Feather," British *Vogue*, April: 33–38.

—— 1989. "Watch This Space," British *Vogue*, September: 271.

—— 1989. "Isaac Mizrahi," British *Vogue*, September: 316.

—— 1992. "Alberta Ferretti," British *Vogue*, June: 86.

Muir, L. 2001. "Call of the Wild," British *Vogue*, October: 58–61.

"The New Chic," British *Vogue*, August 1995: 78–91.

"New Generation Classics," British *Vogue*, March 1986: 400–403.

"The New Rules of Short," British *Vogue*, October 2001: 330.

O'Donnell, K. 2001. "Choo Polish," British *Vogue*, March: 179–182.

"On the Scent of Summer Nights," British *Vogue*, June 1980: 86–96.

"Overheard in the Changing Room," British *Vogue*, March 1998: 210.

"Paris Pleasures," British *Vogue*, March 1986: 255–262.

Picardie, J. 2001. "Is Vintage Old Hat? British *Vogue*, October: 127–130.

Quick, H. 2001. "Candy Girls," British *Vogue*, March: 74–77.

—— 2001. "Couture Report," British *Vogue*, October: 149–152.

—— 2001. "Total Recall," British *Vogue*, October: 163–164.

Reinhardt, M. 1983. "Having a Fling with Fur," British *Vogue*, October: 274–277.

"Shapeliness Nouveau," British *Vogue*, March 1986: 272–286.

"Single White Female," British *Vogue*, January 1995: 68–79.

"Snip: Economy Class," British *Vogue*, October 2001: 269.

"Sole Searching," British *Vogue*, March 1998: 49.

Spencer, M. 1995. "Welcome to the Comfort Zone," British *Vogue*, January: 55.

"Summer Life Silks," British *Vogue*, May 1980: 118–124.

Sykes, P. 1995. 'She Wears it Well," British *Vogue*, January: 53.

—— 1995. "Continental Cool," British *Vogue*, August: 16–19.

"Take It Away," British *Vogue*, August 1995: 108–114.

"Tsars in their Eyes," British *Vogue*, October 2001: 33.

"*Vogue*'s-Eye View," British *Vogue*, August 1986: 123.

"*Vogue*'s-Eye View," British *Vogue*, April 1989: 163.

"*Vogue*'s-Eye View," British *Vogue*, September 1989: 281.

"*Vogue*'s-Eye View of Golden Opportunities," British *Vogue*, May 1980: 103.

Web References

Fletcher, V. 19/11/02. "Topshop Scandal: East End Sweatshops Exposed."
http://www.thisislondon.co.uk/news/articles/2104055.html (26/11/02)

Mintel. 2000. Women's Magazines: October 2000, Executive Summary. http://reports.mintel.com/sinatra/...exec/x/print/42845499&rep code=C521 (19/10/02).

Porter, C. 17/09/01. "From Catwalk to Carnage." http://www.media. guardian.co.uk/mediaguardian/story/0,7558,552685,00.html (28/06/02).

Fashion Theory, Volume 10, Issue 1/2, pp. 225–258
Reprints available directly from the Publishers.
Photocopying permitted by licence only.
© 2006 Berg.

Elegance and Substance Travel East: *Vogue* Nippon

Brian Moeran

Brian Moeran is Professor of
Culture and Communication
at the Copenhagen Business
School, Denmark. A social
anthropologist by training, he has
conducted extensive fieldwork
in the advertising and publishing
industries, particularly in Japan
where he is currently doing
fieldwork on "fragrance cultures."
Among his publications are
*The Business of Ethnography:
Strategic Exchanges, People and
Organizations* (Berg, 2005).
bdm.ikl@cbs.dk

Women's fashion magazines are both cultural products and commodities. As cultural products, they circulate in a cultural economy of collective meanings, providing recipes, patterns, narratives, and models of and/or for the reader's self. As commodities, they are products of the print industry and crucial sites for the advertising and sale of commodities (particularly those related to fashion, cosmetics, fragrances, and personal care). Like women's magazines in general, fashion magazines are thus deeply involved in capitalist production and consumption at national, regional, and global levels (Beetham 1996: 1–5).

The study of women's magazines is interesting and various. On the one hand, there is the pioneering feminist critique by Betty Friedan (1963) who claimed that, in their emphasis on the fulfillment of femininity, women's magazines in the United States (but, by implication, elsewhere as well) merely reproduced what she called "the happy housewife heroine." Another early study is the semiotic analysis by Roland Barthes (1967) who, in *The Fashion System* (*Système de la Mode*), examined the language used in French fashion magazines from the late 1950s into the early 1960s to describe the "written garment" worn by women, and so to analyze the world implied by fashion.

From a rather different perspective, Joan Barrell and Brian Braithwaite (1988) have looked at the history of magazines and the contemporary magazine industry in the United Kingdom from a purely business angle that takes account of such publishing issues as launching, advertising space, magazine distribution, and editorial practices. Another approach is that of historical research—exemplified by Marjorie Beetham, who has traced the emergence and history of women's magazines in Britain from the seventeenth century to the present day (Beetham 1996).

By far the greater part of the research on women's magazines, however, has come out of cultural studies. One comparatively early study was Marjorie Ferguson's *Forever Feminine*, in which the author made full use of her decade's experience as writer and associate editor for a weekly women's magazine in Britain, to produce an account that combined in-depth interviews with editorial staff with content analysis of selected English women's magazines between 1949 and 1980 (Ferguson 1983). Another comparatively early commentator on women's magazines, Janice Winship, combined a feminist, Marxist, and reader's approach in an analysis of *Woman's Own*, *Cosmopolitan*, and *Spare Rib*. Her *Inside Women's Magazines* provided some general ways of understanding the place of women's magazines in contemporary British women's lives, as well as the cultural codes that shape those magazines as a combination of "survival skills and daydreams" (Winship 1987).

This second, very different, approach to the study of women's magazines by scholars associated with cultural studies has sparked a radical shift away from their production, to a focus on textual analysis and reception.[1] Ellen McCracken (1993), for example, has looked at "glossy" women's magazines in the United States primarily as "cultural texts." Although she also brought in the business side of magazine publishing by focusing in detail on the relation between advertising and editorial matter in the women's glossies that she studied, her main aim has been to argue that women readers are "duped" by magazines into becoming unreflective "slaves" of trends in fashion, beauty, and "femininity." Unfortunately, she made such assumptions on the basis of her own readings of particular magazines and failed to talk to those on the production side to find out to what extent the latter consciously intended to dupe, or not to dupe, their readers through the textual matter and promotional advertising—an issue to which I shall return below.

The kind of textual analysis and critique conducted by Winship, McCracken, and others has since spawned an interest in what readers actually think of women's magazines (as opposed to what academics presume they think). For example, Joke Hermes (1995) has conducted in-depth interviews with readers of women's magazines to determine what it is precisely that does (or does not) interest them, makes their contents memorable, helps women with their everyday lives, and so on. This shift in interest among those studying women's magazines may be seen as part of a more widespread trend in cultural studies as a whole, which has, since its early decades as the "Birmingham School," gradually moved from an engagement with issues of production toward a focus on reception, by way of textual analysis.

This leads me to the methodological point that I wish to make regarding this article's discussion of Japanese *Vogue* (*Vogue* Nippon). In the study of cultural productions of all kinds, we cannot properly conduct research on *just* their production, or *just* their reception, or *just* the products themselves. While such research can be—and has been—useful and enlightening, we should recognize that it is always *partial*. As a result, as part of our scholarly endeavor, we need to take account, as best we can, of the *total* social processes surrounding the production, representation, distribution (circulation), and reception (consumption) of such cultural products, as well as of the products themselves. It is the negotiations that take place among and between producers, consumers, and various kinds of "critics" (employed in advertising, PR, journalism, and so on) during a product's move from production to reception, that transform a cultural *product* into a cultural *production*.

At the same time, we should note that we are concerned with the study of cultural production*s*, rather than with cultural production in the singular, which sounds far too monolithic for comfort. What I have to say about Japanese *Vogue*, therefore, may well differ from similar studies of the same magazine elsewhere in the world, as well as from other women's fashion magazines within Japan itself (although it is likely to be very close because of the industry in which the title is found). It is certainly going to contain elements that distinguish it from other cultural productions such as a Britney Spears record album, a Hollywood film, or *haute couture* fashion show (even though it is likely to share certain economic properties with such "creative industries" [Caves 2000: 3–9]). Moreover, what I have to say is extremely limited temporally, since media productions are transient productions, evolving in an ever-spiralling cycle that quickly makes what has gone before "out of fashion." We need, then, to recognize the historical situatedness of all media cultural studies.

Because of particular circumstances surrounding just when and how research for this paper could be conducted, I found myself obliged to start by examining the contents of Japanese *Vogue*, together with assorted marketing statistics and data. This research led to the kind of content analysis of the magazine that I have just criticized above, although it is marked by a much more market-oriented approach than is generally seen in academic studies. Good luck, however, enabled me to travel to Japan and visit a number of those employed in producing Japanese *Vogue* and it is interviews with members of the Japanese title's editorial and publishing staff that are then used to inflect my content analysis.[2] Nevertheless, because I have not had the opportunity to talk systematically to readers of Japanese *Vogue*, the analysis presented here does not systematically take account of the *total* social processes surrounding its path from production to consumption. All I can do is bring to bear, as appropriate, comments made by women during the course of a dozen interviews with Japanese fashion magazine readers in 2001–2.

Vogue Travels to Japan

In 1998, Condé Nast entered into a joint venture agreement with the Japanese financial newspaper, the *Nihon Keizai Shimbun* (or *Nikkei* as it is usually abbreviated in everyday communication) and established the Nikkei Condé Nast Company in order to publish what was the eleventh international edition of the American publisher's flagship title, *Vogue*, under its common concept of "elegance and substance." The first issue of Japanese *Vogue* was duly put on sale in July 1999, with a comparatively expensive cover price of ¥760 and an initial print run of 90,000.

The process of *Vogue*'s internationalization has been somewhat haphazard over the decades since the title was first published in the United States in 1892. After two early expansions into the British (1916) and French (1921) magazine markets, Condé Nast waited until 1959 before launching an Australian edition. The title was then published in Italy in 1965, followed by Brazil (1975), Germany (1979), and Spain (1988). Condé Nast made its first venture into the Asian market in 1996, when it launched Korean and Taiwanese editions virtually simultaneously. Although Tokyo had for some years been the fourth—and only non-Western—fashion capital of the world, it was a further three years before a Japanese edition became a reality.

The reasons for Condé Nast's late arrival in Japan are various, and not entirely clear.[3] One is connected to the fact that, as a family-owned business, there was no pressure from shareholders for the company to expand. Another is that, when a shift toward a business orientation in the magazine market began to take place in the mid-1980s, it did so first in the UK, followed by Italy and then France, so that Condé Nast's shift toward a more business-like integration of *Vogue* with the luxury brand business came via Europe. At the time, nobody in the United States paid much attention to the potential of the Japanese market, even though marketing data made it obvious that Japanese consumers were the main purchasers of luxury goods produced worldwide by companies like Louis Vuitton and Gucci.

Ideally, then, Japanese *Vogue* should have been launched in Japan in the late 1980s. The fact that it was not did have one advantage in that the Japanese magazine market, which was extremely volatile during the early to mid-1990s, had settled down by 1997. It was thus easier to position the title and get the advertisers it wanted. Even so, positioning Japanese *Vogue* was not, initially at least, easy. Comparatively speaking, the Japanese magazine market is still extremely dynamic (more than fifty major new titles were launched in 2002) and extremely crowded. Broken down into numerous categories based on combinations of gender, age, interests, and lifestyles, it includes in the general area of fashion alone magazine groups like "Mrs," "Quality Fashion," "Cosmetics and Fashion," "Young Fashion," "Street Fashion," and "Teen Fashion" magazines. Japanese *Vogue* is classified as a "Mode" magazine and finds itself grouped with eight other titles (four international, four homegrown Japanese): *Elle Japon, Figaro Japon, Marie Claire Japon, Harper's Bazaar, Ginza, Spur, Sweet,* and *Maia*. At the same time, however, it is mapped to overlap two other groups of magazines: one of "Fashion Magazines for Women in their Thirties" (*Grazia, VERY, La Vie de 30 Ans, Domani,* and *RED*); the other of "Quality Fashion" (*Classy, 25 Ans, Miss,* and *Vingtaine*).[4] Compared with the US magazine market's relatively simple separating out of nine fashion-related titles within women's magazines in general and their classification as the "Fashion Magazine Set" (*Allure, Elle, Glamor, Harper's Bazaar, InStyle, Mademoiselle, Marie Claire, Vogue,* and *W*), the Japanese magazine market is overclassified, overcrowded, and thus extremely difficult to sustain a new title in successfully.

Another aspect affecting the positioning of Japanese *Vogue* has been its readership. The publishers of American *Vogue* have prided themselves on reaching a target audience whose lifestyle is defined by "style, affluence, and activity" (Vogue Marketing Data). A database profile of almost 700,000 subscribers carried out in 2000 revealed the median age of American *Vogue* readers to be 42 years—35% were aged between 18 and 35 years; 23% between 36 and 45 years; and 21% between 46 and 55 years; 42% had attended or graduated from college; 40% were single and 60% married—probably to professional/managerial husbands (since 62% of readers' heads of households had this job status); 29% had children. Their median household income was $64,894.

Readers of Japanese *Vogue* are sold to advertisers in a similar, though more detailed, manner. In 2002, the median reader age was 31.7 years, with 66.4% of all the Japanese edition's readers under the age of 35 years, while only 6.1% were over the age of 50. Accompanying this age difference was one in marital status: 62.7% of all readers were unmarried, 37.1% were married, and 24.1% had children. Almost 70%

were employed in one way or another, particularly in the manufacturing industries, mass media, fashion, and cosmetology. The median household income was more than ¥9 million, or a little over US$80,000.

Given that fashion magazines are both cultural products designed to appeal to readers and commodities which carry advertising and, in the process, sell those readers to potential advertisers, it is very important for a publisher to be able to match its two distinct audiences. The expensively produced 56-page Media Data book published by Japanese *Vogue* in 2002 goes about this by depicting a lifestyle image of its readers—the way they spend their money, the kinds of things they own—which will accord with the image that would-be advertisers have of *their* consumers and so induce the latter to place their advertisements in Japanese *Vogue*'s pages. At the same time, though, the magazine's publisher uses its reader data to construct an image for itself of the kind of advertisers it would like to have contributing to its pages. This is found initially in the breakdown of consumer spending into the separate categories of Cosmetics, Fashion, Watches & Jewelry, and Digital & Cars (Japanese *Vogue*'s publisher is clearly not that interested in big-name advertisers like Bayer, L'Oréal, Procter & Gamble, Philips, or Unilever, and the product areas they represent). It is then reinforced by statistical data on "International Travel Destinations" (48% have been to France, 1.3% to Russia); "Frequency of Patronization of Modes of Entertainment" (21.4 video rentals and 6.6 art museum visits annually); "Utilization of Financial Products" (76.2% have savings deposits, 9% stocks, 24.3% life insurance); and more general information like "Own a one-family (detached) home: 45.8%" and "Shop for clothes and fashion accessories once a month, and spend an average of 563,652 yen on the items annually." The magazine's projected image is reinforced by simple, striking image phrases, like "Have at least 10 bottles of perfume: 14%," or "Own a Rolls Royce: 0.1%," splashed across the whole of a double page.

The Media Data book also makes it clear who Japanese *Vogue*'s rivals for advertising dollars are. It publishes information on which other magazines *Vogue*'s readers buy: *Figaro Japon* (27.6%), *Marie Claire Japon* (8.5%), *Gli* (7.8%), *25 ans* (8.3%), *Spur* (23.8%), *Ginza* (12.8%), and eight other titles (one of them *Nikkei Woman*). Here, as elsewhere, the information provided is selective and occasionally makes little immediate sense. The highlighting of a teenage fashion magazine like *JJ*, for example, does not seem that rational, given that Japanese *Vogue*'s publisher has already told its Media Data readers that only 5.1% of the title's readers are under the age of 19. Not all titles in the "Mode" magazine set are included, either. The absence of *Elle Japon*, for example, is particularly perplexing, since it is later used as *the* main magazine for comparison with Japanese *Vogue* in detailing its readers' consumption of cosmetics, fashion, and accessories.

The Media Data book also compares Japanese *Vogue* with rival same-set titles *Elle Japon, Figaro, Japon* and *Marie Claire Japon* in terms of reader image, in order to show that (its own) readers see the title as (in descending order) more leading-edge, classy, tasteful, stylish, sophisticated, global, intelligent, individualistic, trustworthy, and elegant. Japanese *Vogue* also induces a "greater empathy" (though not much in all) than the other titles and only fails to come top in terms of "warmth" where it is seen to be least "ingratiating." A more independent survey shows that the main image categories associated with Japanese *Vogue* are (in descending order of importance): stylish, classy, good sense, *jōhin* (elegance), and—equally ranked—modern, international, and leading edge. Warmth comes out with a zero rating, while characteristics like intelligence, empathy, and trustworthiness all rank very low in readers' general image of the magazine.[5]

Thus the Media Book information—based as it is on a survey of readers of Japanese *Vogue*, rather than of readers of fashion magazines in general—contrasts with surveys conducted by other magazines of its readers, as well as with those carried out more generally by advertising agencies, and merely serves to show how every magazine tries to sell itself to potential advertisers. *Its* readers are always somehow above average (in terms of income, employment, home ownership, education). They are discerning in their shopping habits, frequent the "right" kinds of shops (specialty and department stores), and spend more (or at least a lot) on the products that a publisher wishes to see advertised in magazine's pages.

Japanese *Vogue*'s entry into an already tricky magazine environment was initially complicated by the perception that, in its original form, *Vogue* was much too far removed from reality to be successful in Japan.[6] The market for women's magazines has operated on the principle that titles aim at just *a little bit* above where people actually are in their everyday lives. This is why they sell.[7] So, just *how* the contents of Japanese *Vogue* would be adapted was of considerable interest to those in the trade and, back in the winter of 1997, there was a lot of skepticism about the launch of the new title.

This skepticism was in large part due to the fact that, as publisher of a financial newspaper, Nikkei itself had no knowledge of, or experience in, the women's magazine market and was buttressed by Nikkei-Condé Nast's publication of an unusually complicated table of advertising rates. This contained progressive discounts for long-term advertising (from 4% off three, to 20% off 48, issues), as well as varied rates for single four-color advertising pages depending on their placement in the magazine. Thus, there was one standard—and extremely high—price for a single four-color page ad (at ¥2.35 million), which became ¥2.8m if placed opposite the opening page of the *Vogue* Beauty section, ¥3m opposite the Editor's Letter, and ¥3.4m facing the first Contents page. A back cover ad was priced at ¥4.5 million. Similar differentials applied to two-page spreads, whose price could vary between ¥4.7m and ¥7.6m (see *Appendix 1*). As one senior agency media buyer noted: if Nikkei-Condé Nast were to fulfill its aim of printing 225,000 copies, Japanese *Vogue*'s ad rates worked out at over ¥10 per page—which was ¥4 more than the average ¥6 per ad page rate in most women's magazines at the time.[8]

Another ad-related problem affecting the launching of Japanese *Vogue* was that Japanese advertisers tend to have a slight prejudice against international magazines, and feel that Japanese titles are more appropriate for their readers. Take two similar titles, *Spur* and *Elle Japon*, for example. In the summer of 1997, *Spur* was chock-full of ads, even though there was at the time no basic difference in the contents of the two magazines. Once sponsors found that they could not place their ads in *Spur*, however, they turned to *Elle* (which they saw as equivalent to *Figaro* in terms of advertising status). Even so, *Spur* had a higher print run, and at the time had a much better distribution network that placed it in both bookshops and convenience stores. It may have looked the same as *Elle*, but it ran special fashion features (on Cartier, Dior, and so on) which appealed more to Japanese readers.

Half a decade later, a concern which might at the time have been dismissed as cultural chauvinism seems to have become reality. My own analysis of advertising carried in seven issues of Japanese *Vogue*, from June to December 2002, reveals a singular lack of Japanese advertisers and preponderance of foreign fashion houses. Of the ninety-three fashion advertisers placing ads during these months, fewer than ten were Japanese; of the half dozen regular cosmetics and skincare advertisers, only one was Japanese and even this company—Shiseido—placed on average just one page of advertising a month in a magazine that prides itself on its beauty section, as well as on being a "fashion bible" (see *Appendix 2* for range of product categories advertised).

A Global Fashion Magazine?

The difference in *Vogue*'s targeted readers in two very different countries shows that any fashion magazine's globalizing strategy is subject to a number of cultural and economic constraints which themselves ultimately affect that magazine's contents. The fact that it is unmarried women in their twenties and early thirties in Japan who are comparatively well-off, and not older women married to comparatively wealthy husbands as in the USA, for example, means that Japanese *Vogue*'s overall style is more "youthful" (and may explain the comparative lack of skincare and other anti-aging commodities in its pages). And because these women are au fait with Western culture, trends and styles, and because they tend to travel abroad quite frequently, Japanese *Vogue* can unashamedly present itself as a Western fashion magazine in which not only are almost all of its advertisers European and American companies, but the models used to illustrate both fashion stories *and* beauty pages are Caucasian—often stereotypically blonde and blue-eyed.

This is not to say that Japanese *Vogue* is *only* Western in appearance. On the contrary, it follows Japanese publishing standards in the way it structures and mixes advertising and text pages in blocks. Its editors also make sure to tailor their regular and special features in such a way that Japanese, as opposed to American (or other), interests are addressed (cf. Moeran 1995). Thus the regular Party pages may start out by showing pictures of foreign celebrities at, say, the Cannes Film Festival, but they also make sure to show Japanese celebrities attending their own public events (Louis Vuitton's Omote Sandō shop-opening party, the Omega Awards, and so on). Each issue also has a regular feature, Tokyo Story, which gives photo vignettes of life in Tokyo as seen through the eyes of foreign visitors from the fashion world (Richard Chai, Sonia Rykiel, Enzo Ammadeo, and so on). Similarly, an "In *Vogue*" page may comment on the accessories used in the latest Paris runway collections, but it also contrives to suggest that foreign designers are about to create new accessory trends based on "Tokyo street style" (Japanese *Vogue*, July 2002: 29). Even the captions to the magazine's fashion pages (with its Western models, Western locations, and Western designer clothing) may pay lip service to local tastes. Stories such as "Tribal Fever," "Toys in the Attic," and "A Formal Affair," for example, include such phrases as: "Skillfully mixing a sporty layered look with a Japanese approach" (Japanese *Vogue*, July 2002: 195), and "A dress somehow reminding one of a kimono" (Japanese *Vogue*, December 2002: 260). A more general Asian-ness is found in such phrases as "Silk Road empress" and "Feeling like a Chinese queen" (Japanese *Vogue*, December 2002: 250), and customary fashion exoticism in "A patchwork top with a luxury-inviting Orientalism" (Japanese *Vogue*, July 2002: 201) and "Oriental image" (Japanese *Vogue*, November 2002: 348). Nevertheless, the overall visual impression is of a *Western* fashion magazine.

The monthly Editor's Letter is one place where readers are clearly addressed as *Japanese* readers. The Editor may use the Mediterranean ("One of this season's themes") to contrast the passionate, glamorous, sexy beauty of stars such as Monica Vitti and Monica Belucci with Japanese women's self-engrossing fixation on "cuteness," and to suggest that it may be time for them to start looking for a new kind of beauty (Japanese *Vogue*, June 2002: 37).[9] Or he may tell Japanese men (presumably through their wives and girlfriends) to become sexier (Japanese *Vogue*, October 2002: 59). Or he may use the unveiling of Louis Vuitton's new monogram designed by Takeshi Murakami to comment on the world quality of Japanese design (a theme already taken up in an earlier editorial [2002/7]) and then go on to name the designers who are this season making use of Japanese art and design (Japanese *Vogue*, December 2002: 39). In this way the Editor's Letter almost always relates the world fashion scene to some aspect of Japanese society and culture.

A good single example of this localizing approach can be seen in the December 2002 issue, where the cover theme is of "The Party & The Celeb." In the feature, "Celebrity Circus," the work of a French and American celebrity photographer is featured first, and then followed by that of a Chinese photographer working in Japan. After a double-page spread focusing on New York celebrities, the feature turns to "Parties and Celebrities in Japan" and various celebrities are introduced—from the Imperial family to fashion and literary worlds. The next feature is "Japanese Tea Party," including a booklet insert titled *Manner Book for Guest*, "directly handed down from Masayoshi Sen," the tea master featured. Here, after learning about traditions of the tea ceremony and seeing photographs of aficionados with the tea master, readers can also learn how foreign visitors come to learn about this Japanese art form. In this way, the two features neatly present a fusion of Japan and the Western world.

The kind of approach taken by Japanese *Vogue* is characteristic of all other foreign titles that publishers decide, for one reason or another, to launch in Japan. Just how much they "localize" the contents of their publications, however, depends on Head Office strategy and local markets. Hachette-Filipacchi, for example, tends to favor as much standardization of format and contents of its title *Elle* as possible, whereas Groupe Marie Claire has less of a hands-on approach and believes in a localizing policy that gives local Editors comparative freedom of choice in what they do and do not select for publication in each issue of *Marie Claire*.[10] Japanese *Vogue* appears to veer toward localization in its choice of features, though not of fashion stories which were in 2002 for the most part commissioned by the locally employed Fashion Features Editor, who used a number of trusted freelance fashion editors in Europe and the United States.[11] At the same time, however, it follows a central directive that the magazine should make use of top-quality photography, art, and design—a quality that the Japanese editorial and publishing staff transform into something very special and, perhaps, "Japanese" in their attention to detail and the overall look of the magazine.

Anchorage and Flow

Like Japanese magazines in general, Japanese *Vogue* structures the contents of each issue in a manner that, in contrast its American cousin, can only be construed as "reader-friendly" (see *Appendix 3*). Given the earlier discussion of the magazine publisher's concern to use its reader base to procure advertising, this may seem paradoxical, but it neatly expresses one of the conundrums faced by the magazine publishing industry (and, indeed, many another "creative" industries). Every magazine has at least two audiences—one of readers, the other of advertisers—each of which is indispensable to enable it to remain in print. The two (or, in some cases, multiple) audience property leads to a structural distinction between two different kinds of staff, each concerned with satisfying one audience's needs: the Publisher and related personnel in advertising, PR, sales and marketing, who deal with advertisers; and the Editor-in-Chief and related feature, fashion, beauty, and artistic personnel, whose job is to put together a magazine's pages in a manner that is attractive enough to appeal to targeted readers.

Not surprisingly, given their different primary tasks, editorial and publishing staff may find themselves in conflict over how the products of their work—editorial and advertising pages—are put together in each issue of a magazine title.[12] An Editor's particular concern is with how her magazine's advertisements will be distributed throughout each issue, as well as with which particular ads are likely to be found opposite particular editorial pages. There is also a general point of publication policy about whether single-page ads will be placed on left or right pages of a magazine, since, depending on how it is opened, the reader's eye is more likely to alight on one page rather than the other.

In a remarkably clear contra-distinction to American *Vogue*, the structure of text and ads in Japanese *Vogue* reveals that the reader gets the nod over the advertiser in the editorial–publishing battle over pleasing their separate audiences. As *Appendix 3* makes abundantly clear, American *Vogue*'s primary and obvious concern is with its advertisers. This can be seen in various ways. Firstly, the sheer proportion of ads is overwhelming (60% of all pages). Moreover, the ratio of advertising to editorial pages in the first half of the magazine is close to 15:1 (compared with 2:3 in Japanese *Vogue*). Secondly, there is a marked tendency for ads, rather than editorial text, to be placed on the right-hand (or rectal) pages of each issue since it is on this "static" page (in a Western magazine) that the reader's eye rests.[13] Even important textual material such as that of the Contents pages is placed on the versal page and is not run consecutively, but separated by advertising matter (a characteristic of all feature material in the magazine).

Japanese *Vogue*, by comparison, is a model of reader-friendliness. For a start, it keeps strict pagination—unlike its American counterpart, whose actual page numbers run ahead or behind pages as numbered. Then it makes sure to keep its rectal (which, in Japan, because of the way in which a magazine is opened is the left) page for editorial, not advertising, matter. In the 2002 fashion issue, for example, only three out of 213 left-hand pages were used for single-page ads, while 151 were used for textual material (the rest were for two-page advertising spreads). Ads are structured differently, too. Instead of placing one ad after another for hundreds of pages on end, as do the publishers of American *Vogue*, the Japanese title prefers to place its ads in blocks between uninterrupted features and thus enable a more equal distribution of advertising and editorial matter. For example, in August 2002, after an initial twenty-page block of double-page ads, the Contents are presented on three consecutive left-hand pages, before being followed by the Editor's Letter which itself leads directly into the regular "In Vogue" feature of four pages, followed by "Nostalgia," four more pages of "In Vogue," and then "Blythe Style Child" and Contributors' pages—all on the left-hand page, all with ads facing on the right page. The first substantial textual matter, an uninterrupted six-page feature on the actor Sean Penn, follows. Its end is marked by three two-page ad spreads before the start of a new seventeen-page uninterrupted fashion feature, "City Girl Goes Tyrolean" (Japanese *Vogue*, August 2002). This is then followed by a single (left-page) ad before the next feature begins. And so on. This is a typical issue structure and is designed to maintain reader's interest.

This example has structural implications. One paradox that emerges in the structuring of magazines that rely on advertising as well as cover prices, is that of *anchorage* versus *flow*. As I have had occasion to note elsewhere (Moeran 1996: 227–229), magazine editors believe that it is crucially important to lead their readers from one topic to another, so that the latter actually read through the whole of each monthly issue of their favorite magazine. This they talk about in terms of "flow" (*nagare*). Advertisers, on the other hand, try their best to make readers *stop* at the page on which their advertisement is placed, so that they will notice the goods advertised, the name of the advertiser, and so on. This, following Roland Barthes's (1977) discussion of an advertising image, I refer to as *anchorage*. Anchorage and flow (or, in Barthes's terms, "relay") form a fundamental structuring principle of most forms of commercial media.

One method of anchoring an ad is to have it placed opposite a page of text which in some way reflects the ad itself—usually in terms of product, but also of design (color,[14] grid structure), image, model's gaze,[15] and so on. Women's magazines in general are known to encourage covert advertising of one sort or another by including textual references to a facing-page ad. Some magazines are more "notorious" than others in the ways and frequency that they do this. In general, Japanese *Vogue* is not an obvious "offender," but occasionally such "pandering" to advertisers does take place. For example, a fashion ad for Costume National featuring a fur-lined dress is placed opposite an "In Vogue" page titled "Get Layered," featuring two photos of fur items (Japanese *Vogue*, October 2002: 64–65). Another, "New Skin," featuring a YSL buffalo bag, Dior salmon-skin bag, and stingray-skin shoes by Helmut Lang, is placed opposite a Vivienne Tam fashion ad featuring a patchwork suede and sheepskin waistcoat (Japanese *Vogue*, September 2002: 24–25), while an Anna Sui ad in which the model's calf-length boot is clearly emphasized is found opposite a fashion page featuring long boots (November 2002: 206–207). The placement of a Samantha Thavasa handbag ad endorsed by the Hilton sisters sitting on a motorcycle opposite the monthly "Car Buzz" page may be stretching the self-referential ad-text page idea a bit too far (Japanese *Vogue*, October 2002: 252–253), but the selection of an Inoui ID makeup ad to face the "Essentials of a Makeup Artist" section featuring "world's top artist" Dick Page (Japanese *Vogue*, October 2002: 164–165) is clearly designed to please the advertiser (Shiseido) which does not otherwise advertise at all heavily in Japanese *Vogue*. Besides the ad-text product link, a cursory glance at the caption under Page's photo reveals that he is "artistic director of the newly launched Inoui ID makeup line."

Interviews with fashion magazine publishing and editorial staff all over the world suggest that this kind of anchorage between advertising and text is for the most part fortuitous since the left hand, so to speak, is unaware of what the right hand is doing, and vice versa. And yet, from time to time, even design links do appear. For example, the top half of a "Nostalgia" page depicting the work of Erwin Blumenfeld and Jean Patchett contains a cover photo of the latter from French *Vogue* (1950/1) in which Patchett's face is depicted as an eyebrow, eye, bright red lips and beauty spot (Japanese *Vogue*, September 2002: 31). The Shiseido makeup ad opposite consists of two eyebrows and eyes, with the phrase "Look fully individual" where the lips might have been (Figure 1). While not an exact image repetition, the ad image is sufficiently close to attract attention. Similarly, a Van Cleef & Arpels ad featuring a chain necklace is similar in overall shape to a handbag and strap on the opposite page (Japanese *Vogue*, November 2002: 63) as well as in texture to the overall subject matter, "Lace Up," while the positioning of a round Versace logo matches that of a circular plate of food in "Hot Table vs. Cool Table (Japanese *Vogue*, November 2002: 83). These are probably, however, accidental image alliances and should not be treated as part of a conspiracy theory of covert advertising (McCracken 1993), although they do add to the overall tightness of the magazine's design.

Another mode of anchorage (though also of flow) is the magazine cover. Since fashion magazines in general are so closely involved in, and act as the mouthpiece for, the fashion world, it is not surprising to find headlines in which names of designers and/or fashion houses are mentioned: for example, "500 Questions to Miuccia Prada" (Japanese *Vogue*, November 2002), "Yves Saint Laurent Told by Tom Ford" (September 2002), and "Murakami Takeshi and Marc Jacobs' 'LV Monogram for the 21st Century' Revealed" (December 2002). But a big-name regular advertiser like Louis Vuitton occasionally has sufficient financial clout, it would seem, to get its own cover headline ("LV's Paris-Omote Sandō Personal Trip") for what is a paid *promotional* story, "Have Bag Will Travel" (Japanese Vogue, October 2002: 323–328) (Figure 2).

The magazine cover is, of course, a means by which an Editor "anchors" the contents of an issue in order to make casual browsers at book and convenience stores stop to look through and, hopefully, buy her magazine.[16] At the same time, cover headlines help relay the reader to

other parts of the magazine, by going first to the Contents pages and
then to relevant sections that interest them. In this respect, Japanese
Vogue's Editor tends to use the main headline (always in English) to
signify the overall theme, or "concept," of an issue in the monthly Editor's
Letter. Thus, "Ciao Ciao Bambina" reflects one of the fashion season's
themes—the Mediterranean (Japanese *Vogue*, June 2002: 37)—and a
"passionate," "glamorous" and "sexy" beauty that contrasts strongly
with Japanese women's self-engrossing focus hitherto on a "cute" form of
beauty (cf. Kinsella 1995). The issue's main feature focuses on "*La Dolce
Vita*": Italian beauty, Italian high life, Italian wine, and a photo essay
titled *Vagabondo*, while its fashion pages are headed "Mediterranean

Madness," with separate stories called "Love in Sicily," "Monte Carlo Decadance" (*sic*), "Ciao Ciao, Bambina," and "A Cretan Myth." The monthly History pages are devoted to Cristobel Balenciaga "who made Mediterranean beauty known to the world" (Japanese *Vogue*, June 2002: 102), while the "It's Only Yesterday" essay tells the story of Sawako Goda on the far side of the Mediterranean Sea in Egypt (193–7).

This kind of flow is found—to a greater or lesser coherent extent—in every month's issue of Japanese *Vogue*. The August 2002 edition, for example, published at that time of the year when horror stories and ghosts come into their own in Japan (coinciding with the All Souls' *obon* ancestor festival in mid-August), carries the title "Dress to Kill." The Editor's

Figure 2
Cover, Japanese *Vogue*,
October 2002. © Japanese
Vogue.

Letter informs the magazine's readers that this month's theme is "strange
world," and tells of how this month's fashion photographer, Tim Walker,
uses a kind of surreal imagination in his photo stories where models ski
in a Moroccan desert, food and women's underwear are placed in strange
compositions to illustrate the photographer's mother's home-cooking recipes, and so on. The main feature (084–109) is titled "Phantoms After Mid-
night" and consists of separate sections called "Strange Tales," "Horror
Manga Master," "Surreal Encounters," "Freaky Flicks" and so on.

   One interesting feature of the thematic flow created by the editorial
staff of Japanese *Vogue* consists of inter-issue links. This is found in basic
form in the last fashion story of the October 2002 fashion issue, "Men's

Club" (304–319), photographed in black and white and featuring a female model wearing men's clothes with captions like "Masculine style" and "Man x woman." Since this fashion story is the last main feature of the October 2002 issue before the appended *Vogue M For Men*, it creates a flow linking the two issues of the magazine.

Another example of this form of relaying of content may be found in one of the August issue's "In *Vogue*" pages (Japanese *Vogue*, August 2002: 31), "Newton Women." The subheading comments on how "stimulating are the kind of sexy women appearing in Newton's photos," and the following text refers to Grace Coddington, Creative Director of American *Vogue*, who used to be one of Newton's favorite models (she is pictured below), before moving on to Prada's 2002–03 Fall-Winter Collection inspired by the sexiness pervading Newton's work. Accompanying a catwalk photo are two larger, well-known photos by Newton of Charlotte Rampling.

In itself, this page more or less stands alone, although its theme ("Newton's Law," along with "Dark Romantic" [see below]) is taken up in the *Collection File* booklet and attached gatefold pages later on) (Japanese *Vogue*, August 2002: 140) (Figure 3). In terms of a longer editorial vision, however, the "*In Vogue*" page foreshadows both the September 2002 issue's fashion pages headed "Newton's Law" (with stories called "Sexy Sexy… but Chic," "Fetish Wave," "Ghost Shadows," and "Heavy Metal" [195–247]), and an interview with Charlotte Rampling in the following month's issue, where two more photos of the actress by Helmut Newton are included (Japanese *Vogue*, October 2002: 234–238).[17]

This example reveals how fashion season themes are used by editors to create a flow in their fashion magazines. Here key words and phrases (like "Newton's Law") tend to form the focus of attention since it is these that define each season's characteristics and moods (cf. Moeran 2004). Again, these words can be anchored in a particular issue or used as a more constant theme through a number of issues. The October 2002 fashion issue, for example, is titled "Dark Angel" and revolves around four key words: *dark, angel, poetic* and *romance*. Thus we find throughout the issue's 426 pages such fashion- and beauty-related phrases (in both English and Japanese) as: "romance," "romantic strangers," "dark romanticism" (*kurai romanticism*), "dark romantic style," "poetic romance," "dark poetry," "the darkness of (Belgian) design," "black dress dancing in the dark," "nouveau noir," "angel of darkland," "urban angel," "bike angel," and so on. The fashion story "Misty" depicts "A darkland angel" whose "world of poetic dark romance" is expressed by photographer, Paolo Roversi (Japanese *Vogue*, October 2002: 258). Alexander McQueen's black dress "dances in the dark" (271)[18] while a pair of long black boots reveal the same designer's "dark poetic world" (275).[19] Even the story "Country Blues" takes as its model a girl with "natural dark hair" (282) who is "a bike angel escaped from the city" (278).

Figure 3
"Newton's Law" as fashion
season theme, Japanese
Vogue, September 2002. ©
Japanese *Vogue*.

This emphasis on sombre and spiritual (?) romance is reinforced by the issue's cover of model Natalia Vodianova photographed in a dark blue Junya Watanabe Comme des Garçons dress (Figure 2), and by a preponderance of black-and-white (as well as poorly lit indoor scene) photos in the fashion stories that make up "Don't Be Afraid of the Dark." Moreover, the issue's opening two-page ads by Chanel, Prada, and Fendi, as well as the right-page ads by AKRIS, MaxMara and Donna Karan facing the three Contents pages, are all black and white; while further ads by Anne Klein, Burberry, Dolce & Gabbana, Givenchy, Gucci, Harrods, Helmut Lang, Kenzo, and others are either black-and-white photos or color photos set against an overall black background.

Newton's Law

As Sarah Mower comments in "Return to Roots" (insert booklet, Japanese *Vogue*, August 2002: 16), the vast majority of the 2002–03 fall/winter season's collections were in black and dark brown. This, given the context of their being the first collections shown after New York's 9/11 disaster, was not that surprising. Following on from "Fantasy of the Woods" (Japanese *Vogue*, July 2002: 90), "Sherwood Forest" (August 2002: 29) can be put together as a fashion theme because three collections made use either of dead leaves strewn on the runway or of (photographs of) trees lining it, while other designers (Cacharel) used leaves as a design motif. The section finishes with the phrase, "woods redolent with the atmosphere of darkness and romanticism"—two key words that are at the center of the fashion issue two months later.

But it is also the materials themselves, as well as their colors, that enable a set of images to persist through a season. The adoption of fur by a number of famous couturiers, for example, nicely complements an issue devoted to being Wild at Heart" (Japanese *Vogue*, July 2002: 169–215), and—time and again—such phrases as call of the wild (September 2002: 260), "wild fur" (November 2002: 380), "wilder than fur" (September 2002: 232), "the dynamism of wildness" (November 2002: 359), and "a wild feeling" (November 2002: 343) maintain the theme of wildness—not all of it connected with fur (for instance, "wildly showing one's skin" [August 2002: 76], "wild leather jacket" [September 2002: 25], and "wild, shaggy-knit long coat" [November 2002: 361])—throughout the season.

Methodological Confrontation?

So much for content analysis. What, then, do the editorial and publishing staff of Nikkei-Condé Nast have to say about Japanese *Vogue*? How much is my textual deconstruction merely a subjective interpretation, even though some of the comments made are based on interviews with advertising and publishing staff in Japan and elsewhere over a number of years of research on fashion magazines?[20]

The first issue raised in my content analysis concerned advertising. On the one hand, advertising rates were perceived to be on the high side compared with other fashion magazines with which *Vogue* is linked. On the other, it appeared that only Western fashion houses were prepared to pay those rates. During interviews it emerged that no fashion magazine, in Japan at least, ever gets anything near its published advertising rates, and that a title is extremely lucky if it persuades an advertiser to pay as much as 55% thereof. A good magazine can stretch this to 60%. Both the Editor-in-Chief and the Vice President of Advertising & Marketing in Nikkei Condé Nast expressed their satisfaction, therefore, in obtaining 62–3% of their published rates: that is, approximately ¥1.5 million for a ¥2.35 million four-color page. Independently, each calculated that *Vogue* needed 1,200 pages of advertising a year to cover costs.[21]

In connection with this, both men stressed that Japanese *Vogue* was a brand whose quality had to be maintained at all costs. This was one reason why foreign advertisers were so good: they had a cachet that could not be matched by Japanese brands. At the same time, however, although fashion houses had always produced high-quality images, fashion advertising itself was now at a peak. This meant that *Vogue* had to increase its cosmetics and skincare advertising (something that by October 2004 it was beginning to achieve) and try to attract the top twenty brand names.[22] As the Vice President of Advertising & Marketing put it:

> But once we've done that, what next? Do we go for automobile or alcohol advertising, like American *Vogue*? Or do we aim at airline companies? Or banks and other financial corporations? There's

a danger here of our getting closer to other fashion magazines, so we have to be extremely careful to *select* our advertisers ourselves, and not allow them to select us. That's why, if we were to go for Nissan, for example, we'd make sure that it advertised one of its expensive models, and not a cheap runabout. We have to maintain visual control if we are to prevent the *Vogue* brand from breaking down ... We cannot afford to have our advertisers dictate the content of our magazine to us."

It became clear during this conversation that both advertisers and magazine are engaged in a mutually reinforcing status game: advertisers place their ads in *Vogue* because of the title's brand equity; *Vogue* in part achieves that brand equity by attracting high-status advertisers.[23]

This brings us to a discussion of readers. Earlier I noted the dual- or multiple-audience property of magazine publishing (and creative industry production more generally). This was continually commented on by my interviewees as they struggled to balance the demands of advertisers with reader preferences. One interesting point that emerged here was the fact that the "reader-friendly" layout that I noted of Japanese *Vogue*, compared with its American sister edition, was in part due to the way in which the magazine is distributed and sold. Because American *Vogue* relies so heavily on subscriptions (more than 85% of its one million plus readers purchases the title by subscription), its editor can afford to structure the magazine the way she does, with advertising placed on the right-hand pages and breaking up the editorial matter. In Japan, however, a very large number of readers buy a magazine on the basis of what they read each month while standing in a bookshop or convenience store (called "standing-reading," or *tachiyomi*, in Japanese). This means that, even though it has a comparatively large subscription base, Japanese *Vogue* has to be structured in such a way that it will immediately appeal to a *tachiyomi* reader and persuade her to buy that month's issue—a point confirmed by Japanese readers in my interviews.

Another point that emerged goes back to the status game between magazine title and advertisers mentioned above, and explains both why Japanese *Vogue* does not use Japanese models and why the magazine is in general so Western in its contents. The Editor-in-Chief told me how there was a third target audience for Japanese *Vogue*:

What you should realize about an international fashion magazine is that there's a secret ranking of its contents among those working in the fashion industry. An *A-Class* magazine is one whose fashion stories appeal to and are readily understood by the international fashion village. A *B-Class* magazine is allowed some local content, while *C-Class* magazines are more or less entirely local.

This means that a fashion magazine's fashion pages are crucially important. They *have* to be made abroad for us to get international recognition ... But making fashion stories abroad in the way that we do is extremely expensive. I mean, it costs us something like $2.25 to $2.75 million a year[24] to have sixty stories, ranging from six to twelve pages each, produced. This is an enormous—and in some respects meaningless—sum of money. But what it does do is get international recognition for Japanese *Vogue* in the fashion village—that is, among photographers, models, makeup artists, PR people, and so on. It'd be easy to lift pages from the American and British editions of *Vogue* and pay very little for the stories, but then there would be no *creation*. So far as the fashion village is concerned, it is a magazine's ability to be creative that counts. And it is the fact that we produce such high-quality pages that also attracts advertisers.

So my aim has been to make Japanese *Vogue* part of the fashion village. And that means being treated as an *in*sider, not an *out*sider—which in itself enables us to get quick and immediate access to information and news, because we are seen as an integral part (*nakama*) of the fashion village.

This extract helps explain why, given the lack of overall central control, the various editions of *Vogue* are so different from one another.[25]

That the magazine is structured according to the basic concepts of anchorage and flow, as discussed in my content analysis, quickly became apparent during the course of my interviews and all those I talked to alluded to them in one way or another. Each season's overall concepts were fixed at a two-day meeting following each season's fashion shows, where senior staff discussed everything they had seen over the past four to six weeks and came up with a set of keywords (like "romantic," "menswear-like," "nostalgic 1950s," and so on). Out of these, half a dozen basic "concepts" were selected, based on a particular fashion personality, or on the different materials, colors and clothing styles those concerned had seen in the collections. It was around each of these concepts that an issue was then constructed, in order—as the Editor-in-Chief put it—"to take the reader from front to back cover in an effortless flow."[26]

And how did he reconcile this with advertisers' desire to make readers stop at their pages? Here the Creative Director echoed interviews with magazine staff elsewhere in the world, when he said that he hardly ever knew which advertiser's ad was going to be placed where, and therefore that it was virtually impossible to create the kind of flow between pages that I suggested and pointed out. At the same time, though, he freely agreed that, for a designer, it was the two-page spread, and not each single page, that was important.

This was supported by the Editor-in-Chief who proceeded to make a rather startling admission:

> That's a tricky question you've asked. In fact, I believe my readers actually enjoy looking at ads. This means I *want* to know in advance—and the sooner the better—which ads are coming where in the magazine. Some editors abroad like to pin up the whole of an issue on the wall of their offices, with text stories and fashion features filled in, and ad pages left blank. If I had the space to do this here, I'd do the same. But I'd put in pictures of all the ads *first*, before the text and fashion pages were produced, because knowing what ad is going where helps me construct the text page. You can't really separate the two. It's the two-page spread as a whole that really counts. Each page should play off the other. That's why you can find all sorts of little links between ads and textual matter in terms of layout, content, color, and so on. [He pauses to show me some examples from the latest November 2004 issue.] It definitely doesn't work all the time, of course, but the simplest way to create a link between pages is through color matching. This goes on a lot.

It was clear that the Editor-in-Chief's desire to create visual and/or content links between editorial and advertising pages was an ideal that could only sometimes be practiced, although the fact that Saito is both Editor-in-Chief and Publisher allows him far greater control of this side of the production process than is permitted to most magazine editors. Nevertheless, it was reassuring to hear, finally, that my carefully unearthed data were not misleading and that one puzzle of content analysis could be satisfactorily resolved.

Conclusion

In this article I have focused on Japanese *Vogue* as both cultural product and commodity, and sought to highlight the relationship between editorial and advertising matter. As a methodological position vis-à-vis the study of media more generally, I have argued that we need to take into account the total social processes surrounding the production, representation, circulation, and reception of Japanese *Vogue*, but have here focused my analysis on the first three as part of my attempt to discuss an international fashion magazine as a cultural production.

Nevertheless, I would like at this point to add three reception-related points on the basis of a dozen in-depth interviews with Japanese fashion magazine readers (who were not necessarily readers of Japanese *Vogue*). The first is that, virtually without exception, the women I talked to emphasized the importance of quality in the photographs they saw in their magazines. It was *image* that attracted their attention, and their fascination with images meant that—so far as magazine readership was concerned—it did not matter if the clothes shown in the fashion pages of a title like *Vogue* were practical or not. What was paramount was that photographs should be striking and beautiful—and, in this respect, what emerged was that women themselves expected both anchorage and flow while reading a magazine. In other words, they wanted editorial pages to be so stunning that they would be stopped in their tracks as they flipped through their magazine. This supports the Editor-in-Chief's attention to flow and anchorage when constructing each issue of Japanese *Vogue*. It also suggests that his decision to use high-class foreign photographers for the fashion features was not just to please his third audience—the "fashion village." It was also based on a sound understanding of Japanese readers' expectations.

Secondly, although readers generally agreed that Caucasian models made the clothes they wore look good (because they are tall and slender), they also pointed out that there was a gap between what they, as readers, looked at in the magazines and what they wanted to wear in the streets. In order to be made to feel that they wanted to *buy* a fashion item, they argued, a magazine's fashion pages should use Japanese models to illustrate the clothing shown. This was even truer of a magazine's beauty and cosmetics pages, since readers firmly believed that Japanese women differed from Western women when it came to certain physical features like skin texture and eyelid formation. In this respect, at a *practical* level, Japanese fashion titles, which made use of Japanese—or at least Asian—models, were seen to be more appropriate vehicles for advertising and consumption than foreign titles like Japanese *Vogue*.

Thirdly, although a number of readers admitted that they could never wear the kind of clothes shown in the pages of foreign titles like *Elle* and Japanese *Vogue*, they almost uniformly agreed that fashion magazines—in particular, domestic Japanese titles—showed them how to coordinate clothes and how to make a limited wardrobe go a long way. While one or two women claimed to be utterly uninfluenced by what they saw in their magazines' pages, three or four others said that they would actually telephone a store to find out if it still stocked an item carried in the latest issue of a particular title. Every reader said that she used magazines as a shopping guide in some way or another, although most were careful to stress that their purchases were not dictated by what they saw in the fashion pages. It also became clear in interviews that some women used the magazines, not to see what was *currently* fashionable, but to try to guess what would *become* trendy in the short-term future. At the same time, it transpired that—for all the talk about brand-consciousness among Japanese women—many readers were not in fact that loyal to brands. Rather, they tended to shift preferences for designer items season by season, or as the mood took them. This general link between magazine content and consumption practices validates Japanese *Vogue*'s (and other magazines') overall policy of selling its readers to potential advertisers, but does not provide support for particular styles of consumption of particular items sold by particular advertisers.

In spite of these rather general remarks relating to magazine readers, my main interest in this essay has been to conduct a content analysis of Japanese *Vogue* and then see to what extent this analysis holds up in the light of interviews conducted with staff employed in different areas of the magazine's production. Perhaps because of the long-term nature of the research that I have been conducting over the past fifteen years, and perhaps because of my previous fieldwork among advertising agencies and magazine publishers, I came across no major discontinuities between content analysis and interviews. However, a number of confusing issues were at least clarified—in particular, those relating to the effect of the subscription system on magazine structure; the nature of the multiple audience on Japanese *Vogue*'s fashion pages; and the importance of maintaining visual quality in order to attract advertisers and permit an ongoing play-off between participants' economic and cultural capital.

Brian Moeran

Appendix 1: A Summary of Initial Advertising Rates for Japanese *Vogue* (in '000 yen), 1998

Position	1 time	3 times	12 times	24 times	48 times
Discount			4%	12%	16%	20%
Inside Front Cover spread	7,600	7,296	6,688	6,384	6,080
Second Page two-page spread	7,400	7,104	6,512	6,216	5,920
Two-page spread before Contents	7,000	6,720	6,160	5,880	5,600
Facing Contents 1	3,400	3,264	2,992	2,856	2,720
Facing Contents 2	3,350	3,216	2,948	2,814	2,680
Facing Contents 3	3,300	3,168	2,904	2,772	2,640
Facing Editor's Letter	3,000	2,880	2,640	2,520	2,400
Facing Contributors' page	2,900	2,784	2,552	2,436	2,320
Two-page spread before Beauty	5,600	5,376	4,928	4,704	4,480
Facing Vogue Beauty opening	2,800	2,688	2,464	2,352	2,240
Inside Back Cover spread	4,800	4,608	4,224	4,032	3,840
Back Cover	4,500	4,320	3,960	3,780	3,600
Four-color two-page spread	4,700	4,512	4,136	3,948	3,760
Four-color one-page ad	2,350	2,256	2,068	1,974	1,880

Note: US$1 is equivalent to approximately ¥110.

Appendix 2: Advertising Categories and Promotions in Japanese *Vogue*, 2002

AD CATEGORIES	June	July	August	September	October	November	December	Totals
Accessory	3	1	0	0	2	3	0	9
Alcohol	0	0	0	2	0	1	0	3
Automobile	2	3	0	3	0	3	1	12
Communications/ Media	1	1	8	2	0	2	4	18
Eyewear	5	5	3	3	2	2	1	21
Fashion	27	14	7	26	103	94	34	305
Food & Drink	0	0	0	1	0	0	0	1
Footwear	1.5	2	1	4	7	5.5	4	25
Fragrance	3	1	4	2	0	7	3	20
Haircare	1	1	1	1	1	1	1	7
Handbag	10.5	7	3	5	13	8.5	10	57
Interior/Living	0	0	0	0	0	3	1	4
Jewelry	7	6	8	1	1	9	8	40
Lingerie	0	1	0	0	2	0	0	3
Makeup	6	7	9	7	7	5	10	51
Retail	0	0	0	1	0	0	0	1
Skincare	6	4	5	0	4	2	2	23
Travel	1	0	1	1	0	1	0	4
Watch	7	5	11	2	3	11	14	53
Totals	81	58	61	61	145	158	93	657

PROMOTIONS	June	July	August	September	October	November	December	Totals
Accessory	0	0	0	0	0	0	0	0
Alcohol	0	0	0	0	0	6	0	6
Automobile	0	2	0	0	0	0	0	2
Communications	0	0	0	0	4	0	0	4
Eyewear	0	3	0	0	36	0	0	39
Fashion	0	4	0	12	0	24	0	40
Footwear	0	0	0	0	0	0	0	0
Fragrance	0	2	0	0	0	0	0	2
Haircare	0	0	4	0	0	0	3	7
Handbag	0	5	0	0	0	0	2	7
Interior	0	0	0	0	0	0	0	0
Jewelry	0	2	0	0	0	2	2	6
Lingerie	0	1	0	0	0	0	0	1
Makeup	0	4	0	0	0	0	4	8
Retail	0	0	0	0	0	26	0	26
Skincare	0	0	0	0	0	0	0	0
Travel	0	0	0	0	0	0	0	0
Watch	0	6	0	0	0	0	0	6
Totals	0	29	48	12	40	58	11	154

Appendix 3: Structural Comparison of the 2002 Fashion Issue of American, French, and Japanese Editions of *Vogue*

	American *VOGUE*	French *VOGUE*	Japanese *VOGUE*
	Sept 2002	Sept 2002	Oct 2002
COVER			
Cover Type	Gatefold	Single Page	Gatefold
Model	Kate Hudson	Karolina Kurkova	Natalia Vodnanova
Photographer	Herb Ritts	Inez Van Lamsweerde	Craig McDean
Fashion	Donna Karan New York	Christian Dior	Comme des Garçons
Makeup	L'Oréal	Dior	Calvin Klein
Title Color	White on blue	Black on blue	Black on white
Title Position	Behind model's head	Over model's hair	Behind model's head
Main Cover Headline	Fall Fashion's All-out Glamour	I've Got You Under My Skin	Dark Angel
Topic	*Fashion*	*Fashion/Fur*	*Fashion*
Headline 1	One Year Later	Luxury Tastes: The Haute Couture Collections	Mother and Daughter Exchanging Fashions?
Topic	*Society/Culture*	*Fashion*	*Fashion*
Headline 2	Kate Hudson: Hollywood Royalty...	n/a	Liking the "Darkness" of Belgian Design
Topic	*Celebrity*		*Fashion*
CONTENTS PAGES			
Contents 1 Page Number	46	31	37
Contents 2 Page Number	64	36	39
Contents 3 Page Number	76	n/a	41
MASTHEAD PAGES			
Masthead 1 Page Number	174	42	418
Masthead 2 Page Number	194	52	419
Masthead 3 Page Number	n/a	58	n/a
TEXT STRUCTURE			
First Text	letter from the editor	Arrêt sur image	Editor's Letter
Page number	126/154	64-66	59
Contributors' Page	314	42	97
Beauty Section Start	618	235	355
Number of Pages	12 interrupted	7 interrupted + 6	22 uninterrupted + 4 promotion pages
Fashion Well Page Start	647 (78.7% through magazine)	259 (70% through magazine)	257 (60.3% through magazine)
Total Pages	46	55	62
Fashion Well Theme	Glamour Now	I've Got You Under My Skin	Don't Be Afraid of the Dark
Fashion Story 1	*Let It Shine*	*Emmanuelle*	*Misty*
Fashion Story 2	*Glamour, defined (text)*	*Aristocats (Aristochats)*	*Blacklight*
Fashion Story 3	*Sparkling Star*	*Dune*	*Country Blues*
Fashion Story 4	*The Greatest Show on Earth*	*Silence of the Lambs (Le silence des agneaux)*	*Dark Romance (text)*
Fashion Story 5	*The Shotmaker (text)*	*The Collector (La Collectionneuse)*	*Romantic Strangers*
Fashion Story 6	*Twisted Classics*	*Haute Couture*	*Men's Club*

ADS

Inside Front Cover Ad	Ralph Lauren (*Gatefold*)	Celine (*Two-page Spread*)	Chanel (*Gatefold*)
Ad Category	*Fragrance*	*Fashion Purse*	*Makeup*
Number of Ads to Contents	45	30	35
Ad Facing Contents 1	Honda	Guy Ellia	AKRIS
Ad Category	*Automobile*	*Watch*	*Fashion*
Ad Facing Contents 2	Rolex	Ralph Lauren	MaxMara
Ad Category	*Watch*	*Fashion*	*Fashion*
Ad Facing Contents 3	Clinique	n/a	Donna Karan
Ad Category	*Skincare*	*n/a*	*Fashion*
Ad Facing Masthead 1	Kate Spade	Michael Kors	n/a
Ad Category	*Fashion*	*Fashion/Footwear*	*n/a*
Ad Facing Masthead 2	Cover Girl	Sergio Rossi	n/a
Ad Category	*Makeup*	*Footwear*	*n/a*
Ad Facing Masthead 3	n/a	Custo Barcelona	n/a
Ad Category	*n/a*	*Fashion*	*n/a*
Ad Facing First Page Beauty	Aveeno	Plein Sud	n/a
Ad Category	*Skincare*	*Fashion*	*n/a*
Ad Facing First Page Fashion	Donna Karan New York	Versace	Che Che New York
Ad Category	*Fashion*	*Fashion*	*Accessory*
Inside Back Cover Ad	Max Factor (Single page)	Sam-Rone (*Single page*)	Marginal Glamour (*Two-page spread*)
Ad Category	*Makeup*	*Fashion*	*Fashion*
Back Cover Ad	Concord/Saks Fifth Avenue	Dior	Armani
Ad Category	*Watch/Retail*	*Makeup*	*Fashion*

AD/TEXT

Total Number of Pages in Issue	822	370	426
Total Text Pages	312 (38.0%)	168 (45.4%)	280 (65.7%)
Total Ad Pages	*510 (62.0%)*	*202 (54.6%)*	*146 (34.3%)*
Number Text Pages in First Half	26 (6.3%)	46 (24.9%)	86 (40.4%)
Number Ads in First Half of Issue	*380 (92.5%)*	*139 (75.1%)*	*127 (59.6%)*
Number Text Pages in Second Half	286	122	194
Number Ads in Second Half of Issue	*130*	*63*	*19*
Number Right Pages of Text	77 (18.7%)	68 (36.8%)	72
Number Right Page Ads (facing text)	*80 (19.5%)*	*46 (24.9%)*	35
Number Right Page Ads (facing ad)	*37 (9.0%)*	*0*	0
Number Left Pages of Text	136	100	**151 (70.9%)**
Number Left-Page Ads (facing text)	15	17	*3 (1.4%)*
Number Left-Page Ads (facing ad)	37	0	*0*
Number Two-Page Spread Ads	160 (38.9%)	69 (37.3%)	51 (23.9%)
Gatefold Ad Pages	20	0	5
Back Cover	1	1	1

References

Barrell, Joan and Brian Braithwaite. 1988. *The Business of Women's Magazines*. London: Kogan Page.

Barthes, Roland. 1967. *Système de la Mode*. Paris: Éditions du Seuil.

—— 1977. *Image Music Text*. London: Fontana.

Beetham, Margaret 1996 *A Magazine of Her Own*. London: Routledge.

Caves, Richard. 2000. *Creative Industries: Contracts Between Art and Commerce*. Cambridge, MA: Harvard University Press.

Ferguson, Marjorie. 1983. *Forever Feminine: Women's Magazines and the Cult of Femininity*. London: Heinemann.

Friedan, Betty. [1963] 1992. *The Feminine Mystique*. Harmondsworth: Penguin.

Hermes, Joke. 1995. *Reading Women's Magazines: An Analysis of Everyday Media Use*. Cambridge: Polity.

Inoue Teruko et al. 1989. *Josei Zasshi o Kaidoku Suru: Comparepolitan Nichi-Bei-Mexico Hikaku Kenkū*. Tokyo: Gakiuchi Shuppan.

Kinsella, Sharon. 1995. "Cuties in Japan," in L. Skov and B. Moeran (eds). pp. 220–254. *Women, Media and Consumption in Japan*. London: Curzon.

McCracken, Ellen. 1993. *Decoding Women's Magazines: From Mademoiselle to Ms*. Basingstoke: Macmillan.

Moeran, Brian. 1995. 'Reading Japaneseness in *Katei Gahō*: The Art of Being an Upper-class Woman," in L. Skov and B. Moeran (eds) pp. 111–142, *Women, Media and Consumption in Japan*. London: Curzon.

—— 1996. *A Japanese Advertising Agency: An Anthropology of Media and Markets*. London: Curzon.

—— 2004. "A Japanese Discourse of Fashion and Taste," *Fashion Theory*, Vol. 8 (1): 35–62.

Myers, Kathy. 1986. *Understains ... The Sense and Seduction of Advertising*. London: Comedia.

Winship, Janice. 1987. *Inside Women's Magazines*. London: Pandora.

Notes

1. In addition to the English-language literature surveyed here, we might note that an extremely detailed and competent comparative study of women's magazines in Japan, Mexico, and the United States, based on content analysis, has been carried out by Teruko Inoue and her Women's Magazine Study Group in Japan (Inoue et al. 1989).

2. I would like to take this opportunity to thank the following members of *Vogue Nippon* for taking the time in mid-September 2004 to talk

to me so revealingly about different aspects of their everyday work in editing and producing each issue of their magazine: Kazuhiro Saito, Editor-in-Chief and President of Nikkei Condé Nast; Aya Aso, Beauty Director; Yasushi Fujimoto, Creative Director; Makoto Uesaka, Vice President of Advertising & Marketing; and Mitsuko Watanabe, Fashion Features Director. I am very grateful, too, to Kimmi Fukuda, Personal Assistant to Mr Saito, and Masaya Haraguchi, Media Promotions Group Management Leader in ADK, for helping arrange these interviews, and to Kin'ichi Nakamura, former Director of the Magazine-Buying Division at ADK, for his continued help with my research on Japanese women's magazines over the past fifteen years.

3. The information carried in this and part of the following paragraph comes from my interview with Kazuhiro Saito, Editor-in-Chief of *Vogue Nippon*, September 21, 2004, 1610–1740 hours.

4. Data supplied by ADK advertising agency, Tokyo.

5. Based on information supplied by ADK.

6. The following three paragraphs are based on an interview with Kin'ichiro Nakamura, of Asatsu-DK, in December 1997.

7. As editors of one magazine, *Katei Gahō*, told me, the dream should be realizable.

8. The ad rate table makes it clear that, prior to actual publication, Nikkei Condé Nast intended to have ads facing its two Masthead pages (generally placed at the back, not front, of Japanese magazines), as well as "Talking Back" and "Up Front" sections.

9. One should realize that such comments are themselves subject to the "logic" of the fashion industry. Thus, the main concept for the October 2004 fashion issue of Japanese *Vogue* was "Sweet & Sexy"—in other words, precisely the "cuteness" criticized by the (same) Editor-in-Chief two years earlier.

10. Interviews: Katie Breen, International Editor-in-Chief, *Marie-Claire*; and Fabrizio Lo Cicero, Associate Publisher, *Elle International* (Paris, February 2002).

11. At the time of my research, all fashion stories appearing in each issue's fashion well are commissioned via Gabriele Hackworthy, an Australian Fashion Director working for Japanese *Vogue* out of New York.

12. There seems to be general agreement among Japanese readers that fashion magazines are far too heavy to carry around (something that precludes their regular purchase), and that their weight is attributable to the advertisements, rather than textual material, that they carry.

13. In contra-distinction, the left, or versal, page moves and is therefore not readily focused on by readers. (Interview Alex Fung, Hong Kong Polytechnic University Design School, May 2001.)

14. Color is one of the simpler ways of creating links between pages (e.g. 2002/11: 52–53, 60–61, 64–65, 68–69, 80–81, 88–89, 90–91, 200–201, 294–295).
15. The placing of a left-facing model in an ad on a right-hand page to draw attention to products and text on the left-hand page (or vice versa) is comparatively common (e.g. 2002/10: 64–65, 66–67, 94–95, 170–171).
16. Readers vary with regard to the importance they attribute to the cover in their decision to purchase a particular issue of a magazine. In general, it would seem that editors are the firmer believers in the efficacy of a title's cover.
17. Similar examples may be found in other issues. A Dior promotion, "Call of the Wild" (September 2002, pp. 260–65), harks straight back to the July 2002 issue's theme, "Born to be Wild," while the word "wild" appears regularly in other months' fashion photo captions (cf. "City Girl Goes Tyrolean," August 2002, p. 76).
18. There is, I assume, a conscious allusion here to the film of this title by the Danish director, Lars Von Trier, which was released at this time.
19. Other fashion stories include "Poetry in Motion" (November 2002: 356–367).
20. I should here express my thanks to the former Danish Institute for Advanced Studies in the Humanities and the Danish Research Agency for providing me with both the time and the financial wherewithal to carry out some of the previous research mentioned here.
21. Each also said that, because of its cut rates, *Elle Japon* would need 2,000 pages of advertising a year to cover publishing costs.
22. That is, from Estée Lauder down to Max Factor, but not including Maybelline, or Japanese brands like Sophina.
23. This view was extended by my reader informants who commented not only on the direct link they saw between foreign fashion and cosmetics advertisers, on the one hand, and magazine titles, on the other, but on how these then affected the status of the (in particular, Japanese *Vogue*) reader.
24. ¥250-300 million in local currency.
25. For example, while American *Vogue* is read by women who include extremely rich upper-class New Yorkers, on the one hand, and Idaho and Montana cowgirls, on the other, and so tends toward the lowest common denominator in its contents, a very large proportion of readers of Italian *Vogue* are themselves in the textile and fashion business and thus look for something "edgy" and "different." In this respect, Italian *Vogue* is closer to being a trade, than a commercial, magazine.

26. No attention is paid by the staff of Japanese *Vogue* to what other editions of *Vogue* may be doing. As the Fashion Features Editor laughed: "That would make our work impossible!"

Fashion Theory, Volume 10, Issue 1/2, pp 259–278
Reprints available directly from the Publishers.
Photocopying permitted by licence only.
© 2006 Berg.

Doppie Pagine:
Not Spelling It Out[1]

Judith Clark

Judith Clark is currently joint
London College of Fashion/Victoria
and Albert Museum Research
Fellow in Contemporary Fashion,
and founder of the Judith Clark
Costume gallery. Her most recent
exhibition, *Spectres: When Fashion
Turns Back*, is accompanied by a
book of the same title. The research
for this piece is part of a work in
progress towards an exhibition on
the work of Anna Piaggi for the
Victoria and Albert Museum.
j.clark@vam.ac.uk

The following is a transcript of an interview I conducted with Anna Piaggi and Luca Stoppini, Creative Director of Italian *Vogue*[2] in Anna Piaggi's apartment in Milan on June 16, 2005. The interview was recorded in Italian and translated by me.

Luca Stoppini (LS):   She (Anna) goes to all the fashion shows, accompanied "backstage" by a photographer—who is Bardo Fabiani,[3] and who in the past was Alfa,[4] her husband ... they photograph backstage, and she watches the show from the front row. That is it. Bardo comes back with ...

Anna Piaggi (AP):   Trolleys.

LS: Suitcases of slides and Anna starts to set out themes, she gives the shows a point of view.

Judith Clark (JC):   How long have the photos been "backstage" and not front shots of the shows?

AP: I have to say it became backstage because of a series of rather dramatic events—in the old days Alfa photographed backstage, but a bit later, see, I used to go to the shows with Vern—when Vern died I suddenly felt an emptiness behind me, behind my back; it was an incredible feeling, very strong, because he used to sit behind me, they used to give him the seat behind me, and he helped me take off my coat. In my superficiality I miss that as well—I miss the person who helps me with my sleeves, I miss his physical presence.

       Vern died and I remember the first show I went to and he wasn't there, and I asked a girl from *Vogue*—maybe it was Anna dello Russo—I was sitting in the front row and she was sitting behind me, and I said to her, "Do you mind coming and sitting beside me?" And she said, "why?" and I said, "Just come and sit here" without giving her any reason, and from that moment it had changed, and I decided that I didn't want to be in the main room, I wanted to be backstage, and so, see, it was contingent facts, and then I worked with Alfa backstage and that was all we did, and it was important because we conducted interviews for *Panorama*.

LS: The approach changed.

AP: Yes, the approach changed and from then on, I was front and back. It started for a psychological reason but wonderful work came from it … but times changed, and backstage became difficult, and Alfa then also died. There was a long period of reflection on who, from the available photographers, could replace him. We asked Bardo, and we were right, weren't we?

LS: Yes.

JC: Does Bardo anticipate, intuit what will interest you?

AP: He is a person who … he has a great detachment from it all … he is a great gentleman. He isn't "fashiony"[6] but he has it inside him, he comes from a family.

JC: Yes.

AP: So he sees the clothes with nonchalance he just sees them.

LS: The great thing is that Vern, Alfa, Anna, myself, Bardo; we are all people with large personalities, with our own individual point of view. Each with a very precise point of view—and in my opinion, and I don't know how, this is a genial thing. Bardo has an attitude to fashion that is completely different from what I might expect. He takes photos as though it were not a fashion show; he sees things completely from his perspective. This is the unusual thing—you said something earlier which was "whether he anticipates what we need": no, it would be totally wrong. If we used a fashion photographer we would receive an already interpreted photo which would exclude a lot of possibilities for us; what she [Anna] needs is documentation.

Vern had a lot of documentation, reference; incredible.

JC: Historical?

AP: Vern—on dresses ...

LS: Incredible.

AP: Vern would pick up a dress, let's say an antique dress; he would look at it with these eyes [she squints] with his shortsightedness, he would turn it inside out and hold it against the light, and he would look and say, "The dress was altered 'at home' in 1928," "A seamstress changed the hem in 1928"; those are the sorts of things he would say.

LS: Ten years ago we worked differently.

JC: He (Vern) was self-taught, wasn't he?[7]

AP: Yes, he was self-taught. What was wonderful about him was that he would turn it into a story; it was great, he invested clothes with animism—he believed that they had souls.

JC: I think at the beginning I saw these exhibition tableaux[8] as telling the story of one dress, the story of its story, and so on...

LS: That's what we will do.

JC: ... to create a historical habitat for it [the dress] or for a word. You are extremely well versed when it comes to fashion; self-referential.[9] When you use a title like *Pink Ink!*[10] you expect us to get it.

LS: Yes.

JC: Not only Vreeland's *"Think Pink!,"* but also her *"Pink is the navy blue of India."* It's always a game that goes on, and on if you like.

AP: That is to enter in an animistic[11] way into the concept.

JC: And to read it in a certain way, with a certain attitude. What do you want from the reader? When I read the other sections of *Vogue*, I might admire the photography, but the message is "Buy me." "Go out and buy this and this, at this incredible cost." The Doppie Pagine don't do this: I think "Go and look me up" would be more accurate there. I would want to become an expert in that particular historical moment, motif etc. which now I think—is slightly more expressionistic we are invited to think about a mood belonging to a (hypothetical) event. What do you want the reader to do?

AP: We work instinctively.[12]

LS: No reflection.

AP: You can't analyze it, no, no. It is about sounds, impressions.

LS: No, there is never a strategy. It is what we were saying earlier. There are four or five people's point of view, which are all totally different.[13] I don't know what she sees, and I don't question it either; I don't even want to know. It is as though I do this, and then I pass it to you, and you do this and pass it to her …

JC: You trust each other.

AP: No, certainly we chose to work together, of course. I will tell you something which is absolutely extreme,[14] it is about "squatting."[15] It is about inhabiting space. That's what it is for me—don't you think? Is it true or not?

       I have always said that my role in magazines is to squat—where there is free space, that's where I place myself. Then you expand, you adapt, you synthesize and most of all, you defend yourself, you push against the material.[16]

LS: My work is about contamination.

JC: [to Luca] You choose from a choice.

LS: Yes, from her [Anna's] choice, I choose things that can be used differently.

JC: And then it goes back to her for the words.

LS: I prepare the layout—I have never worked with texts which are already done, not one page of *Vogue*, not one.

JC: So you actually ask for a specific number of words, or even letters?[17]

LS: Sure. She gives me a title.[18]

AP: I had written to you about the April issue, the one with all the fragmented words. In there I talk to you of Barbara Hutton and Sienna Miller. I had interviewed John Galliano and asked him what he was trying to say with the show, and he said it was about a hypothetical meeting between Sienna Miller and Barbara Hutton at Glyndebourne Festival in England, and there is an exchange. I only took the words belonging to their names and I am convinced that that is the story.[19]

JC: Do you care whether the readers know that that was the motivation behind that particular show?

AP: No, because it just is true, it *is* what inspired Galliano. It *is* the reason.[20]

LS: There is a double language—one which is intellectual, of ideas, and one which is purely graphic. Ninety percent of people don't get the first, but I live for the ten percent who do.

       This is *DP* [points to the cover of *Fashion Algebra*], meaning *Doppie Pagine*, but for me it is a drawing, a design. I see the two aspects of it totally disassociated.

AP: This is *Doppie Pagine di Piaggi* [Double Pages by Piaggi]. That is what came to my mind—DPDP—when we needed a title for the pages.

LS: She [Sozzani] is the only Editor to whom I can say, "Let's give this issue a title which starts with a "P"—and she understands why and does it. She doesn't care why, but if I make a demand like this she knows that I need it graphically; I need a "P" on the page. It is an important shape that will go with an image.

AP: She sees things. She has an instinct without which the magazine couldn't be what it is—great instinct. A very particular leadership.[21] It is very unusual, very smooth.

LS: She never goes deeply. She has the same approach that we have. Never go inside; the minute you go inside you lose your instinct.[22]

AP: You can't explain it. You can't explain it. The most I can tell you, which is like an explanation, a paradoxical explanation, is things such as squatting, which actually mean anything. It is more to do with that than any analytical concepts. We couldn't even attempt an explanation. Everyone can imagine it as they please. It is, if anything, a graphic enterprise.

　　In fashion you can identify dresses that have something more to say, more characteristics, more interest for the pages, because this person has chosen this shape, because it has a language and it talks. But these are things that people say, really wanting to lecture, otherwise you don't reiterate it. They are pages created through instinct. They are invented, and they have been invented for *Vogue*. There, there isn't an explanation, only a final result— their existence.

JC: [to Luca] How long have you been doing it?

LS: Condé Nast, 1981.

AP: We have worked together a long time.

LS: Twenty-four years.

AP: When we started you were …

LS: Twenty. I am forty-four this year. I was a textile designer before this.

JC: Did you start with *Vanity*?[23]

AP: Shall I get the sandwiches?

JC: What is the continuous element in her attitude as Editor of *Vanity*, before and after. What is the thread?

LS: It is really her attitude to fashion. Every season a theme comes through. And you can see the contrast between what other magazines do. When it is an ethnic season, everyone goes ethnic. We don't; we always have a different, unique approach. We need more.[24] Hers has been, and mine as well. Which is why I design a magazine that changes all the time—each issue. There is some consistency, but it evolves, the graphics change. I could never stick to one typography, the lettering—I'd get bored.

JC: Her work is always recognizable.[25]

LS: Of course it is.
　　[Sandwiches arrive.]

JC: Do you have any heroes? Who do you use as shorthand to describe a style?

AP: No. You could possibly say Brodovich,[26] but not really …

LS: We have a huge baggage in our heads, and in this job you have a particular frame of reference, most often self-referential, but we have a position.

AP: For Luca it is lettering itself.

LS: Words.

AP: I have a huge advantage of using English as well, foreign words; this is a huge benefit

LS: It makes it much more beautiful.

JC: Is it always English and Italian?

AP: No, you know instinctively.

LS: Titles are always in English.

AP: Yes, titles are almost entirely in English.

JC: Or composite?

AP: Yes, mixing the two.

LS: The whole magazine is this way because I much prefer English. It is more succinct.[27]

AP: Yes.

LS: Italian is so long; in English you summarize with one word. In a relationship or a dialog between two people, I don't like it as it cuts off too many possibilities. Italian is richer—in my opinion—but visually English is our contemporary language. It couldn't be otherwise. There isn't enough space.

JC: What you mean is American English.

LS: You are right, that is shorter spelling.

JC: Soon you will use text message spelling.

AP: It is terrible, but we play. For "Christmas tree" we used "x-mas3,"[28] and we used "U2" once. It can happen.

AP: What do you see in the space?[29]

Afterword

> An image is strong not because it is brutal or fantastic—but because the association of ideas is distant and right.
>
> Pierre Reverdy, *L'Image*[30]

Anna Piaggi has had a long and prolific career as a journalist, editor, and stylist, working in Milan since the late 1950s. She has contributed to *La Settimana Incom* (Istituto Luce) in the "Il vivere moderno" (modern living) section, *Linea Italiana* (Mondadori). She was Fashion Editor at *Annabella, Arianna;* she was Editor-in-Chief of *Vanity* from 1980 to 1983; she has contributed to both *Panorama* and *l'Espresso*. She was a fashion editor for Italian *Vogue* from 1969–71, a trend reporter through her "Box" column from 1974–79, and from 1988 to the present has contributed her *Doppie Pagine*.

Figure 1
Doppie Pagine of Anna Piaggi
(Italian *Vogue*, July 2005).

She is often described as being the most extravagant dresser in Italy, as well as one of the most photographed. She is always both eccentrically and dramatically dressed. Always with touches of contemporary couture. A "look," rather than masquerade. Always unique and always fashionable. Her flair for the styling and anachronistic mixing of vintage couture and costume was drawn, affectionately, by Karl Lagerfeld during the 1970s and collected into a publication.[31]

As an adolescent growing up in Rome, I first came across her work in *Vanity*, a magazine devoted to fashion illustration. I found myself at school redrawing Antonio Lopez's campaign for Missoni, similar to many commissioned by her for the magazine. Anna Piaggi's name started to come into focus for me with the double pages and photos of her around. What I couldn't know then, but know now, is that she was an informing presence in my work as a curator. I wanted ways of talking about fashion. She connected clothes to storytelling. She was my Diogenes Teufelsdrockh,[32] providing found fragments of stories about stories about fashion. The individual words on her pages were like crossword puzzle clues: you didn't necessarily have to get them right, you just had to play the game. She was telling us something about clothes without necessarily telling us what it was.

Fashion's allusions and references to disparate (real and fantasy) worlds is of course acknowledged. The *Doppie Pagine*, starting in the late 1980s, provided accounts that were somehow still not spelled out. Although she resists intellectualization it was, in my opinion, the idiosyncratic conceptual gymnastics of fashion that she was alluding to. You had to be in the know to get it; but what you had to know wasn't clear.

Figure 2
Doppie Pagine of Anna Piaggi
(Italian *Vogue*, July 2005).

Clothes in this account of fashion are not self-sufficient and here my path deviates from material culture studies, or dress history as a form of connoisseurship, and toward ideas about installation design. If connections are the focus and the dress is not isolated, then what she provides is a staggering multitude of perspectives, or curatorial voices, that I suggest are unavailable in the museum world. It is precisely because she remains outside academic thought that she can be free with her references; it is because she doesn't have to prove it that she can call "a fringe" "spaghetti,"[33] and words can be "made to measure" (Piaggi 1998: 127). For Piaggi, a dress requires a word, a monkey a fridge,[34] or indeed another dress to come to life. She relies on juxtapositions.

Two years ago, I was given the opportunity to pay something of a homage to her, albeit architectural, in the exhibition "Malign Muses, When Fashion Turns Back" (MoMu, Antwerp 2004; V&A 2005). It was an attempt to reconcile what I believed to be connections between (fashion) theory and (curatorial) practice, as well as hypothetical links between avant-garde fashion and the museum and historical archive. The "theory" in this case was taken almost as a case study, and quoted largely from Caroline Evans's *Fashion at the Edge* (Evans 2004); the motifs, the translated even misunderstood (by me) leitmotifs of Piaggi's pages I know informed the installation design. The games, haunting, connections, distortion that Evans traces so clearly in her seminal book, reminded me somehow of those games that Piaggi had been irreverently placing before us as collage. We have been told by her, since 1988, of the complex nature of fashion's historicity.

Now I am curating an exhibition dedicated to Piaggi's work and I am faced with the task of communicating something about that work and my sense of what it involves. Anna Piaggi is not interested in a

Figure 3
Anna Piaggi, photographed
at the opening of the Vivienne
Westwood exhibition at the
V&A.

description of the skills she uses, but she is interested in using them. So my project is not to tease out the theory behind her work, but to see how she works. The *Doppie Pagine*, she says (Piaggi 1998: 84) are "a non-system, a free association, a sequence, a vision that transcends the fold of a binding."

Fashion historian James Laver, in *Style in Fashion* (1949), wrote of his work as a sequence of formal associations and juxtapositions; this prefigured Piaggi's approach. Here the connection is between fashion and architectural style:

The method adopted in this booklet is strictly non-scientific, which is a different thing from unscientific. We shall proceed not logically but analogically. There will be no attempt to prove anything, but only to bring related shapes together in the hope of *firing the imagination to a perception of the reality behind surface-pattern*. The whole work, text and pictures included, is what, a hundred years ago, would have been called a suggestive inquiry. It is hardly even that, it is a mere hint, *a signpost pointing to the Unknown* ... Such at least is its intention (Laver 1949).

Cultural theorist Michael Carter quotes the above in his *Fashion Classics* (Carter 2003: 134) and comments:

That sequence of apologies and qualifications is embarrassing to read. Again Laver seems unwilling, or unable, to clear the final intellectual hurdle and get down to practise (and enjoy) the life of a scholar. When we arrive at the pictorial section of the essay our disappointment is compounded. Laver's aim only seems to be to draw attention to the presence of stylistic parallels.

What Carter fails to ask himself is which version of science Laver is using as his negative ideal. Making connections that are not proof of anything and that cannot be tested experimentally—there is no replicable experiment here, only a suggestive resonant impression, which is, in itself an interesting "method."

My intention was to engage with Piaggi's project on its own terms, if possible. The difficulty is that within a discipline desperate for meaning, profundity, and context, we are faced with a manifesto or an anti-manifesto of "instinctive work." This has been her position throughout her career. In an interview for *W* magazine by Andre Leon Talley in 1978, she says: "My nature has always been to be superficial. I never think too much or make statements. I just stay on the edge of things." Being on the edge is not conventionally associated with being superficial.

Piaggi places herself as anti-intellectual, however, more than anyone, she reveals the vast diversity of fashion's muses, showing us its ability to incorporate conflicting ideas into its project. It is as though she pretends to be fashion's unconscious memory.

There seems to me to be an interesting link between Piaggi's pages and art historian Aby Warburg's great unfinished work, the *Mnemosyne Atlas*. Warburg (1866–1929) was a Renaissance scholar and founder of the library and institute that bear his name. The *Mnemosyne Atlas* was made up of themed groupings of photographic reproductions of works of art, pinned to black screens. He famously rearranged the sequences, incessantly shuffling the pattern. Warburg described the project as a "Ghost Story for Grown-Ups." A story that could be told in pictures alone. What he meant by art history without words was not without

Figure 4
Mnemosyne Atlas, Plate 5.
Courtesy of the Warburg
Institute Library, London.

titles and words (indeed there are notebooks full of titles to hypothetical panels), but without explanation.

Piaggi's pages and Warburg's work both have repetitions, motifs that they reiterate throughout. For Piaggi it was Vreeland, fashion itself, the historical avant-gardes. For Warburg it was paganism, nymphs, classical drapery, or the serpent ritual. In both projects, high and low art are first translated into two-dimensional images—a postage stamp carrying equal weight to classical statuary, the importance being located in their juxtaposition.

Both seem to be characterized by the certainty of their starting points; they know where they want to begin: the art of the Renaissance and catwalk fashion respectively. The breadth of their references is always startling.

Figure 5
Mnemosyne Atlas, Plate 77.
Courtesy of the Warburg
Institute Library, London.

They both search for details that were "activated," to use Gombrich's
term, by association with the afterlife of something else (Gombrich
1986: 289). The essence of what people casually call dynamic projection,
fashion's forward momentum—is at its most compelling in these pages.
Their work is not really about "trends" or "artistic movements," which
is how they are usually described, they are not creating consensus or
riding the Zeitgeist—if anything they both want to show how the artist
has resisted his conventions.

A recent study of Aby Warburg (1998, translated into English 2004)
by Philippe-Alain Michaud, *Aby Warburg and the Image in Motion*,
suggests Warburg's method "operated through historical anachronisms
and discontinuities. Using procedures of 'montage-collision,' he brought
together pagan artifacts with masterpieces of Florentine Renaissance

art." He located the sources of the Renaissance in the Dionysian spirit of movement and gesture. His enigmatic landscape was not based on the meaning of the figures, but on their interrelationship, or "violent associations."

What Piaggi calls animism, is what Warburg called his "Gods in exile."

It was the visual image rather than the work of art that he considered the key document of civilization; he was unwilling to look at style in terms of artistic conventions and traditions. The project revealed what he understood by the afterlife of antiquity. What he meant by paganism was the artist's surrender to impulses of frenzy and fear. What Piaggi surrenders to is frivolity.

Some of this is clearer if we read Franca Sozzani's introductory statement to the collected *Doppie Pagine* (see note 1), though the "free variable," translated from "variabile impazzita," lessens its effect and is misleading. *Impazzita* means "mad; out of control; corrupting rather than free." It disturbs the strict algebraic sequence, it undermines it, it questions the rest of the magazine. It captures the restlessness of Piaggi's thought and Stoppini's hand. It is perhaps this restlessness, the unwillingness to settle, which connects Piaggi to Warburg.

"When I dress with a perfect law of contrast I am in a trance" Piaggi said in an interview in W in 1978, once again invoking ideas of the primitive. She ends her book (Piaggi 1998: 291) with the following words: "Pages in pieces. Ready to be reassembled. Diassembled. To continue. Not a retrospective. A geometry. The End."

The spectator has to meet the curator more than halfway. Piaggi implies that the curation of dress is always a collaborative work-in-progress, with the clothes in between the curator and the spectator, there to be reimagined; infinitely reassembled.

Notes

1. The *Doppie Pagine* (Double Pages) are two to three double-page spreads in each issue of Italian *Vogue*. They are conceived by Anna Piaggi, creative Consultant to the magazine. Their subject matter is derived from the catwalk collections and selects a theme, around which a composition made up of catwalk images, reference images, and words is created. The themes vary in scope from, for example, belt buckles to Victoriana. The spreads themselves are the subject of a book (Piaggi: 1998) celebrating ten years' work, published by Thames and Hudson. She continues contributing the pages to the present day. In her introductory statement to the book, the Editor of Italian *Vogue*, Franca Sozzani (who took over the magazine in 1988) wrote:

At *Vogue* I wanted a *Vogue* that was volatile, vivacious, vital and very quick at spotting trends, Vreelandesque in its extravagance, a hothouse of new ideas. I wanted it to be visionary. But most of all *Vogue* had to be like a paper video, a barometer of style. It needed that unexpected something, it needed that famous "free variable" which had to disrupt every issue and all expectations. So were born the DPs by Anna Piaggi.

2. Luca Stoppini is also Creative Director of *L'Uomo Vogue* and *Casa Vogue*. He designs the layout of the *Doppie Pagine*.

3. Bardo Fabiani is a catwalk photographer. His mother Simonetta, an Italian couturier, was born Duchesa Simonetta Colonna di Cesaro, in Rome, Italy. She opened a studio in Rome in 1946 and signed her first collections as Simonetta Visconti. In the late 1940s she dressed many filmstars. In 1953 she married Alberto Fabiani. Fabiani and Visconti followed separate careers until 1962, when they did a joint venture in Paris. Then in 1965 moved back to Rome, where she designed for several years. She retired in 1973.

4. Alfa Castaldi was an Italian photographer. He married Anna Piaggi in New York in 1962. He died in 1995. See http://alfacastaldi.com for his archive.

5. Vern Lambert was an Australian fashion historian. Anna Piaggi met him in London, where he owned a vintage couture stand at Chelsea market in the 1970's.

6. The Italian was *modaiolo*, a colloquial term for fashion victim.

7. Anna Piaggi draws attention to uninstitutionalized skill—i.e. it can't be taught.

8. The meeting was set up for the forthcoming exhibition at the Victoria and Albert Museum, "Anna Piaggi: Instant Fashion" (provisional title) dedicated to the work and archive of Anna Piaggi and curated by Judith Clark. The tableaux are sections within the exhibition, to be themed by Piaggi herself.

9. What would it be to be fluent in fashion when you don't accept facts or theory, what becomes the grammar?

10. I am referring to *Italian Vogue*, December 2004, for which the title of the two double-page spreads was "Pink Ink," extending Diana Vreeland's dictum "Think Pink!" Alternately pink and blue dresses by Prada, Christian Lacroix, Helmut Lang, and John Galliano were juxtaposed. The riddle, or connection, referring to an afterlife of Vreeland's attitude and a humorous reference to traditional catwalk trend reports where colors are stated as fashionable.

11. Animism. It seems a curious concept to introduce. It is a term from anthropology and used by nineteenth- and twentieth-century anthropologists to describe to way in which so-called "primitive tribes" lived in environments populated by spirits. There were benign spirits, malign spirits, and ancestors. It is a very suggestive

concept when related to fashion. Is part of her project creating possible ancestry? It is associated with ritualized oral histories, stylized narration.

12. She says in *Fashion Algebra* (Piaggi 1998: 92) "For me it was important never to lose the thread of my instinct—my instinctive reaction again deep thought." She feels the intrusion of verbal description as a distraction or even sabotage of talent or creativity.

"What the overemphasis on the idea of content entails is the perennial, never-consummated project of interpretation. And, conversely, it is the habit of approaching works of art in order to *interpret* them that sustains the fancy that there is really such a thing as a content of a work of art" (Sontag 1997). Susan Sontag's seminal essay, *Against Interpretation*, is a significant statement of what is in fact a long tradition of skepticism about interpretation, summed up in Wilde's remark: "It is only shallow people who do not judge by appearances."

Another source is Marjorie Garber's book, *Quotation Marks* (2003), and in particular her essay entitled "Historical Correctness," where she makes a case for anachronism as creativity rather than "mistake."

13. It might be interesting, compositionally, to think of them literally as contrasting perspectives.

14. The Italian, *Spietante*, also means "ruthless."

15. "Squatting" is cited also in the introductory words of *Fashion Algebra* (Piaggi 1998) as representing an attitude. It is about using space that doesn't belong to you or that is left over. It is about need, or in Piaggi's case, I believe, ideas being in excess of available space. Nothing for Piaggi is finite, only contained. The association with squatting is provocative.

16. Franca Sozzani was, I think, alluding to this attitude in her introductory paragraph to the book on the initial creation of the *Doppie Pagine*: "It [*Vogue*] needed that famous 'free variable' which had to disrupt every issue and all expectations."

17. He refers to the equal if not greater importance of the layout. A useful analogy might be the futurist idea of "Parole in liberta" (words in freedom). It is, of course, more familiar to Italians. A good definition can be found in Marjorie Perloff's *The Futurist Moment*: "The visualization of the text that is neither quite verse nor prose, a text whose unit is neither the paragraph nor the stanza but the printed page itself."

Piaggi's visual, graphic, onomatopoeic love of words runs through her work. Anna Piaggi wrote all the Prada press releases during the 1990s, writing both the English and Italian versions, changing the meaning if she didn't like the "look/sound" of the word. Her Spring/Summer 1998 release reads:

POSITIVE MOVEMENT
Avant-garde work ethic:
Sewing machines go crazy
Irons become undisciplined,
Nervous are the scissors.
Hems react in unpredictable ways.
'Lightening' darts.
Morphological creases
Become decorations.
Work
Defines aesthetics.

NEW DETAIL-ORING
Positive movement
Of detailing,
Of unexpected finishings,
Of embroidered seaming,
Of frayed trimmings,
Of invented fastenings,
And superimpositions.

POSITIVE REFERENCES
Tight hips on
Streamlined silhouettes.
Hemp plays with gold.
Latex pajamas
Sewn with surgical precision;
Dress in silk denim;
In elaborate "patch"
In geometric or idyllic prints
—a wheatfield—
transfigured by the computer.
Dress-up in light;
Cover-up in beading.
Hyperbolic.
Like THE TOY SHOES.
a.p.

18. Titles from 1988–1998 are recorded in *Fashion Algebra* (Piaggi: 1998). Titles from 1998 to the present include: re-flex (December 1998); sur-face (September 1999); white in-clean-ation (December 1999); bloom boom (May 2001); purely puritan (October 2001); décor-action (April 2003); short-age (October 2003).

19. The e-mail sent from Anna Piaggi to Judith Clark on 07/04/05 included this description (translated from the Italian by Judith Clark):

Here I wanted to "show" [her quotation marks], in a synthetic way, some of the concepts about the collections that were expressed or described to me by some of the designers: John Galliano, Ann Delmeulemeester, Basso & Brooke. For Jean-Paul Gaultier I interpreted what was suggested from the photos. For Galliano the ideas were: Barbara Hutton and Sienna Miller meet at Glyndebourne Festival and a new paradoxical style is created; and for Demeulemeester, in honor of the centenary of Arthur Rimbaud, she reproduced on a T-shirt one of his poetic lines: "Je est un autre." In both cases, what the designers felt became, in detached words, a type of poem ... abstract. But all absolutely real ...

I think it worked well, but my dependence on an art director is fundamental. When I say dependence it is about relying on professional editing, even though, as you can see, my final motto in the far corner of the fourth page is "rebel."

She draws attention to two elements, one that a hypothetical event becomes history, the other is Rimbaud's "I is another" which has become one of the key formulas of modernism. In terms of reference, one as real as the other.

20. It is an important moment as it is to do with the identification and then the authenticity, in her terms, of the reference. What is omitted from the conversation is the fact that on the *Doppie Pagine* are other words that "explain" the mood in "fashion terms," i.e. a color, a posture.

21. Instinct as leadership. It depends on not knowing what you are doing. Piaggi seems to have a primitivist, quasi-modernist view of instinct as authenticity, though this would not be her description.

22. He said this in English.

23. *Vanity* magazine, published by Condé Nast. Anna Piaggi was Editor of the magazine between 1981 and 1984. The magazine was devoted to illustration and her collaborator was the late Antonio Lopez. She maintains her love for illustration, and now collaborates mainly with British illustrator Richard Gray.

24. Details are taken to their logical consequences. A story on lace incorporates all the names for lace, and lace itself becomes hieroglyphic: Turnure, Burano, Arles, Le Puy, Mousse, Flandre, Bruges, Brode (Italian *Vogue*, April 1994).

25. "Recognizable" here was intended with reference to the previous point that Piaggi's work is understood as something outside the norm, for its idiosyncratic references.

26. Andrei Brodovich, the legendary Art Director of *Harper's Bazaar* in New York who would say, when approached by potential employees: "*Astonish Me!*" He is credited with inventing the modern magazine layout in regard to composition and in particular the use of white space.

27. Though the articles are in Italian, all titles in Italian *Vogue* are in English, associating them with the imagery more than with the text. Mysteriously, only the title for the horoscope section has been left in Italian: "Oroscopo."
28. Italian *Vogue*, December 2003.
29. The conversation continues [unrecorded] about the forthcoming exhibition at the V&A.
30. Godard quotes a text by Pierre Reverdy called *L'Image* in Michaud (2004: 289).
31. Piaggi, Anna. 1986. *Karl Lagerfeld: A Fashion Journal.* London: Thames and Hudson.
32. *Sartor Resartus*, Thomas Carlyle, 1831. The book within a book, from which hypothetical extracts are recounted called, "*Clothes, their Origin and Influence*" by the fictional Professor.
33. In May 1991 she entitled the *Doppie Pagine* "Fashion Menu: Pasta." The title was traced on a wooden spoon from Zaire, and decorative details from the Jean Charles de Castelbajac collection were categorized in terms of their approximation to shapes of pasta: farfalle, tortellini, tortiglioni, timballi, pappardelle.
34. Anna Piaggi interviewed by André Leon Talley in *W*, July 21–28, 1978.

References

Carter, Michael. 2003. *Fashion Classics. From Carlyle to Barthes.* Oxford: Berg.

Conti, Quirino. 2005. *Mai il mondo sapra*. Milano: Feltrinelli.

Clark, Judith. 2004. *Spectres. When Fashion Turns Back*. London: Victoria and Albert Museum.

Evans, Caroline. 2004. *Fashion at the Edge*. London: Yale Univerity Press.

Garber, Marjorie. 2003. *Quotation Marks*. London and New York: Routledge.

Gombrich, E. H. 1986. *Aby Warburg. An Intellectual Biography*. Oxford: Phaidon.

Laver, James. 1949. *Style in Architecture*. London: Oxford University Press.

Michaud, Philippe-Alain. 2004. *Aby Warburg and the Image in Motion*. New York: Zone Books.

Perloff, Marjorie. 2003. *The Futurist Moment*. Chicago: University of Chicago Press.

Piaggi, Anna. 1986. *Karl Lagerfeld: A Fashion Journal*. London: Thames and Hudson.

Piaggi, Anna. 1998. *Anna Piaggi's Fashion Algebra*. London: Thames and Hudson

Sontag, Susan. 1966. *Against Interpretation and Other Essays*. New York: Farrar, Strauss & Giroux.

Stimelli, Davide (ed.). 2005. *Aby Warburg. Ludwig Binswanger. La Guarigione Infinita*. Vicenza: Neri Pozzi Editore.

Tafuri, Manfredo. 1976. *Architecture and Utopia*. Massachusetts: MIT Press.

Trilling, Lionel. 1971. *Sincerity and Authenticity*. Harvard University Press.

Fashion Theory, Volume 10, Issue 1/2, pp. 279–288
Reprints available directly from the Publishers.
Photocopying permitted by licence only.
© 2006 Berg.

Vogue Timelines

Janine Button

Janine has worked in the Vogue library since arriving in London from New Zealand in 2001 and has been the Library and Archive Manager since 2002. She is responsible for managing a small team, for organizing the photographic material in the library and for helping with picture research for magazines and books.

American *Vogue* Timeline

■ December 17, 1892, American Vogue launched. Arthur B. Turnure listed as Publisher.

■ 1893–1900. Josephine Redding is Editor-in-Chief of American *Vogue*.

■ 1901–1914. Marie Harrison is Editor-in-Chief of American *Vogue*.

■ 1909. *Vogue* title acquired by Condé Nast.

- June 24, 1909. Condé Nast listed as President of the *Vogue* Company for the first time.

- 1914–1954. Edna Woolman Chase is Editor-in-Chief of American *Vogue*.

- January 1, 1923. Thirtieth anniversary issue of American *Vogue*.

- September 15, 1942. Condé Nast dies. His obituary is listed in American *Vogue*, October 15, 1942: 24–25.

- November 1943, Fiftieth anniversary issue of American *Vogue*.

- 1954–1963. Jessica Daves is Editor-in-Chief of American *Vogue*.

- 1963–1971. Diana Vreeland is Editor-in-Chief of American *Vogue*.

- 1971–1988. Grace Mirabella is Editor-in-Chief of American *Vogue*.

- August 1974. Beverly Johnson becomes the first African-American model on the cover of American *Vogue*.

- November 1988–present. Anna Wintour is Editor-in-Chief of American *Vogue*.

- April 1992. Hundredth anniversary issue of American *Vogue*.

Argentinean *Vogue* Timeline

- 1924–1926. Argentinean *Vogue*.

Brazilian *Vogue* Timeline

- May 1975. Brazilian *Vogue* launched.

- 1990 onwards. Ignácio de Loyola Brandão is Editor-in-Chief of Brazilian *Vogue*.

- 1995. Twentieth anniversary issue of Brazilian *Vogue*.

- 2000. Twenty-fifth anniversary issue of Brazilian *Vogue*.

British *Vogue* Timeline

■ September 15, 1916. British *Vogue* launched. (Cover: Helen Thurlow/British *Vogue*)

■ 1916–1922. Elspeth Champcommunal is Editor of British *Vogue*.

■ 1922–1926. Dorothy Todd is Editor of British *Vogue*.

■ Early April 1924. Cecil Beaton's first photograph in British *Vogue*.

■ 1926–1935. Alison Settle is Editor of British *Vogue*.

■ July 20, 1932. First photographic cover in British *Vogue* by Edward Steichen. (Cover: Edward Steichen/British *Vogue*)

■ 1935–1940. Elizabeth Penrose is Editor of British *Vogue*.

■ April 28, 1937. Coronation issue of British *Vogue*. (Cover: Pierre Roy/British *Vogue*)

■ September 1, 1937. Twenty-first anniversary issue of British *Vogue*. (Cover: M. De Lavererie/British *Vogue*)

■ September 1941. Silver Jubilee issue of British *Vogue*. (Cover: Pierre Roy/British *Vogue*)

■ 1940–1960. Audrey Withers is Editor of British *Vogue*.

 ■ October 1944. First still life cover in British *Vogue* by Irving Penn. (Cover: Irving Penn/British *Vogue*)

 ■ June 1945. Victory issue of British *Vogue*. (Cover: James de Holden-Stone/British *Vogue*)

 ■ June 1953. Coronation issue of British *Vogue*. (Cover: Norman Parkinson/British *Vogue*)

■ May 1956. The first photographs in British *Vogue* by Anthony Armstrong-Jones (Lord Snowdon).

■ July 1958. Retrospective article on British *Vogue* from 1916–1958.

■ Early September 1960. David Bailey's first photographs for British *Vogue*.

 ■ February 15, 1961. David Bailey's first cover for British *Vogue*. (Cover: David Bailey/British *Vogue*)

■ 1961–1964. Alisa Garland is Editor of British *Vogue*.

 ■ June 1962. Jean Shrimpton's first cover for British *Vogue*, photographed by David Bailey. (Cover: David Bailey/British *Vogue*)

- 1964–1986. Beatrix Miller is Editor of British *Vogue*.

- March 1, 1966. Donyale Luna becomes the first cover model of ethnic origin for British *Vogue*, photographed by David Bailey. (Cover: David Bailey/British *Vogue*)

- October 15, 1966. British *Vogue*'s golden jubilee issue. (Cover: David Bailey/British *Vogue*)

- October 15, 1967. Twiggy's first cover for British *Vogue*, photographed by Ronald Traeger. (Cover: Ronald Traeger/British *Vogue*)

- July 1970. First man appears on the cover of British *Vogue*— Helmut Berger with Marisa Berenson, photographed by David Bailey. (Cover: David Bailey/British *Vogue*)

- October 15, 1976. Diamond jubilee issue of British *Vogue*. (Cover: James Mortimer/British *Vogue*)

- August 1981. Lady Diana Spencer appears on the cover of British *Vogue*, photographed by Snowdon. (Cover: Snowdon/British *Vogue*)

- 1986–1987. Anna Wintour is Editor of British *Vogue*.

- December 1987–September 1988. Mark Boxer is Editor-in-Chief of British *Vogue*.

- 1987–1992. Elizabeth Tilberis is Editor of British *Vogue*.

 ■ January 1990. Iconic British *Vogue* cover of five nineties supermodels, by Peter Lindbergh.
(Cover: Peter Lindbergh/British *Vogue*)

  ■ June 1991. Seventy-fifth anniversary issue of British *Vogue*. (Cover: Herb Ritts/British *Vogue*; Supplement cover by Tyen/British *Vogue*)

- April 1992–present. Alexandra Shulman is Editor of British *Vogue*.

 ■ January 1993. Mario Testino's first cover for British *Vogue*.
(Cover: Mario Testino/British *Vogue*)

 ■ March 1993. Kate Moss's first cover for British *Vogue*, photographed by Corinne Day. (Cover: Corinne Day/British *Vogue*)

- June 1993. Corinne Day's iconic photographs of Kate Moss in British *Vogue*.

 ■ November 1993. Nick Knight's first cover for British *Vogue*.
(Cover: Nick Knight/British *Vogue*)

- October 1997. British *Vogue* tribute issue to Princess Diana.

 ■ December 1999. British *Vogue* millenium edition.
(Cover: Robin Derrick/British *Vogue*)

■ May 2000. Fashion meets art issue of British *Vogue*.
(Cover: Sarah Morris/British *Vogue*)

■ December 2000. British *Vogue*'s gold issue.
(Cover: Nick Knight/British *Vogue*)

■ December 2004. Alexandra Shulman awarded an OBE for services
to the magazine industry.

■ March 2005. Kate Moss's nineteenth cover for British *Vogue*,
photographed by Patrick Demarchelier.
(Cover: Patrick Demarchelier/British *Vogue*)

Chinese *Vogue* Timeline

■ September 2005. Chinese *Vogue* launched.

■ September 2005. Angelica Cheung is Editorial Director of Chinese
Vogue.

French *Vogue* Timeline

■ June 15, 1920. French *Vogue* launched.

■ 1922–1927. Cosette Vogel is Editor-in-Chief of French *Vogue*.

■ 1927–1929. Main Boucher is Editor-in-Chief of French *Vogue*.

■ 1929–1954. Michel de Brunhoff is Editor-in-Chief of French *Vogue*.

■ December 1, 1940. French *Vogue* suspended temporarily due to
WWII. It returns in January 1945.

■ January 1945. French *Vogue* Liberation issue.

■ 1954–July 1966. Edmonde Charles-Roux is Editor-in-Chief of
French *Vogue*.

■ January 1967–January 1968. Françoise de Langlande is Editor-in-
Chief of French *Vogue*.

■ February 1968–January 1969. Françoise Mohrt and Francine
Crescent are Editors-in-Chief of French *Vogue*.

- February 1969–January 1988. Francine Crescent is Editor-in-Chief of French *Vogue*.

- December 1971/January 1972. Fiftieth anniversary of French *Vogue* (Salvador Dali cover).

- February 1988. December 1991. Irene Silvagni is Editor-in-Chief of French *Vogue*.

- February 1992–July 1994. Colombe Pringle is Editor-in-Chief of French *Vogue*.

- September 1994–January 2001. Joan Juliet Buck is Editor-in-Chief of French *Vogue*.

- December 1995/January 1996. Seventy-fifth anniversary of French *Vogue*.

- April 2001–present. Carine Roitfeld is Editor-in-Chief of French *Vogue*.

German *Vogue* Timeline

- April 1928: German *Vogue* launched and ceases publication later that same year.

- August 1979. German *Vogue* launched.

- 1978–1984. Christa Dowling is Editor-in-Chief of German *Vogue*.

- 1985. Florentine Pabst is Editor-in-Chief of German *Vogue*.

- 1986–1988. Charlotte Seeling is Editor-in-Chief of German *Vogue*.

- 1988–1989. Benita Cantieni is Editor-in-Chief of German *Vogue*.

- 1989–February 2003. Angelica Blechschmidt is Editor-in-Chief of German *Vogue*.

- September 1989. Tenth anniversary issue of German *Vogue*.

- October 1994. Fifteenth anniversary issue of German *Vogue*.

- October 1999. Twentieth anniversary issue of German *Vogue*.

- March 2003–present. Christiane Arp is Editor-in-Chief of German *Vogue*.

- October 2004. Twentieth anniversary issue of German *Vogue*.

Greek *Vogue* Timeline

- March 2000. Greek *Vogue* launched.

- March 2000–December 2003. Elonora Fetsi is Editor-in-Chief of Greek *Vogue*.

- December 2003–present. Elena Makri is Editor-in-Chief of Greek *Vogue*.

Italian *Vogue* Timeline

- 1964. *Novità*/Italian *Vogue* launched.

- 1965–1966. Lidia Kuster Tabacchi is Editor-in-Chief of Italian *Vogue*.

- November 1965–May 1966. Italian *Vogue* known as *Vogue & Novità*.

- June 1966–onwards. Magazine known as Italian *Vogue*.

- 1966–1987. Franco Sartori is Editor-in-Chief of Italian *Vogue*.

- 1988–present. Franca Sozzani is Editor-in-Chief of Italian *Vogue*.

- September 1994. Thirtieth anniversary issue of Italian *Vogue*.

Japanese *Vogue* Timeline

- September 1999. Japanese *Vogue* launched.

- September 1999–August 2001. Hiromi Sogo is Editor-in-Chief of Japanese *Vogue*.

- September 2001–present. Kazuhiro Saito is Editor-in-Chief of Japanese *Vogue*.

Korean *Vogue* Timeline

- August 1996. Korean *Vogue* launched.

- August 1996–present. Myung-Hee Lee is Editor-in-Chief of Korean *Vogue*.

Portuguese *Vogue* Timeline

- November 2002. Portuguese *Vogue* launched.

- November 2002. Paula Mateus is Editor-in-Chief of Portuguese *Vogue*.

Russian *Vogue* Timeline

- September 1998. Russian *Vogue* launched.

- September 1998–present. Aliona Doletskaya is Editor-in-Chief of Russian *Vogue*.

Janine Button

Singaporean *Vogue* Timeline

- September 1994. Singaporean *Vogue* launched.

- 1994–1996. Nancy Pilcher is Editor of Singaporean *Vogue*.

- 1996–1997. Michael McKay is Editor of Singaporean *Vogue*.

- 1997. Singaporean *Vogue* ceases publication.

Spanish *Vogue* Timeline

- 1918. Spanish *Vogue* launched. (Published in Havana).

- 1923. Spanish *Vogue* ceases publication.

- April 1988. Spanish *Vogue* launched.

- April 1988–December 1989. Maria Eugenia Alberti is Editor-in-Chief of Spanish *Vogue*.

- January 1990–April 1995. Rachele Enriquez is Editor-in-Chief of Spanish *Vogue*.

- May 1995–March 1997. Mara Malibran is Editor-in-Chief of Spanish *Vogue*.

- April 1997–July 2001. Daniela Cattaneo is Editor-in-Chief of Spanish *Vogue*.

- August 2001–present. Yolanda Sacristan is Editor-in-Chief of Spanish *Vogue*.

- April 2003. Fifteenth anniversary issue of Spanish *Vogue*.

Taiwanese *Vogue* Timeline

- August 1996. Taiwanese *Vogue* launched.

- August 1996–present. Sky Wu is Editor-in-Chief of Taiwanese *Vogue*.

- October 2004. Eighth anniversary issue of Taiwanese *Vogue*.

Vogue en Espanol Timeline

- October 1999. *Vogue en Espanol* launched (Latin Americas).

- 1999–2000. Jackie Blanco is Editor-in-Chief of *Vogue en Espanol*.

- 2000–2002. Lilian Arrenovich is Editor-in-Chief of *Vogue en Espanol*.

- 2002–present. Eva Hughes is Editor-in-Chief of *Vogue en Espanol*.